Global Capital, Human Needs and

C000319004

Also by Ian Gough

THE POLITICAL ECONOMY OF THE WELFARE STATE

A THEORY OF HUMAN NEED (*with Len Doyal*)

CAPITALISM AND SOCIAL COHESION (*co-editor with Gunnar Olofsson*)

Global Capital, Human Needs and Social Policies

Selected Essays, 1994–99

Ian Gough
Professor of Social Policy
University of Bath

© Ian Gough 2000, with the exception of
Chapter 2 © The Association for Evolutionary Economics 1994
Chapter 3 © Pearson Education Ltd 1995
Chapter 5 © Baywood Publishing Co Inc 1994
Chapter 6 © Frank Cass Publishers 1996
Chapter 8 © Journals Oxford Ltd 1996
Chapter 9 © Imprints 1996

All rights reserved. No reproduction, copy or transmission of
this publication may be made without written permission.

No paragraph of this publication may be reproduced, copied or
transmitted save with written permission or in accordance with
the provisions of the Copyright, Designs and Patents Act 1988,
or under the terms of any licence permitting limited copying
issued by the Copyright Licensing Agency, 90 Tottenham Court
Road, London W1P 0LP.

Any person who does any unauthorised act in relation to this
publication may be liable to criminal prosecution and civil
claims for damages.

The author has asserted his right to be identified
as the author of this work in accordance with the
Copyright, Designs and Patents Act 1988.

First published 2000 by
PALGRAVE
Houndmills, Basingstoke, Hampshire RG21 6XS and
175 Fifth Avenue, New York, N. Y. 10010
Companies and representatives throughout the world

PALGRAVE is the new global academic imprint of
St. Martin's Press LLC Scholarly and Reference Division and
Palgrave Publishers Ltd (formerly Macmillan Press Ltd).

Outside North America
ISBN 0–333–80239–X hardback
ISBN 0–333–92687–0 paperback

In North America
ISBN 0–312–23599–2 hardback

This book is printed on paper suitable for recycling and
made from fully managed and sustained forest sources.

A catalogue record for this book is available
from the British Library.

Library of Congress Cataloging-in-Publication Data
Gough, Ian.
    Global capital, human needs, and social policies / Ian Gough.
        p. cm.
    Includes bibliographical references and index.
    ISBN 0–312–23599–2
    1. Public welfare—Government policy—Europe. 2. Capitalism—Europe.
    3. Basic needs—Europe. 4. Europe—Social policy. 5. Europe—Economic
    policy. I. Title.
    HV240.5 .G68 2000
    362.5'094—dc21
                                                            00–033345

10   9   8   7   6   5   4   3   2   1
09 08 07 06 05 04 03 02 01 00

Printed in Great Britain by Antony Rowe Ltd, Chippenham, Wiltshire

Dedicated with love to Daniel, Matthew, Lawrence, Deiniol, Ben and Kate

Contents

List of Tables and Figures

Preface

This book bring together essays written in the mid-1990s which share some common themes: the ongoing contradiction between what is good for capital and what is good for welfare, and the ongoing struggle to bridge the gap by means of social policies. Put another way, they address the tensions between normative and consequentialist arguments for the welfare state. Prior to this period my thinking had proceeded along parallel tracks: on the one hand the historical analysis of the political economy of welfare capitalism; on the other hand the normative analysis of welfare via the idea of human need. These two streams were represented by two books published in 1991: *Can the Welfare State Compete?* (with Alfred Pfaller and Goran Therborn) and *A Theory of Human Need* (with Len Doyal).

The essays collected here begin to bridge that gap. They are divided into three groups, each opened by a long keynote essay. The first part opens with 'Economic Institutions and the Satisfaction of Human Needs', a direct continuation of the questions addressed in *A Theory of Human Need*, asking to what extent capitalism, socialism and communitarianism provide acceptable frameworks for the improvement of human welfare. One clear conclusion is that unregulated capitalism provides a poor institutional framework and the next two essays ask what the prospects for welfare capitalism are, or to what extent the structural power of capital is escaping public control. The implications at this stage of the argument are pessimistic.

The second part opens with 'Why Does Need Satisfaction Vary across Nations?', an exercise in cross-national number-crunching, based on theoretically-driven indicators of need. Its finding that democracy, rights and public regulation on balance improve levels of welfare is encouraging – if these are compatible with the new stage of global capitalism. It is followed two comparative studies of social policies and safety nets in peripheral zones of world capitalism: southern Europe and Russia. They illustrate that national histories and institutions continue to play an independent role in shaping social programmes.

The third part opens with 'Social Welfare and Economic competitiveness', which claims that welfare states are instruments for the reproduction not only of social relationships but also of capital accumulation. Even in today's world of hyper- internationalisation, national welfare states can be more or less productive. There is always scope to invent new ways of reconciling the dilemmas of welfare capitalism and the variety of social and national settings provides a natural laboratory for these to be fought over and implemented. The trick is to combine a productive welfare state with a morally attractive welfare state. The ability of Basic Income to bridge this gap is the subject of the concluding chapter.

The introductory essay, previously unpublished, serves to introduce the book as well as developing these themes in its own right.

All the essays have been previously published, with the exception of Chapters 1 and 4. The case for reproducing them here is that they are scattered across very different journals yet exhibit (I hope) interesting linkages. I have fought the temptation to revise arguments and update data. The essays are reproduced here as published except that tiresome repetitions and material irrelevant to this collection have been deleted and all have been forced into a common format.

I am grateful to Kevin Farnsworth for agreeing to publish our joint essay 'The Renewed Structural Power of Capital' here and to Peter McMylor for similarly agreeing to my publishing our joint article as Chapter 7. I also acknowledge with thanks the permission of the following publishers to reproduce the remaining essays:

Chapter 2   The Association for Evolutionary Economics and *Journal of Economic Issues*
Chapter 3   Pearson Education Ltd
Chapter 5   Baywood Publishing Co. Inc. and *The International Journal of Health Services*
Chapter 6   Frank Cass Publishers and *South European Society and Politics*
Chapter 8   Journals Oxford Ltd and *New Political Economy*
Chapter 9   *Imprints*

Sincere thanks also to Wendy Schouton, Sue Scull and Kate Jones for elp in compiling and editing this collection.

Introduction

1
The Needs of Capital and the Needs of People: Can the Welfare State Reconcile the Two?[1]

To what extent are the needs of capital and the needs of people antagonistic? Are either global or universal, or do they reflect national and cultural differences? Can national social policies in an era of globalisation serve either the interests of capital or the needs of people? Can the welfare state reconcile the two? These are the questions addressed in the essays brought together in this book.

The issues are certainly topical. Witness, on the one hand, the triumph of capitalism in 1989, the accelerating integration of investment and financial markets around the world, the Asian meltdown and financial turmoil, the dissolution of national borders and the globalisation of culture; all these are examples of the growing power of capital, where power entails the ability to define, and to impose, one's own definitions of one's needs. Witness, on the other hand, growing inequality in the distribution of the world's resources, climbing death rates and social dissolution in Russia, the near-holocaust of AIDS in southern Africa, the commodification of more and more aspects of life, including education, the growing insecurity of life for many in the richest countries, and the mounting threats to the global ecology. These are all real threats to human needs and global welfare.

Surely, the answer to my last question is 'no'. The needs of capital and the needs of people are irreconcilably opposed and there is little or nothing the welfare state can do about it in today's world. This pessimistic view is encountered every day in the media and academic tracts. Gray (1999: 214), for example, writes: 'The conflict between social democracy and global free markets seems irreconcilable.' I want to take a more nuanced and hopeful position. Let me try to answer the question in three parts: What are the needs of people? What are the needs of capital? Can the welfare state reconcile the two?

The needs of people

You might think it easy to define the needs of people. Are they not present – unfulfilled – in the faces of the hungry in Ethiopia, the orphaned in Honduras – or the abandoned in old people's homes in Britain? Yet the ability of academics to squabble over such apparently straightforward ideas is legendary, and not always to be despised. The idea of need is no exception. So let me begin by summarising some of the arguments Len Doyal and I put forward in our book *A Theory of Human Need* (Doyal and Gough, 1991).

A theory of human need

The word 'need' is often contrasted with wants. We use the distinction in everyday language: 'I want a cigarette but I need to stop smoking' – a regular mantra of mine until I finally gave up. The distinction, it is generally agreed, rests on the nature of the goals referred to. Need refers (implicitly if not explicitly) to a particular category of goals which are believed to be universalisable; whereas wants are goals which derive from an individual's particular preferences and cultural environment. The universality of need rests upon the belief that if needs are not satisfied, then serious harm of some objective kind will result.

Can we then agree on a notion of harm? We define serious harm as fundamental disablement in the pursuit of one's vision of the good. It is not the same as subjective feelings like anxiety or unhappiness. Another way of describing such harm is as an impediment to successful social participation. We argue that we build a self-conception of our own capabilities through interacting with and learning from others. This is an essential feature of our human nature. As Len Doyal put it in an earlier book:

> It is fundamentally mistaken to view yourself as acting with total self-sufficiency – by yourself and for yourself – without reference to anyone else. Social life is an essential characteristic of individual humans, unlike the situation of an individual tree which just happens to be in a forest. Grown from a seed in isolation, a tree is still a tree; but humanity is the gift of society to the individual.
>
> (Doyal and Harris, 1986, p. 80)

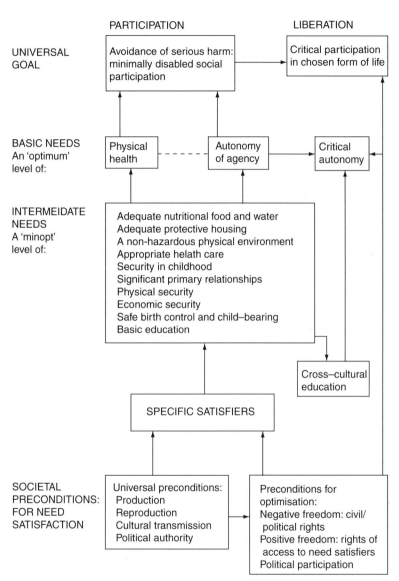

Figure 1.1 The matrix of human needs

Source: Doyal and Gough (1991: 170).

It follows that participation in some form of life without serious arbitrary limitations is a fundamental goal of all peoples. This enables us to define human needs (See Figure 1.1). *Basic needs* consist in those define human needs (See Figure 1.1). *Basic needs* consist in those universal preconditions that enable such participation in one's form of life. We identify these universal prerequisites as physical health and autonomy. Survival, and beyond that a modicum of physical health, is essential to be able to act and participate. But that is not enough. Humans, distinct from other species, also exhibit autonomy of agency – the capacity to make informed choices about what should be done and how to go about doing it. This is impaired, we go on to say, by severe mental illness, poor cognitive skills, and by blocked opportunities to engage in social participation. Health and autonomy are basic needs of all people.

This applies to participation in all and any social groups. At a second level, we can talk of *critical* participation – the capacity to situate the form of life you have grown up in, to criticise it and, if necessary, to act to change it. This more dynamic type of participation requires a second-order level of critical autonomy. Without critical autonomy, human societies would change little if at all, simply reproducing themselves from generation to generation.

Now these common human needs can be met in a multitude of different ways by an almost infinite variety of specific 'satisfiers' – goods, services, activities and relationships that satisfy needs in particular contexts. These do vary over time and place. How, then, can we bridge the gap between universal needs and variable satisfiers? We do this by identifying those characteristics of need satisfiers that everywhere contribute to improved physical health and autonomy. These we label 'universal satisfier characteristics', or *intermediate needs* for short.

We group these characteristics into eleven categories: adequate nutritional food and water, adequate protective housing, non-hazardous work and physical environments, appropriate health care, security in childhood, significant primary relationships, physical and economic security, safe birth control and childbearing, and appropriate basic and cross-cultural education. Nine of these apply to all people, one refers to the specific needs of children, and another to the specific needs of women for safe childbearing. All eleven are essential to protect the health and autonomy of people and thus to enable them to participate to the maximum extent in their social form of life.

Our approach has much in common with Sen's influential ideas of functionings and capabilities. For Sen (1992: 4–7), functionings 'constitute a person's being' and, since functionings are 'intrinsically valuable', they amount to states of *well*-being. Capabilities refer to the set of functionings that is feasible to that person – that she could choose. But what are these functionings? Sen's list includes being happy, being able to choose, having good health, being adequately fed and sheltered, having self-respect, being able to appear in public without shame, and taking part in the life of the community. Though we may well value all these things, it is a rather strange list. It embraces subjective states (being happy) and objective states (being adequately fed), and culturally generalisable conditions (having good health) alongside specifically liberal values (being able to choose). It is not self-evident that all these are 'intrinsically' significant in defining the social good. I consider that Sen needs a theory of need to buttress his notion of functionings (Nussbaum, 1993).

So much for human needs. Since needs are met – or not met – in social contexts, I must now turn to these. All societies by definition comprise institutions directed at production, reproduction, cultural transmission and political authority. But to improve the ways needs are met, some forms of these are better than others. There is not the space here to expound our analysis in any detail. Suffice it to say that the process of identifying appropriate social policies should combine two approaches: drawing on the top–down codified knowledge of experts and professionals, and the bottom-up experiential knowledge of ordinary people in their everyday lives. Either without the other risks harm and waste.

In the essay which comprises Chapter 2 of this book, three procedural or political preconditions are identified as necessary optimally to define human needs: (1) a way of rationally and collectively identifying needs, in part by tapping the latest stock of scientific knowledge, (2) a means of using the experiential knowledge of people in their everyday lives, and (3) the informed, democratic resolution of the inevitable disagreements which will result from these two approaches. At the material or economic level, further preconditions are ideally required to meet these needs: (4) to produce sufficient and appropriate need satisfiers, (5) to distribute them in line with the needs of individuals, households and communities, (6) to transform these satisfiers into individual need satisfactions – a task that predominantly takes place within households, and (7) to ensure that this whole process is sustainable through time.

Thus we argue that universal, objective human needs exist, can be known and charted. Moreover, we contend that there are better and worse ways of meeting human needs. The closer societies approach these procedural and material preconditions, the better are the chances that the needs of its members will be met.

Moral arguments for the welfare state

This leads me on to the moral argument for what I am happy still to call the 'welfare state'. We make this connection in the following stages (Doyal and Gough, 1991: ch. 6):

1 The membership of any social group implies obligations or duties.
2 To ascribe duties to someone presupposes that they are in fact able to perform these duties.
3 The ascription of a duty thus logically entails that the bearer of the duty is entitled to the need satisfaction necessary to enable her or him to undertake that duty. It is inconsistent for a social group to lay responsibilities on some person without ensuring she has the where-withal to discharge those responsibilities.
4 Where the social group is large, this entails similar obligations to strangers, whose needs we do not directly witness and can do nothing individually to satisfy. This will require support for agencies that guarantee to meet the needs of strangers. This is roughly my defini-tion of the welfare state: public rights or entitlements to the means to human welfare in general and to minimum standards of well-being in particular, independent of rights based on property or income. Only the state can guarantee strong entitlements to people of this sort, though this does not require that it directly provides the satisfiers in question – it can regulate, legislate, subsidise and in other ways ensure that other agencies, including private ones, do so.

Michael Ignatieff (1984: 10) put it better than I can:

> Strangers around me have needs, and because they live within a welfare state, these needs confer entitlements – rights – to the resources of people like me. Their needs and their entitlements estab-lish a silent relation between us. As we stand together in line at the post office ... some tiny portion of my income is transferred into their pockets through the numberless capillaries of the state.

Of course, should Ignatieff fall ill or on hard times, he in turn would be the beneficiary.

5 However, our theory entails one major step beyond the traditional confines of the welfare state. This commitment to meet the needs of strangers and to support the necessary welfare structures cannot stop at the borders of any particular state. The idea of universal human

needs leads remorselessly to the global guarantee of their satisfaction. It lends powerful support to contemporary ideas of cosmopolitanism, which sees the entire world as a potential political community – however difficult are the obstacles and however utopian this sounds to our ears today (see Held, 1995: Part IV; Jones, 1999: ch. 5).

Critiques

It is difficult to exaggerate how disliked our whole approach is in some quarters. It goes against the grain of much postmodern thought, which emphasises relativism, authenticity and plural forms of justice. Let me now turn to four critical responses to our book.

First, Drover and Kerans (1993) challenge our 'thin' idea of human need and put forward a 'thick' alternative. A thick approach to need attempts to understand the way people name their needs in specific cultural contexts. It relies on interpretative methods to grasp the full particularity of need in everyday life. This approach is more historic, subjective and authentic. It recognises the role of social movements, which in the 'claims-making process' contest expert and top–down definitions of need and struggle to name their needs through social action. This approach, they claim, avoids the abuses of the concept of need which have been perpetuated by experts; it acts as a corrective to various forms of cultural imperialism which neglect the plurality of discourses that give meaning and moral significance to the lives of individuals within different cultures.

Yet, such a thick account suffers from several problems well summarised by Soper (1993). If we are to give full due to the variety of claims about needs, what saves their approach from being simply an account of struggle over wants and interests? If, as is almost certain, the communally named needs of different groups conflict, how are we to reconcile them in the name of need? In 1997, the Taliban in Afghanistan denied hospital care to women (*The Guardian*, 29 November 1997). Must we accept this in the name of authenticity? Several groups of women in Afghanistan did not. Or, to take another example, if affluent people in the West claim the unlimited use of private cars as a need satisfier, how are issues of global warming and the sustainability of needs at the global level to be addressed?

Drover and Kerans attempt to answer this by drawing on Jürgen Habermas to claim that a group can articulate needs which are universalisable, hence 'true' in the sense that in an ideal speech situation there can be a common consensus. But Hewitt (1993) argues that this requires some shared common background to provide the 'translation bridgehead' between different social movements espousing different cultural preferences and interests. And if this much is agreed, it subverts the priority given to subjectivity and authenticity. At a global level, too, there seems no way of addressing the sustainability of the sum of group-defined needs. In other words, thick needs return us via a different route to the well-established problems of wants, preferences and utility.

A second critique contends that theories of universal need are founded on an individualist notion of agency. Tao and Drover (1997) make this point when contrasting a Chinese notion of need to our 'western' one. They appreciate that we underline the social bases of individual autonomy, the fact that a person's individuality is rooted in their role relationships. However, they claim that this idea is not followed through and that it sits uneasily alongside the idea of critical autonomy, which may entail individuals uprooting themselves and turning against their culture of origin. But we do this deliberately. Their alternative is the rigid set of five cardinal relationships of Confucianism: 'The father is righteous and protective, the mother is loving and caring, the elder brother is fraternal, the younger brother is respectful, and the son is filial.' I am not sure where daughters fit in here. In this rigid relational ethic 'individuals are never recognised as separate entities', they write. This is to go far too far. It is individuals who are born, suffer, love and die! Len Doyal and I do indeed recognise that our individuality is rooted in our role relationships, but this alternative goes too far towards community domination. As much as avoiding ungrounded individualism, a credible theory of need must avoid social constructivism.

Third, thin theories of need, like our own, can be criticised for being too thin to act as a guide for policy. Objectivity and universality can only be achieved at the cost of such a high level of abstraction from real societies, cultures and modes of satisfaction that the theory cannot serve as a practical guide to welfare provision. Now, we explicitly address this question in Part III of our book. Between universal needs and socially specific satisfiers we posit 'universal satisfier characteristics'. As Soper puts it: 'These provide a standard of reference by which levels of deprivation within particular groups can be charted and specific welfare strategies defended as objectively grounded rather than ethnocentrically motivated' (1993: 74). In this sense our theory, while not thick, is certainly thicker than thin! Yet, Soper claims that this smuggles in dubiously objective claims, especially in relation to the prerequisites for critical autonomy. This is further compounded when we insist on the role of bottom–up experiential knowledge in identifying specific satisfiers.

I do not believe that this criticism stands up. The procedures for identifying universal satisfier characteristics rest on two foundations: first, the best available technical knowledge articulating causal relationships between physical health and autonomy and other factors, and second, comparative anthropological knowledge about practices in the numerous cultures, sub-cultures, states and political systems in the contemporary world. Both natural and social sciences play their role in rationally determining policies to meet needs. But in identifying and improving *specific* satisfiers, experiential knowledge grounded in the 'lifeworld' is essential. At the former level, the codified knowledge of physical and social sciences is non-negotiable. At the latter level, the two forms of knowledge should ideally enter into a dialogue within a communicative situation which is as unconstrained and informed as possible. Social policy as an academic discipline embraces both forms of enquiry; but that does not mean that their differing epistemological groundings cannot be distinguished.

Finally, Wetherly (1996) accuses our theory of incoherence when identifying the standards of *basic* need satisfaction. What levels of physical health and autonomy are required to secure minimally disabled social participation? We reject both the 'minimum' and the 'adequate' standard in favour of the 'optimum'. Reflecting the distinction between personal autonomy and critical autonomy, this is divided into two: the 'participation optimum' and the 'critical optimum'. The latter comprises those levels of health and cognitive, emotional and social capacities which permit critical participation in one's chosen form of life. In practice, however, we go on to posit a third variant, the 'constrained optimum': the best level of need satisfaction presently achieved in the world or a feasible better level (Doyal and Gough, 1991: 160–1). Present Swedish levels of health and autonomy, we suggest, provide a practical exemplar of this constrained optimum.

Soper and Wetherly criticise this proposed standard on related grounds. Soper contends that this standard may actually be too high, in that the extravagance of Swedish energy use and socio-economic institutions is not generalisable to all other peoples in the world or to future generations. In so far as this is true, it is accommodated within our definition of constrained optimum. But this raises a difficult issue. We have narrowed our focus from a concern with the universal requirements for minimally disabled social participation to whatever is universalisable across time and place in practice (Soper, 1993: 78). This raises more issues than can be dealt with here, but ultimately 'ought' must imply 'can'. If; due to past industrialism, population growth and environmental degradation, we can achieve less than optimal generalisable satisfaction of basic needs, then so be it. We will forever be living in a world of constraint. Wetherly goes on to claim that this reintroduces relativism. The constrained optimum standard remains 'historically – and so socially, culturally – relative' (Wetherly, 1996: 58). But the 'and so' does not follow. The concept of human need we develop is historically open to the continual improvements in understanding that have characterised human progress. But at any one time, there is a body of best knowledge to which international appeal can be made. Put simply, our theory is relative in time but absolute in space.

If these rebuttals of criticisms of our theory are sound, I would claim that the case for a strong, rights-based and wide-ranging conception of the welfare state still stands. The existence of universal human needs justifies support for an institutional framework guaranteeing sufficient provision of resources to deliver their (constrained) optimal satisfaction. However difficult it is to conceive of this in practice, the institutionalised guarantees to human welfare should be generalised to all the peoples of the world, subject only to ensuring the need-satisfactions of future generations.

The needs of capital

The interests and needs of capital

So much for the needs of people. Now to turn to the 'needs' of capital. Where better to begin than with *Capital* – the greatest work of Karl Marx. He contrasts capital with the simple circulation of commodities.

> The simple circulation of commodities – selling in order to buy – is a means of carrying out a purpose unconnected with circulation, namely the appropriation of use-values, the satisfaction of wants. The circulation of money as capital is, on the contrary, an end in itself, for the expansion of value takes place only within this constantly renewed movement. The circulation of capital has therefore no limits. Thus the conscious representative of this movement becomes a capitalist. His person, or rather his pocket, is the point from which the money starts and to which it returns.... The restless never-ending process of profit-making alone is what he aims at.'
>
> (Marx, 1926: 169–71)

So the prime 'need' of capital, said Marx, is restless, never-ending expansion of its value – the pursuit of profit. This applies whether this thing called capital is invested in industry, agriculture, services, distribution or finance. This activity is quite distinct from consumption where money is expended in order to satisfy wants. Where human wants or needs (at this point we can ignore the distinction) are plural and qualitative, the goal of capital is singular and quantitative. Compared with the complexity of people's needs it is simplicity itself: the goal of capital is to expand profits (I will not say 'maximise') while managing risk. In place of the messiness and multidimensionality of people's needs, there is one overriding goal measured in one dimension – money.

Wetherly (1995: ch. 6) directly applies our model of human needs to analyse the 'needs' of capital, as shown in Figure 1.2. He begins from Marx's starting point that the basic need of capital is profit, a necessary and universal prerequisite for the overall survival of the capitalist system. To produce and realise profits certain intermediate 'needs' must be fulfilled: a system of law (guaranteeing private property), a monetary

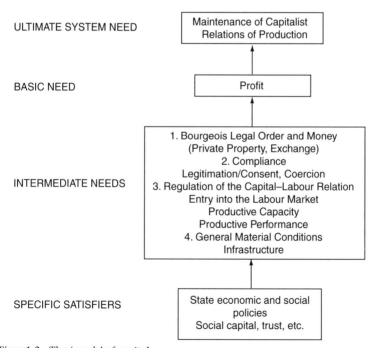

Figure1.2 The 'needs' of capital

Source: Adapted from Weltherly (1995: 203).

system, collective infrastructures such as transport, and some level of compliance of the population in general and the working population in particular. Compliance can be achieved in many ways, varying from informed consent at one extreme to coercion at the other. More particularly, the relation of labour to capital needs regulating to ensure that labour-power is forthcoming to work for capital, that these workers have the appropriate set of capacities and that they do in fact work at a satisfactory level. This reproduction of the labour force applies to the actual labour force, the unemployed, potential workers (e.g. housewives) and the future working population (e.g. children).

These intermediate needs, he goes on, also require specific satisfiers to meet them. These may be provided within the household or community, but all will require a state backed by coercive powers and territorial legitimacy. The state will be pressured to search for workable policies to meet these needs (while at the same time being constrained in its range of solutions by the structural power of capital – see below).

Wetherly's model conveniently compares the needs of capital with the needs of people, but it raises a host of problems. Capital is not an entity in the same way as people, and there is a danger of reifying the category – of imbuing it with lifelike qualities. Moreover, to speak of the 'needs' of capital is to resort to functional explanations of state policies, whereby the consequences of a policy explain its origins. According to Elster (1980), a critic of functional explanations in social science, there is no general mechanism (and few specific mechanisms) equivalent to natural selection in biology, to explain why and how adaptive traits emerge and persist. But Cohen's reply is valid: that, like Lamarck, we may have powerful evidence that features adapt without understanding the mechanisms at work. Marx's theory of 'historical materialism may be in its Lamarckian stage' (Cohen, 1980: 134). In *The Political Economy of the Welfare State* (1979: 37–8) I concluded that 'It *is* useful and helpful to analyse the changing functional requirements of capitalist economies...but it does *not* follow that the state will necessarily perform those functions.'

With this warning in mind, Chapter 3 revisits James O'Connor's analysis of the activities of the state. He contends that the capitalist state will try to fulfil two basic functions: accumulation and legitimation. It must attempt to maintain or create the conditions in which profit-making can succeed, and at the same time control threats to that process by policing the population or in other ways ensuring minimal levels of social harmony. Social policy can contribute to accumulation, in the form of social investment (in training, for example), or social consumption (by enabling families to combine work and child-rearing). And it can provide social expenses, such as relief measures to stave off disaffection and revolt. If social policy is solely influenced by the needs of capital – a big 'if' – these define and limit the scope of its activities.

We may summarise the argument thus far as follows. First, capitalist development pushes the state to search for policies to enable profitable production to continue. The emergence of a propertyless proletariat encourages some forms of social security, the changing division of labour with industrialisation and tertiarisation fosters public education, the growth of cities pushes public authorities towards some forms of urban and public health policies (Gough, 1979: 32–8). But the 'specific satisfiers' adopted will vary according to many other factors, and cannot be read off from the abstract needs of capital. Indeed, the state may not respond at all. Second, the extent to which these capital-driven policies enhance human welfare will vary – sometimes they will, sometimes they will not. Both capitalist and labouring classes 'may see a particular social policy as in their interests, but for quite different reasons. The working class because any policy which mitigates hardship or which modifies the blind play of market forces is to be welcomed. The capitalist class because it reduces working-class discontent, provides an added means of integrating and controlling the working class, and offers economic or ideological benefits too' (Gough, 1979: 66).

Unregulated capitalism and human welfare

Let us now assume a society of unregulated capitalism, where society and state are subordinated to the needs of capital – the pursuit of private profit. This is similar to what Ed Nell (1984) has called 'cowboy capitalism' and Susan Strange (1986) 'casino capitalism'. This can be contrasted with capitalist societies in which the state and/or other civil organisations and movements have more leverage. How well can a relatively unregulated capitalist system satisfy human needs? Chapter 2 addresses these questions.

There *are* ways in which the restless pursuit of profit can serve social welfare, as has been recognised since the time of Mandeville and Adam Smith. First, markets can utilise the dispersed knowledge of millions of separate people, providing them with incentives to act on that information so as to maximise production in response to consumer demand. Almost a century before Marx, Adam Smith (1970: 119) wrote: 'It is not from the benevolence of the butcher, the brewer or the baker that we expect our dinner, but from their regard to their own interests.' This is not an overtly moral set-up – it is greatly reliant on the pursuit of private greed – but it does work! The result of harnessing these knowledges and motives is the prodigious productivity of capitalism today. It is manifestly able to satisfy the wants of many millions of people, not just in the West – and satisfying wants often satisfies needs.

The second strong claim is that the free market system fosters the freedom to choose and to act in the spheres of consumption and production, and thus enhances human autonomy. Related to this, the decentralisation of markets encourages democracy. This can enable groups to organise and press their own conceptions of their needs within the political arena. These are good arguments, especially when contrasted with the state socialist record. The gross abuse and neglect of children in orphanages in Romania and elsewhere stemmed mainly from the lack of a flourishing civil society in which concerned groups and citizens could expose these conditions. There *is* a certain link between markets, decentralisation, freedom and citizen activity.

But arguments in the opposite direction are legion. The unregulated pursuit of profit is poorly equipped to meet human needs for a host of reasons which are too well known and will only be listed here: tendencies to monopoly, unemployment, consumer ignorance, the inability of markets to take wider costs into account such as pollution, the self-defeating production of positional goods whose rationale is simply to enable one to stay ahead of the pack; dilemmas where short-term advantage clashes with long-term (Barr, 1992). More problems arise in the sphere of distribution. As Amartya Sen (1981) demonstrates, unregulated markets cannot, even in the richest societies, offer all people entitlements to basic need satisfiers. The homeless can coexist alongside the luxuriously housed. Indeed, the socially excluded can exist with access to none of the basic satisfiers. More than that, an unregulated market economy generates gender inequality despite the discourse of equal opportunities. Markets paradoxically require altruistic, collective behaviour on the part of women in the household in order to enable men to act individualistically in the market.

Radical critiques go further still. The ability of unregulated capitalism to foster democracy is weak. It will be the rich and powerful who can best organise; and it will be policies to uphold markets that have the best chances of being heard, not those that counterpose common human needs. In the sphere of work the restless never-ending search for profits continually recreates new forms of sweatshop, as in the phone answering rooms that employ thousands of people in Britain in highly controlled environments. Alienation at work persists and is complemented by alienation in consumption. The sheer number of commodities devised is beyond count. Despite, or because of, pervasive advertising, we consumers have inadequate knowledge of their characteristics – and inadequate time to find out. It was estimated in the 1970s that the average American had, by the age of 20, been exposed to some 350,000 television commercials alone. How many is it now? A society driven by profits alone undermines human community, subjects solidarity to an all-embracing culture of possessive individualism. Markets can only meet wants in commodified forms. The benefits of co-operation or leisure are beyond its scope, and indeed are undermined as profit and markets colonise more and more areas of social life. Lastly, it threatens nature as the inherited resources of this world are squandered at a reckless rate. Here the never-ending pressures to expand value are most visibly in conflict with the human needs of the planet's inhabitants.

To conclude. The unconstrained pursuit of profit or casino capitalism may be an efficient system for satisfying *certain* wants of *some* people by means of *commodities*, but that is all. The remainder of our complex web of needs cannot be so satisfied.

Globalisation and the structural power of capital

There is today surprising support for the classic Marxist position that the needs of capital conflict with the needs of people. According to many commentators the domination of capital over state interests and human needs is growing and may be unstoppable. Post-war incursions on the power of capital are short-lived, the argument goes. Whatever the political voice of business and financial interests, whatever countervailing mobilisation and pressures from other interests in society, whatever the political complexion and programme of the government in power, the bottom line is that their room for manoeuvre is constrained by the central structural role of private capital in the modern world.

The reason in a nutshell is 'globalisation'. International trade, foreign direct investment and international financial flows have all expanded, the latter at a dizzying pace, in the last two decades, as cross-border movements of capital have been progressively deregulated. More than 1 trillion dollars are now turned over each day in international currency transactions. Following decolonisation and the collapse of state socialism at the end of the 1980s, few areas of the world remain to resist the logic of capitalist markets and economic enterprises. This in turn is imposing the needs of capital in more and more areas of life and is weakening the resources of states and citizens to fight back.

The new essay in Chapter 4 of this book (jointly written with Kevin Farnsworth) addresses these issues by returning to the idea of the structural power of capital. Capital can rely on two sources of power – voice and exit – whereas other groups in society generally possess only voice (if that). On the one hand, businesses, financial institutions, employers' organisations, business interest organisations, wealthy industrialists, and so on can exert powerful pressures on governments and other policy-makers, through open and hidden channels of communication. But in addition to this, capital is able to exert power without applying such pressure – structural power. We distinguish five sources of the structural power of capital: its control over investment, its increasing mobility over time and space, its assymetrical power over labour and trade unions, its role in financing governments, and its ideological power to shape agendas and colonise wider domains of social life. The internationalisation and globalisation of the circuits of capital extend, but do not create, its structural power.

However, we go on to argue that this structural power is not unbounded; it is variable and contingent on institutions and the power of other groups. To capture this we devise measures of structural power in the major capitalist economies. Our conclusion is that the structural power of capital has recuperated following a decline in the 1970s – as indicated by climbing profits and booming stockmarkets. Britain in the last two decades most clearly demonstrates the renewed power of capital over government and citizens. The private share of investment has risen and the public share has fallen, partly due to privatisation, making more areas of life subject to the dictates of profitability. The countervailing power of citizens has also declined. The weaker are trade unions, the lower are welfare benefits, the looser are labour regulations, the higher is unemployment and the more insecure is work; the less able are citizens to control the power of capital. Most of these have moved in capital's favour over the last two decades.

Putting all this together we can see that the power of private business and financial interests over society, workers and the state has grown since the early 1980s. The world has become more hospitable to the interests of capital owners and controllers. Indeed, it is one of these, George Soros (1999), who has recently expressed this most eloquently.

Can welfare states reconcile the two?

My conclusions thus far are that the unconstrained interests of private capital conflict with and hinder human welfare in numerous ways and that the structural power of private capitalist interests is growing in the contemporary world. This is a pessimistic scenario. Gray writes: 'Global laissez-faire is not a conspiracy of corporate America. It is a tragedy – one of several that have occurred in the twentieth century – in which an hubristic ideology runs aground on enduring human needs that it has failed to comprehend' (Gray, 1999: 217). Are we entering such a dystopian, Blade Runner world? Or can welfare states, defined broadly along the lines introduced earlier, possibly bridge this gap? To coin a cliché – is there a third way? Let me optimistically conclude by presenting arguments and evidence that they can.

The fundamental argument is as follows. First, different forms of capitalism coexist in the modern world despite the deepening of capitalist relations across the globe. The common 'need' of capital is to make profits, but the institutional structures and policy patterns (the 'specific satisfiers') which contribute to this can and do vary. Second, welfare states (defined as earlier on – public rights to human need satisfiers) can enhance the competitiveness of national capitals. 'Human need' sounds passive but this is far from my intention. Need is the reverse side of capacity, and good social policies enlarge the individual and collective capacities of peoples and thus their economic performance. Third, this in turn changes the way that private capitals interpret their interests. Forms of capitalism and forms of welfare state fuse in a relatively stable pattern of 'welfare regimes', with different implications for human needs and welfare. In an increasingly competitive world welfare states can provide a competitive advantage to private capital and at the same time encourage different forms of capitalism with different moral underpinnings and welfare outcomes.

Social policies and economic competitiveness

I begin with the economic impact of welfare states. The relationship between social policy and economic competitiveness is the topic of the essay reprinted in Chapter 8. The competitive advantage of firms depends on their ability to create a value greater than the cost involved. To do this a firm must either provide comparable buyer value but perform activities more efficiently than its competitors (the lower cost strategy) or perform activities in a unique way that creates greater buyer value (the differentiation strategy). In other words there is a choice here. The competitive advantage of nations is different but a similar choice is faced by richer nations with the potential to provide welfare states. They can encourage the cost-or performance-competitiveness of their national firms by cost-cutting, reducing wage costs or social costs, for example. Or they can encourage structural competitiveness by aiming to compete in high quality value-added. The arguments of Chapter 8 brutally summarised, are as follows (see also Gough, 1997, 1999)

Fiscal inputs

In a world of closely integrated financial markets persistent and large budget deficits are harmful, especially when financing current spending or transfers. But when we turn to levels of taxation, there is no convincing evidence that higher levels are harmful, whether the focus is taxes on business or on households. There is no consistent cross-national evidence linking levels of social expenditure or taxation to a variety of indicators of economic performance. On the other hand, there is a consistent *positive* association between levels of social spending and openness to trade.

Welfare outcomes

Poverty, ill-health and high crime rates have economic costs. Less unequal societies enjoy higher growth rates, while adjustment to external shocks is facilitated by lower levels of social conflict and better systems of conflict management. Increasing integration into the world economy requires better systems of social protection. The fiscal costs of high crime and incarceration are considerable. There is an alternative 'unproductive burden of the state' that is not caused by social protection, rather by its absence. The competitive contribution of public welfare is here rather evident.

Social programmes

If good welfare levels are positive for economic performance, but spending on public social protection is indeterminate, perhaps the apparent contradiction can be reconciled at the intermediate level of social programmes. This leads us into the 'institutional fine detail' of different social policies, though it is difficult to draw generalisable conclusions. Much research is at a micro level, for example, the impact of Family Credit on work incentives of lone mothers in Britain. To draw conclusions about whole policy areas over several countries still requires heroic acts of aggregation. My broad conclusions are:

Pensions

Concern over the effects of population ageing on public pension provision is widespread and has already inspired counteracting measures in most countries. European systems have been criticised because they are both generous and pay-as-you-go in nature. A crucial argument for our purposes is that they displace private savings, which in turn reduce investment and future growth rates. However, all stages in this argument can be challenged and cross-national evidence in its favour is thin. The transition costs from pay-as-you-go to funding are very high, while means-testing the basic state pension (the other alternative to the European model) has clear and demonstrable disincentive effects on savings.

Social benefits for the working-age population and labour market regulation

European benefits are in general especially generous compared with the US and Japan, notably sickness benefit and unemployment benefit for some groups. The social assistance safety net is also more extensive and more generous in many, but not all, European countries. The OECD and other bodies argue that minimum wages and extensive employment protection laws (Britain notably excluded) discourage firms from hiring labour and contribute to mass unemployment and social exclusion. On the other hand, countries with generous parental leave benefits encourage women to participate in the labour force and this can outweigh the negative effects: what at the micro level appears to discourage work may at the macro level encourage it. Means-tested benefits, the only realistic alternative to the European social insurance model, can clearly discourage work. In any case, if productivity is the measure of economic performance, and output per hour worked is calculated, European economies exhibit higher productivity levels than the US, while Germany scores as good a rate of productivity growth as America over the last decade.

Education and training

There is near-unanimity now that investment in human capital, through education, child care and training programmes, is important to competitiveness in today's high technology world. The returns to education and training appear to be rising everywhere – alongside the penalties attached to little education, redundant skills and lack of expertise. This is an area where the merits of substantial public provision or finance are more frequently accepted. By driving down labour costs, deregulation may enhance short-term performance competitiveness but at the expense of longer-term structural competitiveness. But this is not just an argument for 'education, education, education'. Children from impoverished backgrounds living in areas of crime and social dislocation where most teachers would choose not to live perform less well at school. Social class and parental interest remain important influences on literacy and numeracy. So social security, urban, housing and health policies are indirectly productive. Human needs are interrelated, lending economic support to a more comprehensive welfare state.

To conclude, social policy is, or can be, a productive force. It is a mistake to treat social policy, even in an era of global markets, as simply a burden on capitalist economies.

Forms of capitalism

My other conclusion echoes that of Esping-Andersen (1994: 725): 'the effects of a welfare state cannot be understood in isolation from the political-institutional framework in which it is embedded.' Systems of social protection exhibit both compatibilities and incompatibilities, both positive and negative impacts on different economic outcomes. The adaptability of welfare systems to changing competitive and international contexts varies with their national contexts. The effect of social policy on competitiveness is contingent on the institutions of the nation state and its place in the global economy.

In other words, different forms of capitalism continue to coexist. As Soskice (1999: 123) writes: 'This is the remarkable feature of advanced capitalism in the 1990s: despite liberalisation of international markets, the predicted convergence to a single institutional framework form has not taken place.' This is because property, markets and firms are 'embedded' in wider social relationships. The forms of embeddedness differ across the world. The three members of the global 'Triad' – the US, Europe and Japan – diverge in many notable ways. The US is closer to the neoliberal model and Europe (outside the British Isles) to the statist-corporatist model. While the nature of British, French and German capitalism differs greatly, I conclude that there is a distinct and dominant European model of 'social capitalism' (Gough, 1997).

What is more, the particular framework of capitalism shapes the way that the systemic 'needs' of capital are perceived and formulated. Granted that capitals everywhere seek to expand profits, and granted that everywhere this requires specific state supports, this does not entail that the institutional structures and the policy patterns (the 'specific satisfiers') will converge. The ways that value and profit can be expanded are many and various. The time horizon over which enterprises calculate can vary, with implications for investment in capital and training. The range of stakeholders can vary from narrow shareholders to a broader spectrum of workers, suppliers and customers. The

European ideal of 'social capitalism' is precisely that business itself will embody broader, socially inspired interests – not as an act of altruism but because it will enable them better to pursue their own goals. To quote David Soskice (1999: 129...) again: 'In the Northern European business world, the interests of business policy-makers will normally be to promote a long-run cooperative institutional framework for companies...By contrast, this would not be in the interests of a business community run by finance people whose expertise lay in hostile takeovers.'

These different forms of capitalism lie closer to and further from our ideal procedural and material preconditions for meeting human needs. Chapter 2 reasons that other forms of capitalism are likely to provide superior frameworks for satisfying human needs. One form, corporatist capitalism, integrates market forces with two other modes of coordination – state intervention and public negotiation. Corporatist capitalism, such as that in Denmark or the Netherlands, thus has the potential to overcome market and state failures in the material realm and to foster some form of dialogic democracy in the procedural realm. The predicted outcomes are more favourable to human welfare than casino capitalism.

Does the available evidence back up these arguments? One important tool for investigating this is comparative cross-national analysis. To what extent do countries with differing degrees of regulation of private capital exhibit different levels of need-satisfaction? The developed western world, let alone the contemporary international state system, provides a rich laboratory here, and this is utilised in other chapters in this collection.

Chapter 5 provides some empirical evidence on a global scale. It analyses data for 128 countries to discern what factors account for the great disparities of human welfare across the contemporary world, using indicators of both basic and intermediate needs. The article concludes that affluence or poverty is only one of several factors explaining cross-national variations in need satisfaction: the degree of economic and political independence, the extent of democracy and human rights, the capacity and dispositions of the state, and relative gender equality all impact positively and independently on a nation's level of welfare. Theo Thomas and I conclude: 'These are encouraging findings. They suggest that social rights and levels of human welfare are best guaranteed by forms of economic development guided by an effective public authority which guarantees civil and political rights to all and is thus open to pressure by effective political mobilisation in civil society.'

Much more research has gone into comparing the countries of the OECD. In an earlier book we showed that on most measures of need satisfaction the US exhibited poorer levels than Sweden, with Britain somewhere in-between. This applies to death rates, health standards, poverty levels and economic insecurity, homicide and physical insecurity, access to health services and respect for human rights. A black child born in Washington DC has less chance of surviving to her first birthday than one born in Kingston, Jamaica (Doyal and Gough, 1991: 287–93).

Welfare regimes

Chapter 8 goes on to speculate that different welfare regimes have different impacts on both human needs and capitalist competitiveness. Esping-Andersen's celebrated concept of welfare regime refers to 'the combined, interdependent way in which welfare is produced and allocated between state, market and family' (Esping-Andersen, 1999: 34–5; 1990). These different forms of welfare provision shape both welfare and stratification outcomes. The latter in turn shape class coalitions and other political alignments which tend to reproduce or intensify the original institutional matrix. Thus 'existing institutional arrangements heavily determine, maybe even over-determine, national trajectories' (Esping-Andersen, 1999: 4). He identifies three basic types of welfare regime: the liberal (the US is an exemplar), the conservative-corporatist (e.g. Germany, Italy) and the social democratic (e.g. Sweden). The concept of welfare regime can be usefully applied to marry our analyses of welfare and capital.

Chapter 8 argues that each regime type generates a different set of problems for or threats to national competitiveness, that these generate different recommended policy solutions, but that these in turn may generate further dilemmas or contradictions. These arguments have recently been more rigorously formulated by Iversen and Wren (1998) as the 'trilemma of the service economy'. The goals of employment growth, wage equality and budgetary constraint increasingly come into conflict: all three cannot be achieved simultaneously and different welfare regimes sacrifice or achieve different combinations of outcomes.

- Liberal welfare states of the English-speaking world achieve budgetary restraint and employment growth at the cost of low wages and working poverty. The dominant welfare threat to economic performance in these countries is of inequality and its effects: instability in demand, a poor quality educational base and deteriorating social capital.

- The conservative welfare regimes of the EU 'core', on the other hand, achieve greater labour market equality, but at the costs of employment growth in the public and private sectors. The threats to economic performance here are high and rising social transfers, high social security charges and non-wage labour costs plus an extensive hidden economy, all of which further discourage employment
- The social democratic welfare regimes of Scandinavia combine low wage differentials and high participation rates at the cost of high levels of state spending on both transfers and social services. The twin threats to this regime are high rates of taxation and high non-wage labour costs threatening domestic capital supply.

Thus different welfare regimes exhibit different configurations of effects on capital and competitiveness. A problem in one may be a solution in another. Moreover, in all regimes powerful interest coalitions will resist measures to adapt their welfare systems to the competitive requirements of nations in the new globalised economy: the solutions are likely to remain path-dependent.

This provides the background for two further comparative essays in this book. Chapter 6 studies the southern member states of the European Union and asks why they fail to respect the needs of the poorest by providing an adequate, national and rights-based social safety net. Working within an historical institutionalist framework, it distinguishes social-structural factors (for example, distinct family and employment structures) and political-institutional factors (for example, clientelist politics and segmented interests). In both cases the Mediterranean countries are distinct, and both explain the absence of a national safety net. Despite pressures from the European Union for minimum social protection schemes, I conclude that a substantive safety net is unlikely to develop in southern Europe. The implication is that national history and institutions can lock nations into path-dependent forms of programme development. These may not be congruent with either the interests of capital or the needs of national citizens.

Chapter 7 ventures beyond the confines of the western world to study enterprise welfare in Russia following the collapse of the Soviet Union, democratisation and the wrenching economic restructuring in the early 1990s. Welfare benefits provided directly by enterprises to workers, families and communities were *the* distinguishing feature of social policies in the state socialist countries. They ranged from kindergartens and housing to cheap food and holiday camps. Surely such an extravagant and commercially irrational system could not survive the transition to a market economy? Based on a study of two Russian cities, Peter McMylor and I discovered a process of divestiture of social assets combined with a pattern of selective retention by some firms for a mixture of ideological and self-interested reasons. The 'horizontal' alternatives to this 'vertical system' – local authorities and NGOs – will need time, money and social trust to develop and thrive. Caught between rampant liberalisation and enfeebled civil society, all vestiges of a safety net are disappearing in Russia. Polanyi's (1957) warnings of the dangers of disembedding markets from social relations are most starkly confirmed in the cradle of the October Revolution.

Towards new strategies for welfare

None of the above lends uncritical support to existing West European-style welfare states. Many present-day social policies are irrational in both economic and social terms. Costly public pension schemes which award generous pensions to higher income groups while providing a very low floor (as for instance in Italy) cannot be justified on either social or economic grounds. Trends in contemporary labour markets, such as rising numbers of never employed, growing part-time temporary and casual work, the divergence between 'work-rich' and 'work-poor' households – these are transforming the context of work and family life at the end of the century and social policy must adapt. Some form of income top-up like the Working Familes Tax Credit, or more radical income-mix schemes, may be essential to combine social welfare with effective labour markets. But underlying these necessary reforms is the solid commitment to meet the basic needs of strangers through rights-based benefits and services.

The most holistic and best articulated alternative to existing post-war welfare states is Basic Income, and the last essay in this book reviews perhaps the most sophisticated case on its behalf yet made – by Philippe Van Parijs in *Real Freedom For All?* (1995). A Basic Income welfare state would replace all government transfers and some services with an unconditional income paid to all citizens, irrespective of present income, commitment to work or household membership. Its supporters contend that it, and only it, would adjust social policy to a world of competitive pressures, scarce jobs, wrenching social change and plural lifestyles. Van Parijs makes a strong case that Basic Income can remarry the goals of equity and efficiency and can maximise real freedom for all. Clearly, the Basic Income debate is central to the concerns of this book. Like this book it makes a case for a renewed social policy which is both moral and consequentialist. Yet, I want to argue that it is the wrong way forward.

First, Basic Income advocates, like van Parijs, see work as the antonym of leisure and see little merit in work *per se*. I, on the other hand, see participation in the core activities of social life (which include alongside caring, teaching work, learning and governing) as a defining condition of human flourishing. It is not enough to pay citizens a minimum income without enabling them to participate in socially significant activities, including paid and unpaid work. Similarly, the divorce of rights from duties in van Parijs's argument contradicts the strong link we wish to make between the two (see above). All persons who can, should have the right – and the duty – to contribute in some way to the common wealth. Beneath these differences, I argue in Chapter 9, is a contrast between a fundamentally individualist, libertarian world view and one which recognises the social bases of our individuality.

My second criticism is that Basic Income is historically and institutionally naive. It resembles neoclassical economists in recommending a 'one model suits all' solution to the myriad of new risks, problems and opportunities facing people in today's globalising world. It does not recognise the role of institutions and path dependency in shaping social policies and their welfare outcomes. The implications of the arguments so far are that different policy packages are needed to enhance human welfare in different welfare regimes. These may well include a solidaristic tax-financed national health service provided for all, inheritance taxes, low-wage subsidies for service work, extensive parental leave benefits, lifelong education vouchers, and so on. The case for a one-off universal capital grant given to all citizens on attaining adulthood should also be investigated. And indeed, the case for unconditional cash benefits to certain groups is sound. But these packages will vary according to welfare regime and form of capitalism.

Conclusions

Let me try to pull these sections together and draw some conclusions.

First, I want to maintain that common human needs provide a universal and morally compelling measure of human welfare. The argument is that all persons, whatever their goals in life and whatever the social setting of their lives, require certain objective preconditions to participate as healthy and autonomous persons. Our theory of human need also lends support to the idea that citizens should have rights to a common provision of basic need satisfiers and to a minimum level of living. The institutional guarantee of need satisfiers to strangers enables them to participate and fulfil the duties of good citizenship. It is not only that rights imply duties, as present-day communitarians stress, but that the common duties of social membership presuppose rights to the satisfaction of basic needs. However, these entitlements should be extended beyond the nation state to regional bodies and eventually the global level.

Second, capital also has interests in common, notably the drive to make profits. These 'needs' of capital are also global in extent and considerably more powerful. The drive to seek advantage in markets has transformed the world and almost every community within it, and shows no signs of letting up. Liberalisation of financial markets in the 1980s and 1990s has expanded the structural power of capital over states and citizens. This universalism, however, does not by any means coincide with our moral universalism. Indeed, there is a fundamental conflict between the needs of unregulated capital and the needs of people.

But third, well-designed welfare states can enhance the productivity and competitiveness of national capitals. In guaranteeing the satisfaction of human needs, social policies can also serve the goal of profitability. The basis for this is a broader view of what constitutes the productive forces of a society. We must move beyond simply financial and physical capital to include human, social and natural capital. This is not to argue that meeting needs always has an economic pay-off; of course it does not. And, where it does not, the moral argument for human welfare trumps the consequentialist case for appeasing capital's needs. But in many areas of life meeting needs enhances capabilities and thus economic performance, as even the World Bank now recognises.

Fourth, different national welfare regimes articulate different ways of relating the needs of capital and the needs of people. There are global competitive pressures on all governments and welfare systems, but they call forth distinct policy responses – a basic lesson of comparative research. Policy remains 'path-dependent', which is a social science way of saying 'history matters'. This perspective warns against the wholesale application of neoliberal nostrums to the European social model or the Nordic model – or the Russian model for that matter. Evidence for it is weaker than many economists make out, and many of the policies could not be transplanted anyway.

Fifth, these different patterns of economic and social policy react back onto the way that capitalists perceive their own interests. The 'needs' of capital can be served by a range of perceived interests and policy strategies (within limits). Even in a world of more and more closely integrated markets and institutions, there is no inevitable convergence towards 'casino capitalism'.

My last conclusion is implicit rather than overt. Entitlements to need satisfaction must move upwards towards supranational bodies. The welfare state in the twentieth century in practice equalled the nation-state, but this is no longer an acceptable equation. This is one area where both moral argument and material pressures are pushing towards supranational solutions. Yet the most common reaction is despair: globalisation as the enemy of human welfare. There is reason for this if globalisation remains a market phenomenon. The answer must be some form of global governance of capital.

Writing twenty years ago I argued that the welfare state is a contradictory unity. 'It simultaneously embodies tendencies to enhance social welfare, to develop the powers of individuals, to exert social control over the blind play of market forces; and tendencies to repress and control people, to adapt them to the requirements of the capitalist economy' (Gough 1979: 12). The global capitalist environment has been revolutionised, but the dilemmas remain the same. Welfare systems can serve the needs of capital, or the needs of people, or some combinations of the two. Different welfare systems and broader welfare regimes have different priorities. But so long as they remain contradictory, there is hope that capital's needs will not drown out the needs of people. There is more than one outcome to the negotiated compromise between the needs of capital and the needs of people.

Notes

1 An expanded and amended version of my Inaugural Lecture at the University of Bath, 21 January 1999. It also incorporates some material from my Introductory Lecture 'Moral and Consequentialist Arguments for the Welfare State' given at the International Conference in honour of Professor Abraham Doron at the Hebrew University, Jerusalem, 9 June 1998. Thanks to Kevin Farnsworth and Paul Wetherly for perceptive comments on the second part of this essay.

I
Capitalism and Welfare

2
Economic Institutions and the Satisfaction of Human Needs[1]

The purpose of this chapter is to evaluate different economic systems using as a criterion their ability to satisfy human needs. The conceptual basis is the theory of human need developed in Doyal and Gough (1991), summarised in Chapter 1. To assess the potential of economic systems to satisfy human needs, thus defined, I use a family of theoretical approaches from different disciplines broadly labelled 'new institutionalist' or 'new political economy'. The economic systems to be investigated are distinguished according to their dominant organising principle: the market, the state and the community. Recognising that 'pure' models of each are historically and logically impossible, I evaluate combinations of institutions that are as close as possible to the pure model: minimally regulated capitalism, state socialism and variants of communitarianism. After summarising my conclusions at that point, I then, in the next three sections, go on to consider three variants of 'mixed economy' capitalism: statist capitalism, corporatist capitalism and neoliberal capitalism. Again I evaluate each according to our criteria of need satisfaction, before drawing some general conclusions.

Since this is an extremely ambitious project, it has necessary limits that should be emphasised. First, the sole criterion according to which economic systems are compared is the optimum satisfaction of universal human needs. Second, the focus is on need satisfaction within, not between, nation-states. It excludes global linkages between nation-states. Effectively, this limits my focus to the developed world, though I believe that some of the arguments are relevant for developing nations too. Third, it is concerned only with the ability of economic systems to satisfy present levels of need satisfaction: issues of economic sustainability and intra-generational redistribution are left to one side. These are serious limitations, but they are made necessary by the scope of the investigation that remains. The chapter is necessarily broad and relies on secondary sources to buttress many of its claims.

Need-satisfaction as a measure of welfare outcomes

This chapter attempts to evaluate socioeconomic systems and institutions according to the anticipated welfare outcomes enjoyed by their citizens. Welfare outcomes are conceived in terms of the level of satisfaction of basic human needs. This approach thus differs from much contemporary research in both comparative social policy and economics. The former has sought to explain variations in 'welfare states' by analysing specific welfare inputs, such as levels of state expenditure on social security, or more recently, welfare outputs, such as the specific social policies or the 'welfare state regimes' that characterise syndromes of social policies.[2] Much economics research, on the other hand, has concerned itself with the final outcomes of policies but has traditionally defined these rather narrowly, such as, for example, rates of economic growth, monetary stability, rates of unemployment employment and productivity growth (Strümpel and Scholz 1987; cf. Putterman 1990). Freeman (1989) undertakes a much broader and more sophisticated evaluation of four 'political economies', yet he still restricts his evaluative criteria to two: growth rates and distributional equity.

Both these approaches tend to ignore the final impact of all these factors on the levels and distribution of well-being of the populations concerned (though this gap has been recognised by some such as Alber et al. 1987). The major reason for the lack of progress here is an inability to agree on concepts and measures of well-being that have cross-cultural validity. The post-war period has witnessed a growth in research that utilises concepts such as the 'level of living', 'social indicators', 'basic needs' and 'human development' and that has informed comparative evaluation of welfare outcomes in the Third World. However, this work has had little impact due in part to the changed political and economic climate of the 1980s. It has also been criticised as lacking a unifying conceptual framework (Sen, 1987) and more particularly for incorporating western cultural and political biases in the very notions of universal need and social progress (Rist, 1980; Doyal and Gough, 1991: ch. 8). Though some of these issues have been addressed in some of the philosophical literature on need, there has existed a barrier between this literature and the more applied development literature.

The absence of a theoretically grounded and operational concept of objective human need has inhibited the development of a common calculus for evaluating human welfare. On the contrary, there is a widespread scepticism that human needs exist, or a belief that all needs are relative. Typical of the first view are neoliberals, such as Hayek and Flew, together with the dominant strand in neoclassical economics. The second view, that needs exist but are relative, takes a variety of forms. For many Marxists, human needs are historically relative to capitalism; for various critics of cultural imperialism, needs are specific to, and can only be known by, members of groups defined by gender, race, and so on; for phenomenologists and some social researchers, needs are socially constructed; for postmodernist critics and 'radical democrats', needs are discursive and do not exist independently of the consciousness of human agents (Doyal and Gough, 1991: ch. 1). Clearly, if any of these perspectives are correct, then any common yardstick of welfare is unattainable and cannot be used to compare and evaluate different economic institutions and systems.

Our theory attempts to overcome these limitations. The theory is both substantive and procedural: *substantive* in defending, conceptualising and operationalising the idea of universal human needs; *procedural* in recognising the inevitable social determination of products, policies and processes that satisfy needs and thus in recognising the necessity for procedures for resolving disputes in as rational and democratic a way as possible. Our substantive theory is summarised in Chapter 1. My purpose here is to investigate *theoretically* the contribution of different social institutions to the satisfaction of these needs, which leads me on to the procedural dimension of our theory. Here, we identify universal *procedural* and *material* preconditions for enhancing need satisfaction (Doyal and Gough, 1991; chs. 7 and 11). These are attributes of social systems, and it is these with which I am principally concerned in this chapter.

Procedural preconditions relate to the ability of a group to identify needs and appropriate need satisfiers in a rational way and to prioritise need satisfiers and the need satisfactions of different groups. In the face of radical disagreements over the perceived interests and needs of different groups, how can this best be achieved? To answer this we draw upon the works of Habermas and Rawls to sketch out certain communicational and constitutional preconditions for optimising need satisfaction in practice. Habermas outlines a theory of communicational competence that emphasises the importance for the rational resolution of debates – including debates about need satisfaction, of the best available understanding and of truly democratic debate (Habermas, 1970; Roderick, 1986). With modifications to his three principles, we argue that Rawls (1972) identifies the constitutional framework that will enable citizens to engage in such debate.

In what follows, I will summarise our procedural preconditions under three headings.

P1. *Rational identification of needs.* Needs are defined, and distinguished from wants, by appealing to an externally verifiable stock of codified knowledge, for example, knowledge about nutrition, child-rearing or environmental control. The ability to tap and rationally to utilise this stock of codified knowledge – to engage in collectively identifying common human needs – is a first precondition for improving need satisfaction.

P2. *Use of practical knowledge.* At the next level, appropriate need satisfiers have to be selected. Here we argue that the codified knowledge needs to be complemented by the experientially grounded understanding of people in their everyday lives. For present purposes, we will assume that this knowledge can be tapped in one of two basic ways. First, there is participation in market relations, where these are relatively unconstrained by contingencies of power or ignorance. Second, there are various forms of political participation and 'claims-making' (Drover and Kerans, 1993) – the process whereby people collectively identify their dissatisfactions, name their felt needs and make claims against a variety of institutions.

P3. *Democratic resolution.* If a rational policy to identify and prioritise need satisfiers must draw on both codified and experientially grounded knowledge, then the inevitable disagreements that result must be confronted and resolved in a forum as open, as democratic and as free of vested interests as possible. This is the third procedural precondition by which different socioeconomic institutions will be evaluated.

Next, 'material preconditions' refer to the capacity of economic systems to produce and deliver the necessary and appropriate need satisfiers and to transform these into final need satisfactions. We argue that there is a strong moral case for codifying the intermediate needs identified earlier in the form of state-guaranteed rights. However, the *de jure* codification of social or welfare rights is no guarantee of their *de facto* delivery. To assess the latter, we develop a cross-cultural model of material production (Doyal and Gough, 1991: ch. 11) that yields four material preconditions for improved need satisfaction. These are:

M1. *Production.* The greater the total quantity and quality of need satisfiers produced, the greater the potential need satisfaction. The
efficiency by which need satisfiers are produced is thus the first of
our material preconditions.

M2. *Distribution.* Next, need satisfaction is maximised if these satisfiers
are distributed in line with the needs of individuals. This normally
entails individuals in households, though for certain collective
satisfiers the unit of consumption is different and larger.

M3. *Need transformation.* These satisfiers are then transformed into individual need satisfactions, a process that predominantly takes place
within (various sorts of) households. This, we argue, will reflect the
distribution of satisfiers within the household, in particular the
degree of equality between men, women, and children. Final levels
of need satisfaction will also be affected by the direct effect of
production processes and the quality of the natural environment
on human welfare.

M4. *Material reproduction.* The above processes take place through time,
requiring that the stock of capital goods, natural resources, and
human resources be at least maintained in order to ensure further
rounds of production and need satisfaction in the future. Though
difficult issues of sustainability are raised here, a theory of human
need must encompass material reproduction and must extend
beyond short-term horizons.

However, I have already indicated that to simplify the analysis, this
fourth material precondition is unfortunately omitted here. Thus I am
left with three procedural and three material criteria with which to
evaluate different economic systems.[3]

A theoretical framework for macro-social analysis

Different economic arrangements are to be evaluated according to these
criteria. To do this requires a set of theories and associated knowledge
with two major characteristics. First, they should be broadly applicable
to a variety of socioeconomic systems, yet be sensitive to the institutional variations between them. Second, they should bridge the central
fault-line in social science between the disciplines of economics and
sociopolitical science. I will use for this purpose a body of works that
can be grouped under the labels of 'comparative political economy' and
'the new institutionalism'. This body of work has arisen at the conflu-
ence of economics and socio-political science as a critique of the

dominant paradigms in each: rational choice theory in economics and functionalism/behaviourism in sociology (Cammack, 1989). It represents a return to the central concerns of classical political economy of Smith and his followers and to the critique of that political economy by Marx. Both were concerned with the relation between the economy and the state and with the effect of such relations on human welfare (Esping-Andersen, 1990: ch. 1; Gough, 1979: ch. 1). It also embraces the economic sociology pioneered by Weber (Holton, 1992). Let me briefly consider both strands separately.

On the one side, institutional *economics* emerged, initially in the United States with the work of Commons and Veblen, who were dissatisfied with neoclassical economics and desired to reformulate the discipline in at least three directions.[4] First, technology and preferences are no longer conceived of as exogenous. The economic environment is recognised as affecting access to information and the way that information is processed. This undermines the view that individual agents are continuously maximising or optimising in any meaningful sense since their preferences are continually adapting in the light of their experience. Therefore, second, the neoclassical assumption of equilibrium is replaced with the idea of agents learning and acting through real historical time. Economic life is characterised by structural, not just 'parametric' uncertainty, which imposes on actors a reliance on routines and habits. These durable patterns of behaviour define social institutions. The third characteristic of institutional economics is thus a recognition of the role of institutions in economic life and a rejection of essentialist arguments about 'the market'. Self-seeking action and institutional structures combine to generate a process through time characterised by long periods of continuity punctuated by rapid breaks or institutional shifts. This paradigm also directs our attention to the institutional contrasts between different economic systems.

Within *social and political science*, developments from a very different starting point have resulted in a rather similar set of propositions. In explaining state activity within capitalist societies, the dominant paradigm was some form of structuralism, whether framed by the requirements of industrial society and its economic, demographic and bureaucratic correlates, or the requirements of capitalist society for the performance of accumulation and legitimation functions. In both cases, the economy was conceptualised as isolated from social and political institutions, and the latter were accorded no sources of autonomous development.

One attempt to overcome some of these problems can be traced to central European scholars such as Polanyi (1957)[5] and Schumpeter (1976), for whom the interdependence of the market economy with the state and the community was a *sine qua non*. Another source of alternative thought has been the work of those scholars who, in the tradition of Mill and de Tocqueville, recognise the impact of democracy on state development. More recently, there has been the project of 'bringing the state back in' with its emphasis on the state as an autonomous or independent actor, with certain specific interests, that can act creatively to define problems and develop policy (Evans et al., 1985; Skocpol, 1985). All these approaches attach little weight to the role of particular classes or social agents in explaining state activity (Esping-Andersen, 1990: ch. 1). A common idea is that of institutional persistence and its corollaries. Institutions are enduring, which means that at any time any particular institution, including state structures, can be 'suboptimal' or, to use a more explicit and loaded term, 'dysfunctional' for the system as a whole (Cammack, 1989).

Another strand in the reaction to structuralist perspectives in social and political theory has identified social classes as a key political agent. Developing from social democratic theorists of the Austrian School, this strand has emerged as the class mobilisation thesis associated with various Scandinavian writers (Korpi, 1983; Esping-Andersen, 1985). Another source has been a 'contradictory' Marxist analysis that stresses the role of class conflict in shaping social and state development (Gough, 1979). Alongside and partly critical of these, a broader, more diffuse institutionalism has developed in recent years which recognises the role of other institutions, including firms, other economic organisations and bodies representing class interests. This sociological institutionalism varies according to whether or not it countenances an explicit role for structural or environmental forces alongside institutional behaviour in explaining policy developments.[6]

One prominent characteristic of all these socio-political or 'historical-structural' schools of new institutionalism is a view of institutional change as discontinuous, contested and problematic. Another is the situation of societal and state-centred variables within a more systemic framework. For example, according to Hall (1986), the major components in explaining changes in public policy are the organisation of capital, labour, the state and the political system, and the position of the nation within the international political economy. Within this field, however, institutions resist change and develop in a path-dependent manner.[7]

Taken together, these 'new institutionalist' theories mark a convergence between economic and socio-political analysis, which provides a fertile framework for a macro-social analysis of economic institutions. In particular, they enable comparisons to be made of different socioeconomic systems and different stages of development. It is this framework of institutionalist thinking that I will use to derive hypotheses concerning the impact of different economic systems on levels of need satisfaction.

A taxonomy of economic institutions

Economic debate and policy prescription today are dominated by the respective merits of markets and public planning, so much so that it is tempting to focus on free market capitalism, centrally planned economies, and various sorts of market-planning mix. However, this would neglect a third set of economic relationships currently being rediscovered in the economics literature, that can be gathered under the label 'community'. The list of writers thus distinguishing *three* fundamental forms of economic organisation is long. It includes economic historians (Polanyi, 1957: ch. 4; Boswell, 1990), political scientists (Streeck and Schmitter, 1985), sociologists (Bradach and Eccles, 1989), organisational theorists (Powell, 1990) and institutional economists (Thompson et al., 1991). Table 2.1 illustrates the key concepts identified in some of these taxonomies.

Drawing on Polanyi (1957) and Putterman (1990: ch. 1) we can substantively define the economy as the sphere of social activity in which people produce, distribute and consume the material requirements to meet their wants and needs. This generates recurring interactions among elements and agents in the system. According to all the major

Table 2.1   Taxonomies of economic systems

Author	Principle	Market	State	Community
Polanyi	Forms of integration	Market exchange	Redistribution	Reciprocity
Streeck/ Schmitter	Principles of coordination	Dispersed competition	Hierarchical control	Spontaneous solidarity
Bradach/ Eccles	Economic control mechanisms	Price	Authority	Trust
Powell	Forms of economic coordination	Markets	Hierarchy	Networks

representatives of classical political economy, including Smith and Marx, a major feature of such interaction is a division of labour, both within 'enterprises' and between them. This division of labour raises productivity, but in turn requires some mechanism or mechanisms for coordinating the actions of the numerous interacting agents. It is to this fundamental question that the three solutions identified above have emerged over the course of human history.[8]

First, I look at markets. Here private agents exchange entitlements to goods and services with each other. Where a large number of such commodity exchanges regularly take place we can identify the social institutions of a market. This form of coordination entails private rights in the use, consumption, disposition and fruits of economic resources and goods and the rights to transfer these rights, except the ownership of labour (Putterman, 1990: 59–60). The prices or terms at which these exchanges take place is determined solely by the free negotiation of the parties concerned. Thus, economic coordination is decentralised, *ex post* and unconscious.

The second form of coordination is by authoritative regulations issued in hierarchical organisations. Where these organisations are themselves coordinated by authoritative regulation backed by coercion, we may speak of a state system of coordination. Such a system normally entails state ownership of the means of production, apart from labour. Co-ordination here is thus centralised, *ex ante* and conscious.

The third ideal-type form of economic coordination is more difficult to specify. Nowhere in the modern world does it provide a general mode of economic coordination, though it exists within certain sectors such as some voluntary organisations and social movements. When 'community' is advocated as a normative model of a desirable economic system it appears in different guises. Excluding those who explicitly identify community with pre-modern, hierarchically organised, status-bound societies,[9] we are still left with a great variety of views. First, there is the idea of communism held by radical socialist thinkers such as Marx, Morris and Kropotkin (Miller, 1989). This idea has been revived in the last three decades in response partly to the belief that developments within capitalism are laying the foundations for communitarian economic relationships (in, for example, the work of Gorz (1982) and van der Veen and van Parijs (1987)). Second, at the opposite pole, there is the libertarian view of community espoused by Nozick (1974). Here membership of a community is voluntary and self-chosen. Third, there are new attempts to conceptualise a 'democratic communitarianism' drawing upon the currents of decentralised socialism, personalist Christian democracy, ideas of corporatism and civic humanism (Boswell, 1990). This strand tends to equate community in the modern world with national citizenship (Miller, 1989). The last two conceptions have been explicitly concerned to augment those of market and state, not to replace them.

However, underlying these differences are some common themes distinct from the other two modes. Economic coordination within communities is by democratic negotiation. Solidaristic sentiments of loyalty and reciprocity within social groups facilitate such consensus-building. The opposition between separatist individualism and state collectivism is overcome by a new focus on the quality of human relations. Coordination may thus be conceived as decentralised, *ex ante* and conscious.

In the next three sections I will evaluate the potential contribution of these three forms of economic coordination to the satisfaction of human needs. The intention is to try, so far as is possible, to abstract from real-world complexities by considering these three economic systems as 'ideal types'. However, this is not strictly possible. According to the 'impurity principle' any actual socioeconomic system will contain, alongside its dominant principle, at least one other economic structure based on different principles for the whole to function (Hodgson, 1984: 85–9 and 104–9). Thus, market economies must incorporate a system of authority and operate within a set of specific social relationships. A pure market society is a logical contradiction. Similarly, a centrally planned economy encounters contradictions that can only be resolved via decentralised market and civil relationships. In these two cases, then, I consider models that incorporate the minimum degree of 'impurity' or contamination by other principles, drawing on empirical and historical evidence where appropriate. The third form of economic coordination, via community networks, poses different problems since it has not existed as an even modestly self-sustaining form in the modern age. I will consider briefly conceptions of community as an overarching principle of economic coordination before again pointing out the dependence of such a principle on the other two modes of economic coordination.

Free market capitalism

The defining characteristic of a free market economy is that economic coordination is decentralised, emerges as a result of various individual actions and is not consciously controlled. Free market capitalism is used here to refer to a combination of this form of coordination and private property ownership. It is this that I will now briefly evaluate according to the societal preconditions for optimising need satisfaction sketched earlier.

Our first procedural precondition is excluded by definition. There is no collective sphere of economic decision-making. Free market capitalism is an economic system that responds to consumer wants backed by money – a system in which literally nobody makes decisions on the composition of output and its relation to human needs. Against this it can be argued that capitalism extends, to the maximum feasible extent, people's freedom to negotiate about human needs. If individuals are sufficiently well informed and have the freedom to act on that information, then it can be claimed that subjectively defined wants will closely approximate generalisable human needs.

The second procedural precondition – that the practical knowledge of people be effectively tapped in identifying improved need satisfiers – constitutes a strong claim for markets. Markets make use of the dispersed knowledge of millions of actors, and the continual process of discovery that they are free and able to make engenders the restless innovation and productivity of capitalism.

The third condition – a democratic forum within which debates over how best to meet needs can take place – is also claimed for capitalism. The conjoint development of capitalism and of certain forms of representative democracy in much of the world stems from the decentralisation of decision-making and power in market society. Furthermore, decentralised 'claims-making' is facilitated if citizens have the rights and capacities to form associations to press their own perceptions of needs and satisfiers within the political arena.

Against these claims must be set much recent analysis of unregulated markets and their political implications, which is relevant to our first procedural precondition. Wants can diverge from needs in significant ways, abetted by market society. Markets are an inefficient source of knowledge and can interfere with the communication processes necessary for human needs to be identified and agreed upon. For example, it can be in the interests of individual producers to supply distorted information if this will maximise profits and if they are able to do so. The sheer number of commodities produced in developed market societies means that consumers have inadequate knowledge of their characteristics and insufficient time to find out. Furthermore, it has been argued that unregulated market society undermines communal ties around which less individualistic conceptions of need can form. If wants are endogenous to the economic system, this undermines any simple view of the market as a response mechanism to autonomous consumer desires.[10]

Unregulated markets can also distort the nature of democratic debate within the political sphere. It is rational for actors to attempt to pursue their interests within the political sphere, resulting in democratic abuses such as clientelism and worse. On the other hand, markets offer commodified need satisfiers to those who can afford them, and that undermines their incentive to participate in political debate over alternatives. Opportunities for exit reduce voice. Last, the reliance of all existing market societies on a gendered division of labour constrains the ability of women to participate in democratic fora (Bowles and Gintis, 1986: chs. 4–5). The implication of these critiques is that either authoritative regulation or collective sentiments or both are necessary correctives to the unconstrained pursuit of individual self-interest in market settings if human needs are to be recognised and prioritised.

Turning to material preconditions, the claims of market capitalism are strong. Markets not only utilise the dispersed knowledge of millions of separate actors, but they also provide them with incentives to act on that information in such a way as to maximise efficiency at a moment of time (Hayek, 1948; Gray, 1992: ch. 2). Though the strong claims of Pareto efficiency require unrealistic assumptions, the argument that markets enhance productive or 'x-efficiency' remain. The ability of capitalism to produce goods in prodigious quantities and to innovate totally novel kinds of products is of considerable relevance in assessing its contribution to the satisfaction of human needs. However, it is not real-world capitalism that is investigated here, but a model of a minimally regulated market economy.

This model has several major weaknesses according to a long history of economic analysis. The failures of unregulated economic markets to satisfy consumer wants are so well known that I will not detail them here. They include tendencies to monopoly, the inability of markets to supply public goods, the self-defeating production of positional goods and the inefficiency, or diswelfares, caused by the tendency of markets to meet wants in commodified forms (Penz, 1986). Laissez-faire capitalism may be an efficient system for satisfying *certain* wants by means of *commodities*, but that is all. There are further limitations stemming from the untrammelled pursuit of individual self-interest. This engenders profound uncertainties, results in 'prisoners' dilemma' situations where all lose out in the absence of cooperation, and encourages opportunism and short-termism, which harm longer-term conceptions of self-interest.

Second, the distribution resulting from the operation of unregulated markets cannot, even in rich societies, offer entitlements to basic need satisfiers to all citizens (Sen, 1981). Regarding our third material pre-condition, need transformation, market society will tend to dissolve non-capitalist relations, including those between the sexes. However, recent scholarship contends that gender inequalities are perpetuated via the conjunction of paid and unpaid work and the institution of mono-gamous marriage. A market economy requires altruistic, collective beha-viour on the part of women in the household because their unpaid labour provides a flexible cushion that permits men to respond to market signals (Elson, 1988). Thus, formal equality coexists with gen-dered inequality, that in turn affects the levels and distribution of need satisfactions in society (Pateman, 1988; Bowles and Gintis, 1986: ch. 4). Furthermore, capitalism can harm those needs directly met in relations either at work or in the community. The autonomy of workers may be undermined once firms and factories become established institutions in market societies and the technical division of labour is extended (Wood, 1982). At the same time, the erosion of community bonds creates new diswelfares for which more and more commodities cannot necessarily compensate (Hirsch, 1976).

To conclude, then, a minimally regulated, free market capitalist society suffers from many drawbacks as an institutional setting within which human needs can be satisfied. On both procedural and material grounds it is found wanting. As Polanyi has argued, a strict market economy (even with the concessions to the existence of other institu-tions made here) is neither desirable nor logically possible. The implica-tion of much institutional economic analysis, as well as of political science and sociology, is that to realise their procedural and material potential market relations need complementary regulation by public authorities and by networks of more solidaristic relations in civil society – what Etzioni calls the 'social capsule' (Etzioni, 1988; cf. from different standpoints Wolfe, 1991, and Gray, 1992). It is much more interesting to investigate various forms of mixed economic systems. But before I do that I should turn to another relatively homogenous economic system – a centrally planned economy.

State socialism

Here the dominant form of economic coordination is planning by a central authoritative apparatus. Though this rules out private property ownership, it does not entail any single form of collective ownership.

However, in historical practice (except in what was Yugoslavia), *de jure* ownership of the bulk of capital and land has been vested in the central state. Again, the extent to which this economic system presupposes a specific political form of the state is disputed. However, in all real-world cases since 1917, and before the revolutionary reforms of 1989, representative democracy was denied and official communist parties exercised a pervasive and powerful role in the state apparatus. It is these forms of property ownership and state that will be assumed in what follows.[11]

State socialism, inaugurated in 1917, had as its conscious goal to replace market-determined production for profit by planned production for human needs. Of course, such a system can have, and has had, different goals, such as victory in war or crash industrialisation. Moreover, Marx and his followers drew a distinction between communism and socialism, between the terminus and a station along the way. But let us accept, for the purposes of this argument, that Marx's slogan 'To each according to his needs' is indeed the final goal of socialist society. How well is the model state socialist economy sketched above able to realise this goal?

It forms a stark contrast with the previous model of unregulated capitalism. Centralised planning to meet needs takes centre-stage, whereas citizen participation, whether as economic or political actors, is marginalised. In light of our procedural preconditions, there are benefits and disadvantages. On the one hand, codified knowledge can in theory be utilised effectively to identify needs and to marshall resources to meet them, especially in conditions of underdevelopment and scarcity. On the other hand, there are few sites where the experientially grounded knowledge of people can be utilised. They are denied a creative role in the economic sphere. They are also prevented from making claims in civil society and within the workplace. Finally the absence of civil and political rights undermines the capacity of the political process rationally and democratically to adjudicate on different ways of improving need satisfaction.

All these are clear procedural defects. What is more, the one positive feature, a planning apparatus committed to improving human welfare, has in practice severe limits. The political elite is relatively insulated from other points of view, that results in a distortion of the codified knowledge upon which planning is based. The bureaucratic planning apparatus acquires considerable power to pursue its own interests, establishing in the process what has been called a 'dictatorship over needs' (Feher et al., 1983).

As regards our material preconditions, state socialism exhibits several advantages in principle over unregulated capitalism, at least at low levels of development. The planning apparatus can prioritise the production of basic need satisfiers such as basic education, primary health care, basic foodstuffs or family planning services. Entitlements to these can be ensured via such measures as a radical redistribution of land assets, full employment policies and direct public provision of services (though regional variations in distribution are often harder to combat). Need transformation can also be enhanced via policies to educate and improve the status of women, to control births, and to provide alternative forms of child care.

Against this must be set the case that central planning encounters growing problems of coordination, and notably so as economic development proceeds. Centralised planning, even aided with the most modern computers, cannot effectively coordinate economic transactions in a modern economy where the number of different products runs into the millions. The result is that large-scale projects and homogeneous products are given priority at the expense of many essential yet disparate need satisfiers. Compartmentalisation of interests within the planning apparatus interferes with the adjudication between projects. More problematic, at the enterprise level it is extremely difficult to set targets to motivate managers and workers to produce what the plan requires. Where targets are expressed in physical terms, factories have an incentive to distort products in order to achieve target specifications. This results in shortages and poor quality, that embraces many key need satisfiers such as housing (Nove, 1983).

At the distribution level too, the commitment to work-related rewards can discriminate against those, especially women, with a more tenuous link with paid labour, while special nonmonetary benefits for the elite undermine overall equality. There is no countervailing system of distribution to that determined by the official economy (Szelenyi, 1978). Despite a formal commitment to political and economic equality for women, the structural properties of state socialism deny this in practice. Shortages and the attendant queues add to the double burden stemming from a gendered division of domestic labour. Not only does this harm the need satisfaction of women, it can interfere with the effectiveness of the need transformation process and thus the overall levels of need satisfaction.

As with market economies, analysis and evidence suggest that a relatively pure command economy is neither desirable nor feasible, according to our need-related yardstick. This is perhaps more surprising since both the intent and ideology of state socialism have proclaimed the meeting of human needs as an explicit and high-priority goal. Yet the conclusion is clear: markets and networks in civil society are necessary to overcome the deficiencies of a pure central planning model. And indeed, this is what was found in all state socialist societies between 1917 and 1989, albeit it in distorted forms. All exhibited, alongside the official economy, what Markus (1981) calls 'second' and 'third' economies. The second economy was comprised of self-employed and private production units together with 'moonlighting' and other unlawful enterprises. The third economy embraced the system of 'tolkachi' – networks of informal relations between and within the bureaucracy and state enterprises formed to overcome the mutual problems that they faced.

Community, communitarianism, communism

If community as a generalised system harks back to a mythical past, communism reaches forward to a utopian future. As developed by the utopian socialists and even their critic, Marx, it is a society of absences: without markets and money, without state, without hierarchical, horizontal and sexual divisions of labour, without inequality and scarcity. The tension between individual self-interest and collective interest is overcome through the transformation of social relations and human identity. For many critics, this vision is not logically realisable: it is 'evasive, confused and problematic' (Soper, 1981: ch. 9). In particular, it overlooks the constraints stemming from human psychology, human biology and the limits to the biosphere. Yet the last two decades have witnessed a renewed interest in communitarian alternatives, partly in response to a view that technology and other trends make possible a post-industrial society of one form or another. These take on board some of the above critiques, but hold on to some of the basic tenets of a communitarian position: principles of spontaneous solidarity, relations of reciprocity and small-scale communities with participatory democracy. An example is Gorz's (1982) vision of a dual society, which combines a 'heteronomous' domain of work and authority alongside an autonomous domain of self-determined activity, where the latter is dominant.

In terms of our procedural preconditions, such a model has one major advantage. It permits what Miller calls 'dialogic democracy', a form of negotiation in which genuine learning takes place including learning about basic needs and how to meet them. People's experiential knowledge can be tapped, but sectional interests can be negotiated in a forum that would encourage the reaching of a democratic and rational consensus (Miller, 1989: ch. 9; Doyal and Gough, 1991: ch. 7). Moreover, such democratic negotiation would extend beyond the formal political arena to embrace work relations and certain other relations within society.

It is likely that such an arrangement would also permit the utilisation of both codified and experiential knowledge in the domain of production. The deficiencies of markets and state planning can be mollified if networks and negotiation generate alternative sources of information and motivation. This is more probable if they are based on relations of trust, reciprocity and moral obligation (Boswell, 1990: ch. 2). Such a moral solidaristic community could prioritise the production of need satisfiers, distribute them according to urgency of need, and re-order interpersonal relations to develop gender equality and more effective need transformation. In this way, collective needs can be asserted over individual wants as the dominant goal of a communitarian economy.

Against this must be set several fundamental problems. First, if such communities are 'all-embracing' like medieval monasteries, they risk coercing their members into agreement about the ends of life and the goals that individuals ought to value and pursue. Individuals are 'engulfed' by the community – in other words, one of their basic needs, autonomy, is severely restricted (Plant et al., 1980, ch. 10; Miller, 1989: ch. 9).This can be overcome if membership of communities is voluntary, as Nozick (1974) recommends. But then another problem is faced: some individuals – 'misfits' and outsiders – would not be accepted by any community. Excluded from the only social systems that offer participation and sustenance, it is almost certain that their need satisfaction would be threatened. A more general procedural problem arises because solidaristic communities create distinctions between insiders and outsiders, which inhibits the fostering of universalisable interests and thus the identification of true human needs. To overcome this requires some higher level of authority that is separate from and superordinate to the separate communities.

In terms of our material preconditions, communitarianism appears at first sight superior to the other two alternatives. But again, this is to simplify the relations of modern economies (or implies turning one's back on the whole process of modernisation and the progress in meeting needs that this has sustained). Most communitarian solutions pay insufficient attention to the problem of coordination. For Gorz, local exchange of the products of small-scale enterprise would be via the medium of 'labour-time vouchers'. But as Nove (1983) has argued, either this requires very small-scale production, in which many of the productive advantages of contemporary capitalism are lost, or the value of the vouchers would need to fluctuate according to supply and demand, in which case they would be indistinguishable from money. Intercommunity relations on a broader scale are still more intractable.[12] Moreover, communitarian advocates like Gorz tend to evince a romantic view of unpaid, communal and household labour, ignoring much recent feminist scholarship and its argument that 'community is fundamentally a gendered concept' (Finch, 1984: 12).

For these and other reasons not adequately covered here, 'communities', even democratic and need-prioritising ones, cannot by themselves mobilise the resources necessary to optimise the need satisfaction of their members. I have spent a short time on this third set of economic institutions to disabuse any lingering belief that 'community', 'reciprocity', 'networking' or 'negotiation' can by themselves provide a third alternative to economic organisation and a surer way to meet human needs. It also sets the scene for an integration of community with market and state, as proposed by some recent writers.

Summary so far

Table 2.2 summarises the pros and cons of the three 'pure' or paradigmatic systems of economic coordination as frameworks for the optimisation of need satisfaction. We may summarise their deficiencies another way by returning to the ideas of need that they each embody. Free market capitalism essentially equates needs with wants, an equation that is logically flawed and morally untenable (Doyal and Gough, 1991: chs. 2 and 6). State socialism by contrast operates with an idea of universal and objective need but equates this with the views of the party and state functionaries. Need is identified with one particular form of codified knowledge, which reflects constellations of power incompatible with the pursuit of truth. Communitarian models interpret need as those interests defined by particular cultural groups or communities. They thus make relative the idea of universal human need and denude it of an evaluative or moral role. None of the three systems embodies a notion of human need that is universal and objective, yet open-ended and cumulative.

I now turn to see how far this ideal can be realised within various forms of mixed or 'impure' economic systems. I focus here solely on mixed *capitalist* systems, that is, where markets have a dominant role in

Table 2.2 Evaluation of three 'pure' economic systems

Criterion	Market: unregulated capitalism	State: state socialism	Community: communism
P1. Rational identification of needs	Absent. Unregulated markets weaken 'social capsule'/ collective ethic	Prioritisation of, but dictatorship over, needs	Rational use of codified knowledge but incorporation of individuals
P2. Use of practical knowledge	Markets tap but distort dispersed knowledge	Absent and discouraged	Rational use of dispersed knowledge within, but not between, communities
P3. Democratic resolution	Representative democracy weakened by market exit and inequality	Certain social rights but absence of civil and political rights	Widespread dialogic democracy but absence of codified rights
M1. Production of need satisfiers	Efficiency in commodity production but market failures and absence of non-commodity forms	Prioritisation of need satisfiers but information and motivation failures	Prioritisation of need satisfiers but coordination problems between communities
M2. Distribution according to need	No entitlements to need satisfiers	Entitlements distorted by abuse and labour market links	Entitlements to need satisfiers within, not between, communities
M3. Effective need-transform-ation	Potential for autonomous learning harmed by inequality in work and unpaid household labour	Autonomous learning restricted at work, in consumption, and via unpaid household labour	Greater free time plus autonomous domain but gendered/ household inequalities?

economic coordination and where private ownership of the means of production is the dominant form of property ownership. According to the tripartite model developed above, this generates two fundamental forms of capitalist mixed economy. The first is *statist* capitalism, where market coordination is accompanied by a substantial degree of state steering of the economy. The second is *corporatist* capitalism where the market is accompanied by coordination via networks of negotiation between key economic actors. Where both of these are absent, or weakly developed, or deliberately undermined we may identify a third variant: *neoliberal* capitalism.

I now look at each of these in turn. Though we are here moving from 'as pure as possible' economic systems to 'impure' or mixed systems, I continue to abstract from the complexities of the real world and to analyse models of idealised mixed systems. A real-world economy, such as Germany's, will in practice exhibit features drawn from all these in a bewildering array.

Statist capitalism

Statist capitalism may be interpreted as a return to seventeenth- and eighteenth-century mercantilism. But it can claim at least three intellectual and historical sources since the emergence of industrial capitalism in Britain in the later eighteenth century. First, and most important, is the continental European perspective of statism associated with the writings of Weber, Hintze, List and Wagner, among others (Skocpol, 1985). This stresses the existence of 'states' (as distinct from 'governments') that develop extensive capacities and a wide range of roles. These states engage in relations with other states, promote economic development deemed essential for the competitiveness of second-order industrialising countries, and develop social policies to enhance social integration. This case for statist capitalism is essentially integrative and developmental. Second is the 'socialised liberalism' of Anglo-Saxon thought, beginning with J. S. Mill and continuing in the writings of other 'reluctant collectivists' such as Keynes and Beveridge. Here the case for state intervention may be typified as pragmatic and reactive. Third is the strategy of welfare statism developed by Fabian social thought and social democratic politics in the twentieth century. Here the state's role is proactive and egalitarian. These three strands – conservative, liberal and socialist – have thus generated different conceptions of the economic and social role of the state. There has been no single route to statist capitalism.

To help define the concept of statist capitalism further, we need to consider in more detail the distinctive roles of the state in economic and social intervention. These can be classified in various ways. According to Putterman (1990: ch. 2.5), capitalism can be modified by means of four types of intervention. First and, he argues, least contradictory to the essence of capitalism, is to correct for market failures such as monopoly, externalities and the inability to provide public goods. Second is to modify the distributive results of market mechanisms combined with private ownership via an assortment of redistributive policies. Third, there is a set of reactive macroeconomic interventions intended to correct for systemic market failures in the factor markets for capital and labour, of which Keynsianism is the best-known example. This third form indicates that the market cannot be self-regulating in important areas of activity. Fourth, there are proactive interventions to steer the economy in a desired direction. These last, including indicative planning and specific industrial policies, attempt to provide direction to economic activities at the industry or enterprise level. I will define statist capitalism, as an ideal type, as a system where all four levels of state intervention are practised.[13]

Let us now evaluate statist capitalism according to our procedural and material preconditions for optimising welfare. In theory, it can overcome the deficits of laissez-faire capitalism. In terms of our procedural preconditions, collective interests can be defined in a non-utilitarian way and asserted over powerful sectional interests. State planning can provide the means to prioritise certain basic needs as goals of policy and can act to modify or steer the market where it prevents their achievement. Democratic, educational and administrative processes can supplement, or where necessary override, self-interested action in the market to impose universal, need-oriented values over the pursuit of private wants and sectional interests.

In the material domain, market failures can be compensated or regulated to improve the composition of output in a welfare-oriented direction. Thus, monopoly and externalities can be taxed or regulated by public authority. At the same time, the strengths of markets as mechanisms for identifying need satisfiers, notably those that take the form of commodities and are congruent with wants, are retained. At the distribution stage, the lack of entitlements of the poor and the maldistribution of resources according to need can be corrected by using the familiar instruments of the welfare state. These can include not only taxation, social security benefits and public services, but also wage and price, and training policies designed to alter the distribution of primary incomes. Last, the effectiveness of the need transformation process can be improved in at least two directions. Equal opportunities legislation, public support for child care and other family-support policies can diminish gender inequalities, while employment programmes of various kinds can reduce unemployment and thus directly enhance economic participation with benefits for individual autonomy.

These potential benefits of a 'mixed economy welfare state' have come under attack in recent years from proponents of the New Right, who contend that government failure is always and everywhere both more likely and more pernicious than market failure. In practice, they contend, none of our procedural preconditions is met in a mixed economy, even if they were desirable. State intervention is not rational because it cannot concentrate the dispersed knowledge of actors in a single body; to imagine otherwise is to suffer a 'synoptic delusion'. Nor is such intervention universal in intent, since governments are susceptible to numerous pressures from organised interest groups seeking to advance their own interests and these pressures are self-reinforcing. At the same time, state action weakens the effectiveness of markets and thus their ability to identify those needs that are congruent with wants. State intervention also generates inefficiency and 'sclerosis' in production to meet needs, both directly within the public sphere and indirectly by harming the efficiency of the private sector in a variety of ways. Thus, democratically managed capitalism negates its own goals and undermines the material basis for satisfying its citizens' needs.

Many of these criticisms have in turn been criticised by writers within the institutionalist school. The public choice models of Downs, Olson and others do not in fact predict human behaviour very well. People often act unselfishly or in 'unproductive' ways by voting in elections, by not cheating when nobody is looking, and so on. Furthermore, these neoliberal critics adumbrate an essentialist view of the market and the state. Neither is situated in relation to the other, or in the context of the moral and social order of which it is a part.[14]

Nevertheless, a new institutionalist analysis would recognise certain elements of truth in the neoliberal critique and add some more defects of its own. An interventionist state entails a danger of clientelist politics, wherein special interest groups can lobby or 'capture' state agencies to pursue their specific interests. This danger is especially pronounced when state intervention expands from the first to the fourth of the categories above – from parametric regulation to enterprise-specific regulation. Rather than the state representing the public interest and imposing generalisable goals over sectional interests, sectional interests may extend the pursuit of their goals through political as well as market means (Skocpol, 1985; Rueschemeyer and Evans, 1985). By definition, this will impede the identification of universal needs. At the same time state, intervention may lack legitimacy and stability. Neither bureaucratic nor technocratic rationality is adequate once state intervention shifts from allocative to productive activity (Offe, 1975; Mayntz, 1983).

Turning from procedural to material preconditions for improved need satisfaction, statist capitalism is still vulnerable, although it exhibits several advances over minimally regulated capitalism. States may lack either the willingness or the capacity to intervene in the appropriate ways (or both). The former requires a minimum degree of autonomy from dominant forces in civil society, thus making it vulnerable to the problems discussed above. It also requires bureaucratic capacities, including material resources, a bureaucratic *esprit de corps* and access to relevant expertise, which are not always forthcoming. Moreover, where they are forthcoming, they may well generate further limits. The limits of bureaucratic state regulation are by now well rehearsed. The lack of detailed, 'thick' information, or experiential knowledge, leads to the formal application of rules which can generate inefficiencies (Rueschemeyer and Evans, 1985). Where the state is directly delivering need satisfiers in the form of public services, this can lead to the abuse of clients and the provision of inappropriate satisfiers (Doyal and Gough, 1991: ch. 14). Together these procedural and material defects can generate an authoritarian, corrupt and (what is referred to in Brazil and elsewhere as) an 'anti-welfare state', which acts to protect the interests of powerful groups at the expense of the needs of the mass of the people.

At best, a proactive state is no more than a means for the achievement of a needs-oriented policy: it may be a necessary condition, but it cannot be sufficient. Statist capitalism may be more conducive to meeting human needs than unregulated capitalism, but the answer is indeterminate in the absence of further information on the direction and nature of state policy. To answer this we must turn to the nature of civil society and the case for a third mode of economic coordination.

Corporatist capitalism

Institutionalist economics argues that successful market relations need to be 'embedded' within not only a system of public authority, but also a network of relations in civil society. Market transactions in conditions of uncertainty require a degree of trust between the parties that they will behave according to the agreement (Bardach and Eccles, 1991). On this basis, networks of relationships that sustain trust are featured as a third form of economic coordination. In contrast to market or hierarchy, these coordinate through less formal, more cooperative and negotiated means. These in turn enhance a longer-term perspective and a broadened conception of self-interest, which help reproduce the networks over time.[15]

The other major contributor to a renewed interest in such a 'third way' has been the emergence of democratic 'corporatism' notably in

Western Europe in the 1960s and 1970s, which has been theorised by Schmitter, Lehmbruch, Streeck and others (see Williamson, 1989 for a survey). There are two basic components: first, the centralised organisation and representation of major interest groups in society, and their mutual bargaining, and second, the regular incorporation of these groups into the policy-making process via bargaining with the state and political parties (sometimes called 'concertion'). Katzenstein (1985: 32) adds a third feature of democratic corporatism: an ideology of social partnership that integrates differing conceptions of group interest with vague but firmly held notions of the public interest.

This third form of economy has been conceptualised as a distinct 'associative' logic of social order by Streeck and Schmitter (1985) and as a 'democratic communitarian' third way by Boswell (1990). Both recognise various historical antecedents, including Durkheim's writings on solidarity and corporations, personalist Christian democratic thought, the doctrines of the Roman Catholic Church (in particular the papal encyclicals of 1891 and 1931), and the associationalism of Saint Simon and early socialists. Boswell has done most to theorise this third way as a derivative of communitarian thought. Rejecting all-inclusive communities, for reasons similar to those advanced above, he argues in favour of fostering 'fraternity' and participation in larger groups. He claims that the nation-state is still the prime site of such community identification today (Boswell, 1990: ch. 3). This is close to Miller's (1989: ch. 9) argument that nations are the only possible form in which an overall community can be realised in modern societies, so long as this community is sited within a political organisation of citizenship.

Economic forms of such a national community can be fostered in various ways, including corporate public responsiveness and collaborative industrial relations. In all these examples, 'external colloquy' is the crucial element that prevents organisations from pursuing their own narrow goals and from defying the public interest. Perhaps the most notable modern-day example of this 'public cooperation' is corporatist participation in certain European countries. This parallels Streeck and Schmitter's (1985) characterisation of 'associationalism' as a distinct model of social order in the modern world.[16] Here collective actors of functionally defined interest associations are constrained and enabled to relate and negotiate with each other. 'The central principle is that of concertation, or negotiation within and among a fixed set of interest organisations that mutually recognise each other's status and entitlements and are capable of reaching and implementing relatively stable compromises (pacts) in the pursuit of their interests' (Streeck and Schmitter, 1985: 10).

To explain the emergence and persistence of these structures of 'public cooperation' or 'responsible associative governance', two distinct approaches have typically been adopted drawing on Durkheim and Marx respectively. The first looks for features in the social structure that enhance solidarity, such as the continuity of organisations, their numbers in relation to the size of the nation, the background proximities between decision-makers and the salience of communitarian beliefs (Boswell, 1990: chs. 5–9). The second, however, explains them in terms of class structure, power and conflict. Workers have an incentive to unite and pursue collective action to overcome their individual powerlessness in the labour market. The two dominant power resources that they can construct are trade unions and class-based political parties. According to Przeworski (1986), it would be rational for a workers' movement, under plausible assumptions about the behaviour of capitalists and workers, to pursue a strategy of accommodation with capital. Thus corporatism is another label, and a confusing one, for societal interclass conflict and bargaining (Korpi, 1983; Esping-Andersen, 1985, 1990).

On the basis of this second perspective, Katzenstein (1985: ch. 3) distinguishes two fundamental forms: *liberal corporatism* and *social corporatism*. The former is found where powerful and centrally organised business communities confront relatively decentralised and weak labour movements. The latter is found where there exist strong, centralised and politically powerful labour unions, with or without an equivalent business community.[17] The work of Esping-Andersen (1990) suggests that liberal corporatism is often combined with the influence of Christian democratic ideology, whereas social corporatism is the associate of social democratic ideology. Thus, the two explanations may be combined to explain in different ways the persistence of two distinct forms of corporatism, concertation and public cooperation. Both, however, envisage corporatist arrangements as a complement to the role of market and state. Most analyses also assume a substantial proactive role for the state. Assocationalism is thus, in practice, combined with statism to form a hybrid third form of capitalism.

What, then, are the pros and cons of corporatist capitalism as a procedural and material framework for the improvement and optimisation of need satisfactions? At a procedural level corporatist capitalism offers several advantages. By encouraging reciprocity, shared norms and trust, it nourishes a rational yet democratic process of identifying collective interests and thus, potentially, universal human needs. By retaining the informational mechanisms of the market it enables practical knowledge to be tapped. Yet by fostering dialogic democracy, it discourages a short-term view of economic self-interest and the incentive for those with money to exit while enhancing the mechanisms of voice. Furthermore, Offe and Wiesenthal (1980) argue that in the process of class struggle and bargaining workers' organisations can only achieve their interests by partially redefining them. This 'dual logic of collective action' means that the labour movement interprets material well-being broadly, moving beyond sectional economic interests toward something approaching a conception of broader human needs. This suggests that institutions of social corporatism will tend to pursue need-related goals to a greater extent than those of liberal corporatism.

Against this must be set several risks. In the absence of a universal framework for public cooperation, corporatist practices can degenerate into cartels, particularism and clientelism. Both a relatively autonomous state and a shared normative framework are necessary to counteract these threats. Bargaining between organised groups by definition excludes unorganised groups, that are likely to comprise those whose needs are most clearly ignored and whose 'claims-making' needs to be most encouraged. This also contributes to an imbalance of power, which undermines the effectiveness of democratic practices. It is probable, however, that social corporatism promises a more inclusive and equal system of interest representation than liberal corporatism and is therefore less open to these criticisms. Lastly, the national basis of associationalism today threatens to exclude outsiders, such as migrant workers, from the benefits of citizenship and participation.[18]

Our material preconditions for need satisfaction are more likely to be met in several respects than under the previous economic systems considered here. By supplementing market and state mechanisms with networks of interest intermediation, corporatism offers several gains in the production of need satisfiers. Information passed through networks is 'thicker' than information obtained in the market and 'freer' than that communicated in a hierarchy (Kaneko and Imai, as quoted in Powell, 1991; cf. Elson, 1988). Longer-term perspectives will also foster the production of more efficient services and programmes to meet needs. According to Streeck and Schmitter (1985), 'private interest government' more effectively combines policy formation with policy implementation and thus enhances the delivery of specific need satisfiers.[19]

As regards distribution, democratic communitarianism is likely to prioritise policies to eliminate poverty, defined as a degree of deprivation that seriously impairs participation in one's society (Boswell, 1990: ch. 3). In so far as this is so it will aid the distribution of satisfiers according to need. Social corporatism is likely to go further and add a more radical redistribution to its agenda. The emphasis on worker participation is likely to promote the pursuit of need-related policies within the production process. However, the impact of corporatist capitalism on the need transformation process is at best neutral or indeterminate. In so far as it prioritises production-based interest groups, it could act to marginalise women and the household sphere. The historic influence of Catholicism in European variants of liberal corporatism has imparted a bias against gender-equality policies that is absent in social corporatism.

Neoliberal capitalism

The 1980s have witnessed a reaction against *both* statist and corporatist capitalism on the part of those arguing for a restoration of minimally regulated capitalism. This combines elements of liberal and conservative thought in a novel combination, dubbed 'the free economy and the strong state' by Gamble (1988). This New Right programme is of course associated with the Thatcher and Reagan administrations in the United Kingdom and the United States. In many Third World countries, it has been imposed from the outside via IMF-led structural adjustment programmes.

I will deal with this third form of contemporary capitalism briefly, since it seeks to re-establish a system of minimally regulated capitalism that has already been surveyed. However, it does introduce a new element: the paradoxical development of the powers of the state in order to 'roll back the state'. This stems in particular from the argument of public choice theory, that interest group, bureaucratic and electoral pressures generate a continually expanding but inefficient set of state interventions in the economy and society. Thus, the modern democratic state subverts the freedom of the market order (Dunleavy and O'Leary, 1987: ch. 3). To overcome this requires a strategy to reduce the powers of both the state apparatus and organisations in civil society. Thus, two characteristic policies flow from this: on the one hand, deregulation, privatisation and tax cuts, and on the other, a restatement of the rule of law and a reduction of the powers of trade unions and other institutions that lie between the state and the individual (Gamble, 1988: ch. 2).

It is likely that such a combination of policies will prove to be harmful to our procedural and material preconditions for need satisfaction. The advantages and deficiencies of minimally regulated capitalism have already been rehearsed. To the negative overall balance must here be added, however, the deliberate use of state power, not to further collect-ive, generalisable goals, but to buttress the pursuit of individual interests and the market order. Furthermore, state power is also used to disperse the networks of corporatist negotiation that might form the alternative basis for the emergence of generalisable interests. Bereft of the counter-vailing power of public authority and of networks of public cooperation, we would predict that this form of capitalism will serve less well as a societal framework for improving human need satisfaction than cor-poratist capitalism and many forms of statist capitalism.

Conclusion

Table 2.3 summarises the pros and cons of the three mixed forms of capitalism. Neoliberal capitalism, I predict, would be no more conducive to human flourishing than minimally regulated capitalism. Indeed, its defining feature according to Gamble (1988) – a combination of 'free market and strong state' – promises a poorer performance. It is bereft of both the countervailing power of public authority and the networks of public cooperation. This form of capitalism has a poor chance of realis-ing the procedural and material framework for improving human need satisfaction identified earlier.

The potential impact of statist capitalism on human well-being is, I conclude, indeterminate. While it has a potential to correct for the tunnel vision and market failures of minimally regulated capitalism, it also contains a potential for authoritarian, clientelist and bureaucratic features that distort both procedural and material effectiveness. At best, a proactive state is no more than a means for the achievement of a needs-oriented policy: it may be a necessary condition, but it cannot be sufficient. Statist capitalism may be more conducive to meeting human needs than unregulated capitalism, but the answer is indeterm-inate in the absence of further information on the direction and nature of state policy.

In principle, corporatist capitalism permits the dominant market mechanism to be regulated by both public action and social constraints collectively negotiated by key economic actors. Thus, it has the poten-tial to overcome market and state failures in the material realm and to foster some form of dialogic democracy in the procedural realm. Against this must be set the danger that unorganised groups will remain excluded from the corporatist decision-making bodies, and thus that their needs will be overlooked or overridden. Though this danger is

Table 2.3   Evaluation of three mixed economic systems

Criterion	Statist capitalism	Corporate capitalism	Neoliberal capitalism
P1. Rational identification of needs	Identification of certain collective interests but elite domination	Social capsule and collective ethic favour identification of needs	Absent. Both market and state weaken 'social capsule'/ collective ethic
P2. Use of practical knowledge	Indeterminate potential to improve market effectiveness	Potential to combine market and network knowledge but exclusion of unorganised	Market-based knowledge fostered; claimsmaking discouraged
P3. Democratic resolution	Wider domain of public sphere but bureaucratism/ clientelism	Nurtures dialogic democracy but exclusion of unorganised	Market and state used to restrict democratic public sphere
M1. Production of need satisfiers	Potential to overcome market failures but bureaucratic failures	Potential to overcome market and bureaucratic failures	Efficiency in commodity production but market failures and absence of non-commodity forms
M2. Distribution according to need	Indeterminate potential to redistribute according to need	Social entitlements to basic need satisfiers likely	No social entitlements to need satisfiers
M3. Effective need-transformation	Indeterminate potential to improve labour and gender inequality	Social corporatism: potential to improve labour/ gender inequality	Market and gender inequalities in labour and household

greater under liberal corporatism, it is still present under social corporatism, particularly for groups identified according to extra-economic criteria such as women and ethnic groups.

To arrive at some definitive ranking of these different sets of economic institutions is not possible in the absence of explicit trade-offs between our six preconditions. While we argue that Rawls (1972) and the work of some of his followers, such as Pogge (1989), provide some important signposts to help in answering this question, we do not pretend to advance a comprehensive solution (Doyal and Gough, 1991: chs. 7 and 11). My own view is that the weight of argument emanating from institutional or political economy theory favours corporatist capitalism on both procedural and material grounds, and within this category it favours social over liberal corporatism. Neoliberal capitalism appears to offer the poorest framework for optimally satisfying universal human needs, while statist capitalism is indeterminate.

Let me conclude by noting the two ways in which this analysis could be advanced. One is normative and entails enquiring whether feasible alternative socioeconomic arrangements could perform better than social corporatist capitalism in meeting human needs. It is important to repeat here that only mixed *capitalist* systems are considered here. The claims of market socialism or the economics of partnership, for example, are not investigated.[20] The second route is empirical. It entails constructing operational indicators of these idealised economic systems that can be applied to real-world national economies. These can then be correlated with the historical record of substantive need satisfaction of different nation-states. In this way, the conclusions reached in this paper can hopefully be tested against real-world evidence (see Chapter 5).

Notes

1   First published in *The Journal of Economic Issues* 28(1), 1994, pp. 25–66. Reprinted from the *Journal of Economic Issues* by special permission of the copyright holder, the Association for Evolutionary Economics.
2   For a survey of research on the former, see Wilensky et al. (1987). For a critique and the case for a focus on policy outputs, see Alber et al. (1987) and the work of Esping-Andersen (1990).
3   For the moment, too, we leave open the question of whether all six of these societal preconditions are compatible, or whether there are conflicts between any of them.
4   See Hodgson (1988) and Etzioni (1988). The labels are confusing here. 'The new institutionalism' usually refers to modifications of neoclassical economics, which take into account such factors as the dynamic nature of all economic life as an adjustment to uncertainty (Hayek, 1948, and the Austrian School) or the problems stemming from information and transaction costs and the incentives these give for the establishment of durable economic institutions (Coase, 1937, 1960; Williamson, 1985). These all, however, retain a commitment to rational, maximising individuals as the basic units of analysis, a feature explicitly rejected by the American institutionalist school of Commons, Veblen and others described in Mayhew (1987).
5   However, Polanyi can be criticised for failing to 'embed' the concept of the market itself within social relations and for thus retaining an essentialist idea of markets. See Lie (1991).
6   Examples include Katzenstein (1985), Hall (1986), and Weir et al. (1988). For a general analysis, see March and Olsen (1984).

7   As Cammack (1989) notes, this second strand is close to an 'integrated Marxist account' that combines class organisations and a relatively autonomous state acting within a field or general logic of international capitalism. Nor does the first strand necessarily entail the second, or vice versa. Yet, as Cammack points out, some notion of systemic prerequisites, or 'environmental incentives', is necessary if one is to assess the extent to which institutions are functional or dysfunctional. For this reason, and because the two are so often intertwined, I will take the two strands together as constituting the structural-historical strand of new institutionalism.

8   For a related but different taxonomy, see Sjöstrand (1992). As I will argue below, no real-world economy or mode of production relies solely on only one of these mechanisms; and this applies also to most real-world institutions such as the family.

9   As do Streeck and Schmitter (1985). As a result of this identification they posit a fourth 'associative' model of social order distinct from that of 'community'. However, I will argue below, following Boswell (1990), that their associational order can be considered as a subset of a broadly communitarian mode of economic coordination.

10   This paragraph draws in particular on Hodgson (1988: chs. 7–9), Penz (1986), Liess (1976), Hirsch (1976) and the essays in Ellis and Kumar (1983), notably those by Crouch, Ellis and Heath, and Kumar.

11   This section draws on Westoby (1983), Nove (1983), Feher et al. (1983), Nove and Nuti (1972), Kornai (1980), and Hodgson (1984: ch. 11).

12   One person to address these issues is Devine (1988), who proposes a comprehensive system of interest representation at national, regional, industry and enterprise levels, coupled with an institutionalised form of 'negotiated coordination' to determine all investments and capacity changes in production units. He also specifies the roles of a democratic state in regulating the economic system. However, if this system is designed to *supplant* market-determined prices in many parts of the economic system, it is extremely likely that familiar problems of interest group behaviour would be encountered. For example, the demands such a committee system would make on citizens' time would encourage many, especially the least organised, to opt out. If it is advocated as a third form of coordination to *supplement* state and market relations, then it has much to offer in developing a mixed form of economic system discussed below.

13   On this basis, Katzenstein (1985: 20) regards Japan and France as exemplars of statist capitalism in the developed capitalist world, though his conclusion is dependent on the existence of the third category of corporatist capitalism discussed below. See also Shonfield (1965: chs. 5 and 7) on France.

14   At times, this generates a marked inconsistency between the analysis of interest group formation and the requirement for restraint and virtue in the public sphere, an inconsistency that Hayek overcomes by advocating traditional values and a 'strong state' to restrain the rationalist pursuit of self-interest. This recognises and reinstates the interdependence of markets on state and community, but in a way that threatens our third procedural precondition.

15   Complementarity, accommodation and reciprocity are said to characterise successful network relations in economic production such as those in Japan.

See readings in Thompson et al. (1991) and Hodgson (1988). It is interesting that the genesis of reciprocity is explained in two different ways, corresponding to the division between economic and sociological/anthropological paradigms discussed above. On the one hand, game theory shows how cooperative behaviour can enhance individual interest-satisfaction. On the other hand, anthropologists emphasise the normative standards and obligations that sustain exchange relations. The centrality of cooperation and networks is agreed, but for very different reasons (Powell, 1991).

16   Streeck and Schmitter (1985) are explicit that associations signal a fourth order of economic coordination distinct from market, state and community. However, elsewhere they see them as a series of pragmatic adjustments within capitalist society (1985: 23), with historical antecedents in late medieval cities (1985: 10). They also share several features in common with the community order, for example, a logic of interdependence between actors, compared with one of independence in markets and dependence in hierarchies (1985: 11) and a central role for negotiation between roughly equal entities – the difference being that the entities are organisations rather than individuals. For these reasons, and in the light of Bowell's (1990) arguments, I consider that they are better conceived of as modern forms of community order within mixed capitalist economies.

17   Kohli (1987) argues that the balance of class forces also explains differences in the alleviation of poverty between three states in India, considering that the Communist regime in West Bengal acted like a third world social-democratic government. Penz (1993) considers that this, along with similar historical examples of class conflict, invalidates the 'consensual' perspective developed here. However, the fact that inter-group bargaining develops out of protracted class struggle does not undermine the fact that a new mechanism of coordination has evolved. Moreover, as in the rest of this chapter, my arguments on social corporatism do not translate directly and without mediation to real economies in the real world.

18   For an interesting debate on some of these issues, see the paper by Cohen and Rogers (1992) and replies to it in a special issue of *Politics and Society.*

19   More recently, Streeck and Schmitter (1991) have argued that the age of national corporatism ended in the 1980s in the face of shifts in the global economy, the demise of national sovereignty, and the decay of traditional interest associations. For indirect evidence that corporatist national policy regimes continue to persist, see Pfaller, Gough and Therborn (1991). More strongly, it is contended that corporatism is a national form without any international equivalent in the advanced capitalist world let alone the Third World. In the introduction to this paper I note that I cannot tackle these international issues here though they are undoubtedly of profound importance for the viability of the negotiated coordination model. The answers to these points do not undermine the case for corporatist capitalism as a framework for satisfying human needs but they do raise questions about its feasibility.

20   These issues are well explored in Elster and Moene (1989) and Meade (1989).

3
The Fiscal Crisis of the State: The Contribution of James O'Connor[1]

The Fiscal Crisis of the State by James O'Connor was published in 1973. Yet the book has a direct relevance for understanding social policy today. By 1993 the British budget deficit had reached £50 billion, or about £1000 government borrowing for each person in Britain. Substantial tax increases and spending cuts were announced to help bridge this fiscal gap. Understanding the fiscal crisis of the state remains of first-rank importance to all students of social policy.[2]

The Fiscal Crisis and welfare capitalism

The Fiscal Crisis of the State contends that the modern capitalist state tries to fulfil two, often contradictory, functions: to aid capital accumulation and to buttress the legitimation of its social relations. Corresponding to these functions, state expenditures have a two-fold character, labelled social capital and social expenses. Expenditures on social capital are required for profitable private accumulation. They in turn consist of two categories: social investment expenditures, which increase the productivity of a given amount of labour, and social consumption expenditures, which lower the reproduction costs of labour power. Either way these state activities are indirectly productive of surplus value and hence profits. On the other side are social and military expenses required to maintain social harmony, which are not even indirectly productive of surplus value and profits.

O'Connor points out that many expenditures will contain more than one of these three elements. For example, 'welfare' payments (in the American sense) are a social expense to control the 'surplus population' (O'Connor's early label for what some now term the underclass), whereas social insurance is an investment in the productive sector of the labour force. Education and training embraces elements of social investment, social consumption and social expenses. Nevertheless he considers that each domain of public expenditure has a major function.

Using this framework O'Connor uses the rest of the book to answer two questions: what has determined the growth of the state, notably the US state in the twentieth century? And what are the fiscal and political consequences of this growth? In a nutshell his respective answers are: the expansion of monopoly capital, and a 'fiscal crisis' – the tendency for government expenditures to outrace revenues.

The Growth of the Welfare State

The answer to the first question depends on O'Connor's analysis of American capitalism. Modern America consists of three sectors, each employing about one third of the paid labour force: a monopoly sector, a competitive sector and the state sector. The first is distinguished from the second by such factors as large scale of production, a faster rate of growth of productivity, higher and more regular wages and greater density of unionisation. The third, state sector is rather oddly defined to include those industries from which the state procures goods and services, such as arms manufacturers and construction contractors, as well as government departments and public agencies. It combines features of the other two sectors, exhibiting a low rate of growth of productivity but with security of employment and wage levels closer to the monopoly sector. This represents an early statement of the 'dual economy' thesis with the added merit that the state sector is recognised as distinctive in its own right.

How does the interrelation between these three sectors generate tendencies to rising state expenditures and fiscal crisis? Briefly the process is as follows. Due to the increasing social character of production in modern capitalism, state investment and consumption is more and more necessary to ensure profitability and hence private accumulation. Examples would include public investment in communications and transport, education and training, research and development. This public spending raises total demand and income which benefits the monopoly sector. Yet despite this, O'Connor argues that demand for monopoly sector products does not grow as fast as capacity, resulting in surplus capital and a surplus population. These in turn call forth higher state expenses: the surplus capital necessitates a growth in military spending to protect overseas markets and the surplus population necessitates more programmes of welfare relief. The net result is that all three types of expenditure rise in parallel as the state tries to secure both accumulation and legitimation.

Yet this is too simplistic and 'functionalist' an account of O'Connor's book, suggesting as it does that the state necessarily undertakes various activities simply because the consequences of not doing so would be harmful to monopoly capitalism. Alongside these 'structural' explanations there is also a political dimension developed in Chapter 3 which considers the actual mechanisms that transform these 'needs' into state services. Here O'Connor develops a standard Marxist account of the state which combines its structural location within the capitalist relations of production alongside a recognition of the political means by which interests are represented within the political system. To represent the collective interests of capital as a whole, rather than the particular interests of industries or regions or whatever, a 'class-conscious political directorate' is needed. It is the executive branch of government which provides this directorate, and O'Connor analyses its growth and development in the United States in an uncontroversial way. One feature of this which he highlights is the centralisation of the budgetary process in an attempt to manage particularism and to strengthen class politics. This chapter offers a detailed account of aspects of the US political and budgetary process, with some recognition that other countries differ in certain respects.

In Chapters 4–6 O'Connor applies this framework to explain the expansion of state social investment, consumption and expenses in modern America. In each case a variety of structural and political factors are deployed. Structural factors which necessitate state social investment include the growing interdependence of production, the riskiness of investment, and the 'free-rider' problem that individual firms will always underinvest in training and skills in the context of a free labour market. State social consumption has to offset the decline of family, private aid and mutual benefit societies. Welfare programmes are required to mollify and control the surplus population which is growing due to the inequality and disequilibrium of capitalist growth. Other state expenses include the military costs of global policing and the need for public anti-pollution policies to clear up the mess occasioned by private capital accumulation. In places in *Fiscal Crisis* these structural influences appear to be over-determining, as when O'Connor writes: 'The welfare–warfare state is one single phenomenon, and military and civilian expenditures cannot be reduced significantly at the expense of one another' (p. 236).

However, alongside these structural factors which predispose the state to develop its role O'Connor also examines the political pressures for it to do so. These include special interest industrial lobbies, such as high-way contractors and the military-industrial complex, as well as benefits to keep the self-employed and small businesses sweet. Social insurance is mainly advocated by the organised working class but is actively supported by monopoly capital because it lowers the reproduction costs, and hence the relative money wages, of these workers. In the case of 'collective' social consumption (things like schools, urban renewal, housing subsidies, etc.) there is an interesting account of the political split between suburb and city and its implications for the American welfare state. In the suburbs social services are well developed and meet the preferences of local citizens; in the cities they are of poor quality and are introduced to control the population. The drift of the more affluent to the suburbs accentuates these inequalities and results in what O'Connor calls 'the exploitation of the predominantly working-class city by monopoly sector workers and middle-class and capitalist-class suburbanites' (p. 129).

The upshot is an analysis which combines class and sectoral aspects: alongside class exploitation there is also the exploitation of the competitive sector by the monopoly sector. In the United States at least, political interests are fractured along both lines and this shapes the pattern of welfare services provided. So the expansion of the modern capitalist state, and *ipso facto* of the welfare state, is explained by a combination of structural predispositions and political pressures. With a well-functioning political directorate the two can be aligned. However in American reality the demands of the executive are built on top of the host of special interest demands on Congress, so that a further twist is given to the rising spiral of state expenditures.

The Fiscal Crisis

'The fiscal crisis of the capitalist state is the inevitable consequence of the structural gap between state expenditures and revenues' (p. 221). Clearly, before we can make sense of this we need to consider the revenue side of the public accounts. There are only three sources of finance for the public sector: taxes, borrowing and the surpluses of state enterprises of various sorts, and Chapters 7 and 8 of *Fiscal Crisis* are devoted to these. State enterprises and productive activities are weakly developed in the United States but much more extensive in Europe, as O'Connor recognises. However, even in countries like Italy, he claims, they contribute little to government revenues since their prime purpose is to subsidise private capital through the provision of cheap inputs like electricity and transport. State borrowing is not a long-term alternative since interest payments add to future expenditure. It is adopted only in 'abnormal' times, as when the United States faced popular hostility to raising taxes to finance the Vietnam War.

This leaves taxation. The growth of the welfare/warfare state is also the growth of the modern tax state. Taxes can be levied on expenditure, income or capital, and on corporations or households. The conflict over the distribution of this burden is just as much a part of class struggle as the conflict over wages and profits – indeed 'the oldest form of class struggle' according to Marx. The result, according to O'Connor, is that rising taxation cannot match rising spending. To simplify the argument in Chapter 2, higher taxes mean, on the one hand, a lower growth of real incomes or higher unemployment, especially for competitive sector workers, which engenders further calls for state welfare expenses. On the other hand, it generates a tax revolt and more industrial conflict with the organised, monopoly sector workers, who have to be bought off with higher social consumption. So taxation is part of the problem and cannot be viewed simply as a solution.

One 'solution' to the fiscal crisis of the state would be the development of a 'social-industrial complex'. This is a shorthand for making state expenditure more indirectly productive by transforming unproductive state expenses into productive state capital. It entails developing more 'rational' social policies to train workers, develop a national health insurance scheme, invest in urban renewal, and so on – the sort of policies advocated by successive Democrat challengers for the Presidency but rarely implemented. The reason is that the social-industrial complex requires a new balance of forces between classes, sectors and the state, and this is unlikely to develop in the United States. Monopoly capital must develop a more cohesive, class-based outlook, competitive capitals who oppose it must be weakened, and the trade unions must be coopted but prevented from appropriating all the gains from this strategy. It is an American version of corporatism.

In places in Chapter 2 the 'social-industrial complex' also appears to refer to the direct improvement of productivity in state services, through such means as intensified management control of work patterns and what we would now call 'quasi-markets' to replicate market pressures within the state sector. However, this too is claimed to exacerbate class conflict in the public sector.

In the absence of this, another scenario is a tax revolt: resistance to 'tax exploitation' 'when those on whom the burden falls feel that the tax structure is inequitable and/or when the purposes of state expenditures are rejected' (p. 228). But this too is counterproductive in the longer run and is likely to divide the working class. O'Connor does not consider the possibility that this could set up a reinforcing cycle whereby the state divests itself of social functions whilst the middle classes exit and go private.

The last alternative is that movements of state workers and state clients will grow to challenge the fiscal crisis and argue for more radical solutions. The book offers an early examination of the specific features of public sector workers, especially in the social services. On the one hand, they are educated to value the needs of clients, and their work requires a degree of professional autonomy. On the other hand, they are the immediate victims of the fiscal crisis, whether social workers in New York or teachers in country school districts. Moreover their work situation is increasingly rationalised as they are proletarianised: 'A contradiction arises between the formal and informal requirements of their employment' (p. 241). The roots of public sector radicalism lie here.

At the same time clients of state services are also victims of the cuts and restructuring. Most are in a weak position to respond but in so doing they are forced to raise qualitative issues and avoid crude economistic demands. In this way their interests begin to ally with those of state sector workers. This perspective is taken further in later writings on the democratisation of the state where O'Connor distinguishes between struggles to establish *de jure* democratic control over hitherto appointed state bodies, and *de facto* democratic control by the users over these elected representatives (1978). The last chapter of *Fiscal Crisis* and these other writings reflect O'Connor's activist struggles alongside various public sector and welfare client groups.

It will be apparent that there are several similarities between O'Connor's neo-Marxist theory of fiscal crisis and that of the New Right (Pierson, 1991: 147–52). Yet they differ in at least three respects. First, the New Right explains the fiscal crisis in terms of rising expectations coupled with the pursuit of self-interest within the political arena. There is no recognition, as there is in O'Connor, that rising state expenditure is a response to systemic requirements flowing from modern developments in the economy, the family and civil society. Second, the welfare state for O'Connor is not necessarily unproductive, ineffective and despotic (Pierson, 1991: 48). Part of it is and part of it isn't; his is a more nuanced approach. Third, the ultimate cause of the fiscal crisis for several neo-conservative and neo-liberal writers is modern democracy, whereas for O'Connor it is monopoly capitalism. The ultimate solution therefore is not a constitutionally-bounded domain of popular choice, but socialism.

An assessment

Fiscal Crisis has contributed to our intellectual understanding of the welfare state and to our political understanding of social movements in and around the state. Against this, his work has encountered a series of problems centred in particular on his concept of crisis. Let me consider its positive and negative impacts in turn.

Fiscal Crisis serves as a model of a mature political economy analysis of the welfare state. O'Connor moves beyond the divisions between economics, sociology and political science and makes a genuine attempt to synthesise their insights. The economist would stop at the prediction of a public sector borrowing requirement, the political scientist at the analysis of government coalitions and the sociologist at growing sectoral divisions in modern capitalism. But O'Connor relates each of these to the other. Attempts to cut public spending to balance the budget may stimulate social divisions and tensions which change the balance of political pressures on the state and call forth more welfare spending. This may not only interfere with the original economic policy goal, but also undermine economic performance by substituting unproductive for productive state programmes; and so on. The book forced, and still forces, students of social policy to locate their work in a broad perspective. It forestalls spurious claims that social policy can assert intellectual autonomy from other disciplines.

Second, *Fiscal Crisis* represents an early attempt to develop a Marxist theory of welfare state development which avoids the twin problems of functionalism and idealism. O'Connor's Marxism interprets the 'welfare' state as the product of emerging capitalist relationships and their constraints. There is little room here for an idealistic view of social policy as a collective response to human need, or for the role of pioneering social reformers. Yet, O'Connor skilfully avoids (much of the time – see below) the opposite danger of a functionalist account of welfare state development where the state responds – always and appropriately – to the 'requirements' of the capitalist system as a whole. Politics plays a role, and O'Connor is alive to the specific features of the American political system which influence its public policy responses. *Fiscal Crisis* is a rather eclectic but invigorating mix of Marxist theory and North American radical social science drawing *inter alia* on Galbraith, Piven and Cloward and Baran and Sweezy. The analysis is both integrative and nuanced, wide-ranging and detailed.

Third, and perhaps most important, the state is not interpreted simply as an unproductive incubus on the capitalist economy, a feature of much orthodox Marxism up to that time[3] and of much neoclassical economics even today. The welfare state is not only a means for managing aggregate demand, redistributing income and promoting legitimation; it can and does make a productive contribution to the accumulation of capital and thus to overall economic performance. Here O'Connor goes beyond Keynesian theory to argue that the form of state intervention is important. It matters whether the state sets people to work digging holes and filling them up again (an example of Keynes), building missile systems, teaching skills or paying the dole. The productive contributions of these activities differ. Put another way, the modern state must pay attention to the supply-side as well as the demand-side aspects of its activities. It is interesting that the 'efficiency' aspect of the welfare state is increasingly appreciated now in orthodox economic theory (Barr, 1992). O'Connor made sure that Marxists could no longer overlook the productive contribution of social policies to modern capitalist development.

Fourth, this process, O'Connor contends, is not a smooth one. The state activities generate a fiscal crisis, which is at the same time a political and social crisis. All the available solutions to this crisis generate further problems. The welfare state is not a neutral, technical fix, but part of the problem itself. The 'crisis' in this second, broader sense is an ongoing historical phenomenon, the outcome of which cannot be foreseen because it depends on the struggle between classes. In this way it helps us to understand the emergence of Thatcherism and Reaganism in the 1980s (though O'Connor does not explicitly argue this himself). The New Right in both countries can be interpreted as a successful counter-mobilisation against the power of unions, 'social democracy' and the new social movements. But neither offered a solution to the problems of economic failure and lack of competitiveness because they were blind to the positive productive role of state action. The resulting policies were maladapted to the requirements of modern capitalism and paradoxically they both worsened the original fiscal crisis (see Gough, 1991).

Nor should we ignore the practical impact of his work. In 1981 he wrote: '*The Fiscal Crisis of the State* was intended to be a practical and theoretical intervention into the debates and social struggles raging in the US in the late 1960s and early 1970s. Practically, *Fiscal Crisis* was meant to help shift the American left's focus from industrial workers to the radical possibilities of state worker and state client organisations and actions' (1981: 43). His prediction of a growing public sector militancy and social movements in and around the welfare state were prescient.

His analysis of the way that social service workers must perforce augment traditional trade union demands with more qualitative issues
centred on their work relations was important in combating crude
economistic views about class struggle in the public sector. His thinking
on the 'democratisation of the state' contributed to the theory and
practice of participatory democracy and bottom-up struggles within
the welfare field.

If I move on to some problems, these should not be divorced from the
merits and positive impact of his work discussed above.

One problem arises because the *Fiscal Crisis* appears to take for granted
the underconsumption model of the capitalist economy of the *Monthly
Review* school, notably of Baran and Sweezy (1968). A central argument
of his is that the demand for monopoly sector products does not grow as
fast as capacity, which results in surplus capital and surplus population
(pp. 24–5). This then calls forth, as we have seen, rising military and
welfare spending; together the result is the Marcusian warfare/welfare
state and further fiscal crisis. Quite apart from the functionalist over-
tones of arguments like this, why should monopoly sector capacity
expand faster than demand? O'Connor's answer is that its capacity is
enhanced by state capital which socialises the cost of some investment,
whilst its demand is hampered by the slow growth or stagnation of
competitive sector wages. No evidence is given for this last stage in the
argument.[4] Later on he refers to 'the unfortunate "functionalist" for-
mulations of the basic thesis of *Fiscal Crisis*' (1981: 47) and stresses the
historical and conjunctural role of class conflicts.

Second, an implication of the above argument is that the social
expenses of legitimation increase faster than accumulation expenditures
under advanced, monopoly capitalism. Now this is not borne out when
the composition of post-war state spending in the US and other capitalist nations is explored. In an early attempt to do this I concluded that
'an increasing proportion of … [state expenditures] are productive
expenditures' (Gough, 1975: 80). Since then Miller (1986) has made a
careful analysis of US public spending from 1952–1980. He plausibly
allocates different items of state spending to O'Connor's categories:
Medicare, Medicaid, public assistance, unemployment insurance and
other social welfare are regarded (along with non-welfare items like
military defence) as Social Expenses, while OASDI, education, labour
training, housing and health expenditure are regarded as Social Capital.
The share of unproductive social expenses for legitimation fell from 72
per cent of total public spending in 1952 to 56 per cent in 1960 to 47 per
cent from 1972 to 1980. He concludes: 'According to O'Connor's

analysis, the ability of the state to support accumulation in the 1970s should never have been greater' (Miller, 1986: 246).

A third critical point concerns the origins of the fiscal crisis. Why, if borrowing is only a sporadic solution to funding state spending in modern capitalism, is there a chronic tendency to fiscal crisis? Why, in a context of economic growth, cannot rising spending be matched by rising taxation? His main answer is that a tax revolt develops, chiefly because of the conflicting interests of monopoly sector and competitive sector workers. This is an interesting insight with relevance to modern economies beset by a growing dualisation in the labour market. Yet there is plenty of countervailing evidence that in many countries the tax levy on households has grown *pari passu* with state spending without engendering a tax revolt. In the US, Miller argues, the 'tax exploitation of the working class' has risen since the early 1950s. Following O'Connor's comments on the incidence of various taxes between Labour, or households, and Capital he shows that 'labor's share of the tax burden has not remained constant, but has, in fact, steadily increased over the post-war period' (Miller, 1986: 243). In other words, there appears to be no systemic barrier to financing the welfare state out of higher taxes, which moreover are levied on wages and consumption, not profits and capital.

Fourth, more general criticisms have been levied against the very concept of a fiscal crisis. Moran (1988) provides a lucid survey of crisis theories of the welfare state, including O'Connor's. He distinguishes three usages of the term 'crisis' : catastrophe (a crisis caused by an external blow), turning point (crisis as a moment of resolution of difficulties) and contradiction (crisis as a situation of being trapped between conflicting imperatives). O'Connor's use of the term has varied, though his core idea is of fiscal crisis as an ongoing contradiction within capitalism. Moran concludes (1988: 412): 'There is no crisis of the welfare state . . . Welfare states have proved resilient in the capacity to command popular support, to mobilise resources and to weather economic storms.' The genuine fiscal difficulties of 1975–81 were the result not of an underlying contradiction, but of external shifts in the global economic system. Capitalism has notably demonstrated that it can adapt and learn from past problems. According to Taylor-Gooby 1991: 1): 'In the event, the predicament of welfare capitalism was resolved and growth restored through a policy mix of welfare cuts, industrial protection and fiscal discipline varying from country to country.'

Once we move away from a reliance on crude expenditure figures, it is apparent that national responses in the 1980s diverged between retrenchment, restraint and maintenance. This is borne out in a study of welfare statism in five countries since the mid-1970s by Pfaller, Gough and Therborn (1991: ch. 8). We show that in the US and Britain there were both direct attacks on social programmes and deterioration in welfare outcomes; in France and Germany there were few reductions in social programmes but some worsening of welfare outcomes due mainly to rising unemployment; whilst in Sweden, neither programmes nor welfare outcomes deteriorated. Interestingly these different responses correspond to the three 'welfare regimes' identified by Esping-Andersen (1990): English-speaking liberal, Continental corporatist and Nordic social democratic. Since he explains the development of these regimes in terms of class coalitions, this offers some indirect support for O'Connor's view that the resolution of the fiscal crisis depends on the class balance of forces.

However, the main implication of this theoretical and empirical work for *Fiscal Crisis* is that it undermines its generality. Most of O'Connor's work is specific to the US and cannot be directly applied to all advanced capitalist nations. Now O'Connor is often clear about this, and sometimes signals that things may be different elsewhere. But he also writes that 'many of the ideas presented can be adapted to the experience of other advanced capitalist countries' (1973: 6). A comparative analysis of advanced capitalist economies qualifies and rejects some parts of his work. It forces us to reinterpret what is a rich and insightful treatment of state expenditure in the USA in the late 1960s into a more general, but necessarily comparative, theory (Gough, 1975)

Fifth, a still more general problem has been raised by some: it is that fiscal crisis tendencies are not specific to capitalist states but apply equally well to communist or state socialist countries (Bell, 1976). Moreover Campbell (1993) shows that they also exist in the post-communist states after 1989. This has been put most forcefully by Klein (1993) in 'O'Goffe's tale', a conflated caricature of the main ideas of O'Connor, Offe and myself. Klein writes (1993: 9): 'The same conflicts, contradictions or crises afflicted the Communist welfare states as the Keynsian welfare states. The real difference lay in the fact that while the capitalist societies of the West were able to cope with the supposedly irreconcilable contradictions, the communist regimes of the East collapsed under their weight.' He draws from this the lesson that a statement purporting to be about a class of societies must be tested against a counterfactual to avoid solipsism. This is especially the case since industrialisation theories, such as Wilensky's (1975), provide alternative explanations which apply to all developed societies, capitalist and state socialist.

With Klein's accusation of an untheorised neglect of the non-capitalist world, I, speaking only for myself, could agree. But it is less plausible to argue that communist and capitalist welfare states faced the same contradictions and crises. Rather, the official economy in the Soviet bloc was so inefficient that there was much less surplus for the socialist state to appropriate, whilst the underground economy could not be legally recognised and therefore taxed (see Campbell, 1993). And, whatever the consensus which emerges as to why the state socialist systems collapsed so precipitately, I can think of nobody who would lay the whole burden of the explanation on the fiscal crisis of the state. Klein's attempt at a demolition job is in turn too determinist and all-embracing. There is still a need for a theory of the fiscal limits to social policy in capitalist societies, albeit one which pays attention to the great differences within this group of nations.

In conclusion, *The Fiscal Crisis of the State* continues to provide a mature political economy of the state in advanced capitalism. Unlike orthodox economics, it is aware of the impact of the public sector on social cohesion as well as tax burdens. Early on it alerted us to the productive role of the welfare state. Its defects are a rather functionalist view of crisis and a lack of awareness of national divergences in patterns of state-capital relations, of what we now call 'welfare regimes'.

Notes

1 A shortened version of 'O'Connor', a chapter in *Modern Thinkers on Welfare*, edited by Vic George and Robert Page, Harvester Wheatsheaf, 1995.
2 Perhaps this is the place to record the debt I owe to O'Connor's book and the influence it had on my own work (Gough, 1975, 1979).
3 I have discussed the Marxist concept of productive and unproductive labour and its relationship to state services elsewhere (Gough, 1972, 1975, 1979: chapter 6 and appendices B and C). O'Connor's subsequent contribution to this topic (1975) I do not find particularly clarifying – he redefines all labour as simultaneously productive and unproductive – and reveals some inconsistencies which surface in *Fiscal Crisis*, notably where he conflates selling costs and taxation as equivalent unproductive claims on the surplus (eg. 1973: 232).
4 It is true that in the USA the wage share has fallen and real wages have stagnated since the early 1970s, which would appear to be a vindication of O'Connor's argument. However, this stagnation did not occur in most other western countries. What was hypothesised as a general feature of advanced capitalism turns out to be a particular feature of US capitalism.

4
The Enhanced Structural Power of Capital: A Review and Assessment
with *Kevin Farnsworth*

Introduction: the issue[1]

Though it is implicit in literature surrounding the globalisation debate, theoretical discussion of the structural power of capital is waning. Yet in reality, we shall argue, it is more and more pervasive. Lockwood (1999: 63) has remarked on one of the paradoxes of contemporary social theory: 'the abandonment of Marxism as a means of understanding the dynamics of advanced capitalist democracies has coincided with the ever more extensive and intensive development of capitalist production relations'. It seems that only capitalists – business, the City, Wall Street, George Soros – still believe in class conflict and capitalist power.

When the power of capital is recognised, many political scientists look to capitalist *agents* for explanations of their influence rather than to the *structural* power of capital. Of course, capitalists – businesses, financial institutions, employers' organisations, central industrial bodies, and so on – do play a crucial role in the policy process. Capitalists are undoubtedly able to influence policy-makers and agents within the state through their actions, and are able to participate directly within the institutions of the state. However, in this chapter we choose to ignore this particular form of power. We want to stress the other, *structural* power of capital – the ability of capital to influence policy without having to apply direct pressure on governments through its agents – the power of 'exit' rather than 'voice'. We recognise that in practice the two forms of power are intertwined. Where 'investment strikes' are threatened within the political realm in order to influence the actions of both state and labour, the use of the threat is always action-based, though the power on which the threat is based may be structural.

The plan of this chapter is as follows. In the first section we discuss theorisations of power and of the structural power of capital. The second section outlines five sources of structural power before returning, in section 3, to the problems caused by the heterogeneity of capital and the variability of its power. On this foundation we then, in section 4, develop indices of the structural power of capital and apply these to data for Britain and the other G7 countries over the last two decades. This enables us to draw some preliminary conclusions about trends and variations in the structural power of capital in the heartland countries of the modern capitalist world economy.

Theories of power and the structural power of capital

Power and structural power

'The fundamental concept in social science is Power', wrote Bertrand Russell (1960: 9), 'in the same sense in which Energy is the fundamental concept in physics.' Ever since Weber, the idea of power has been explicitly discussed within sociology and political science, but not orthodox economics, and it is not our purpose here to review this literature in a systematic way. Weber defined power as the ability of a man or group of men to realise their own will in a communal action even against the resistance of others who are participating in the action. In the early post-war period, this intentionalist view of power influenced American political scientists such as Dahl (1961). This was critiqued by Bachrach and Baratz (1970) on the grounds that it ignored the mobilisation of bias and non-decision-making, which excludes from the political agenda potential issues over which there is an observable conflict of values or interests.

Lukes (1974) developed a 'three-dimensional' view of power which went beyond Bachrach and Baratz in two major ways: first, he argued that the bias of the system is also sustained by 'the socially structured and culturally patterned behaviour of groups and the practices of institutions' (Lukes, 1974: 21–2). Second, he claimed that power can be exercised in the absence of conflict through the ability of one group to shape the wants or preferences or subjective interests of another group. Lukes argued that research must study both the objective structures and the motivations and conduct of individual actors. This was taken further by Giddens' (1979) theoretical development of 'structuration': the idea that structures determine the boundaries of action, and are themselves the consequence of human action.

An alternative view of power stems from Marx's analysis of capital, the privileged role of the capitalist mode of production and of the capitalist class within capitalist social formations. This resurfaced in the late 1960s in Miliband (1969), was critiqued by Poulantzas (1969, 1973), and led to a subsequent debate (summarised in Urry and Wakeford, 1973). Much of the debate between Poulantzas and Miliband focused on the differences between structural and action-centred accounts of the power of capital. The former emphasised the determination of state policies by the 'objective relations' of the socio-economic system; the latter claimed that the nature of the state elite and its strategies could not be dismissed from any account of the exercise of power.[2]

Developments in both Marxist and Weberian writings on power, as represented in the works of Isaac (1987) and Mann (1986, 1993) respectively, suggest some convergence between these two approaches. According to Isaac, power refers to an enduring capacity to act, which may or may not be exercised on any particular occasion. Social power refers to those capacities to act possessed by social agents by virtue of the enduring relations in which they participate. In this Marxist-inspired approach, the distribution of power is structurally determined, while the exercise of power is a contingent and indeterminate outcome of inter-action between the relevant parties. Social power in both senses must be understood as relational (Isaac, 1987: ch.3). According to Mann, power is the ability to pursue and attain goals through mastery of one's environment. Following Parsons (1960), Mann distinguishes two forms of social power: mastery over nature (collective power) and mastery over other people (distributive power). He then builds on Weber to define four universal sources of power with distinctive organisational forms: ideological, economic, military and political – his IEMP model. He maintains forcefully that there exists no unitary society, this referring only to a space within which these four networks of power overlap and intertwine. Each is instituted by the other in ways which persist in enduring patterns but which permit the requisite diversity to foster innovation and change. In the two impressive volumes so far published he has applied this model to account for the human history of power up to 1914, and in sundry other papers he has begun to apply the model to the contemporary world (Mann, 1986, 1993, 1997).

If these two authors are representative, it is clear that there has been considerable convergence in contemporary theorising of power from originally distinct Marxist and Weberian starting points. This continues when we turn to analyse economic power and the power of capital. For Isaac, the modern capitalist era is characterised by a structural separation between the relations of production and states. Given this, the only plausible interpretation of relative autonomy is that each is characterised by institutional specificity and causal effectivity. States help constitute capitalist class relations while capitalist relations structure and constrain states (Isaac, 1987: ch. 5). Such mutual constitution by distinct power sources is a crucial theme in Mann, as we have seen. The economy here embraces the two aspects famously distinguished by Marx: the sphere of production, in which people wrestle with nature to produce goods and services, and the sphere of exchange, which provides a thread linking people over long distances and with no other relations between them. The former is intensive and authoritative, the latter extensive and diffuse. But both are entwined and active in determining economic power. Mann here draws on Marx's legacy, going so far as to call the resultant economic organisations 'circuits of praxis'.

Thus recent theoretical work on power from both Marxist and Weberian-inspired perspectives supports three conclusions. First, that structural power can be conceptually separated from agency power. Second, the former does not entail the structural determination of the exercise of power. Third, the structural power of a specific set of institutions, such as economic institutions, is always relative to the power of other institutions.

The structural power of capital

The focus of this essay is the more specific idea that capital exercises a unique form of structural power in the modern era. This sounds like a quintessentially Marxist idea but has also been argued from other perspectives. We shall consider each in turn.

Przeworski and Wallerstein (1988: 11) present a pithy, if contentious, summary of the Marxist perspective as follows.

> The central and only distinctive claim of Marxist political theory is that under capitalism all governments must respect and protect the essential claims of those who own the productive wealth of society.

Whatever the political voice of business and financial interests, whatever countervailing mobilisation and pressures from other interests in society, whatever the political complexion and programme of the government in power, the bottom line is that their room for manoeuvre is constrained by the central structural role of private capital in all capitalist societies. The natural state of play in capitalist societies is for the scales of power and influence to be tipped in favour of capital.

This power imbalance arises from the very nature of the capital–labour relation according to Marx, as reinterpreted by Offe and Wiesenthal (1980). In normal times, capital is advanced, employs labour to produce a product, sells the product and makes a profit. The capitalist can save labour, and increase profits, by investing in new technologies but workers cannot live without employment, unless public or collective agencies step in as a substitute source of income or direct consumption. As capital developed and concentrated into larger corporations and cartels, the historical reaction of workers was to form 'combinations' or trades unions to fight collectively for what they could not obtain individually. In turn this stimulated the formation of employers and business associations. By the post-Second World War era, both sides were organised within civil society and their political voice appeared roughly in balance, if always variable and contested. Both sides could exercise *agency* power, notably over the state.

But this masked a more fundamental inequality. If both forms of collective organisation were stripped away, the *individual* capitalist would still retain important sanctions – the capacity to invest and employ workers – whereas the individual worker would not. Both sides can exercise agency power but only capital disposes of structural power. This argument was resurrected most forcefully in the 1970s by a series of writers from a Marxist background, such as Block (1977, 1980) and Offe (1975, 1984). We shall return to the detailed reasons below.

Business's control over investment was also central in the work of Charles Lindblom. Lindblom, a founder of modern pluralist political thought, argued in 1977 that 'Jobs, prices, production, growth, the standard of living, and the economic security of everyone all rest in their [business persons'] hands'. Consequently, no government could be indifferent to their actions. However, governments cannot command businesses to invest, so they must 'induce rather than command'. As a result, dispute over fundamentals is rare: private enterprise, private property in productive assets, a large measure of enterprise autonomy – all these are excluded from public debate. This stems not so much from the overt exercise of business power as from its structural position in market economies. 'Business interest-group activity, along with its electoral activity, is only a supplement to its privileged position'. Lastly, there is the third level of power over people's preferences: 'citizens' volitions serve not their own interests but the interests of businessmen' (Lindblom 1977: 172, 193, 202).

Others also talk of structural power. Certain globalisation theorist privilege an economic logic and see new transnational networks of production, trade and finance bringing about the de-nationalisation of economies (Held et al., 1999: 3). For Strange, writing in the international relations tradition, structural power refers to 'unconscious power', 'the power to determine frameworks within which states relate to each other, to people and to corporate enterprises' (Strange, 1988: 25). This power is not unique to the economy, but in practice, she claims, the power of credit and production is growing: 'Where states were once the masters of markets, now it is the markets which, on many crucial issues, are the masters over the governments of states' (Strange, 1996: 4).

Thus there has been an undercurrent of interest and thinking about the structural power of capital throughout the 1980s but, despite much vague and vogueish talk of globalisation, this has not made it to the mainstream. Empirical research on the structural power of capital has also been scarce and has petered out in the 1990s.[3]

Part of the explanation for this irregularity of structural explanations lies in a seemingly inherent weakness – their inability to explain power variations between different nation states (Pierson 1995). How can evident differences in the power of national business and financial interests – vis-à-vis the state, labour, citizens or the capitalisms of other countries – be explained, if all dispose equally of an unvariegated structural power? And how do we account for changes in relative power over time – from the Great Depression to the hegemonic 1950s, through the upheavals of the 1970s to the restoration of capital's hegemony in the 1990s – if deep down it is all structural and unvarying? The answer of Marsh (1986), Bowles et al. (1989) and Pierson (1995) is not that the idea of structural power should be dismissed, but that it should be viewed as a variable, not a constant force. It is this view of structural power that we want to develop and assess here.

Sources of the structural power of capital

We rehearse here five sources of the structural power of capital commonly put forward in the literature: control over investment, capital mobility and the possibilities for exit, power over labour, state revenue dependency and ideological hegemony. These are analytically distinct, but in practice are interrelated and, in general, mutually reinforcing. Furthermore, all are relative to the power of other institutions in society and will vary across time. However, we shall set out the sources of power as starkly as follows, introducing qualifications and variability in the subsequent sections. We shall draw mainly on the neo-Marxist accounts referred to above in this section.

Control over investment

The first and unanimously agreed source of the structural power of capital is control over investment and thus the accumulation of means of production. The source of this form of structural power lies in the many and varied investment decisions taken on a daily basis by individual businesses. Przeworski and Wallerstein (1988: 12) have expressed the sequence of arguments here most concisely:

> Investment decisions have public and long-lasting consequences: they determine the future possibilities of production, employment and consumption for all. Yet they are private decisions. Since every individual and group must consider its future, since future consumption possibilities depend on present investment, and since investment decisions are private, all social groups are constrained in the pursuit of their material interests by the effect of their actions on the willingness of owners of capital to invest, which in turn depends on the profitability of investment.

Hence governments, workers and citizens are dependent on investments made by businesses. The pursuit of personal or 'national' interest must accordingly take account of their impact on investment decisions. 'In a capitalist society, the trade-off between present and future consumption for all passes through a trade-off between consumption of those who own and don't own capital and profits' (Przeworski and Wallerstein, 1988: 12).

'Exit' and international capital mobility

If the source of this power is control over investment, its exercise is dependent on the possibilities for exit. It is the ability of capital to not invest or to invest in another jurisdiction that realises this inherent source of power. This power, many now agree, is strengthening in the current period due to the process of 'globalisation'. Once an extensive, if not yet world-wide, international economy had emerged by the last quarter of the nineteenth century, the structural power of capital was enhanced to a qualitatively different level through the opportunities to invest across national boundaries. Following decolonisation and the collapse of state socialism in 1989/91, few areas of the world remain to resist the logic of capitalist markets and economic enterprises. International *trade* has expanded far faster than world output since 1945. Then from the mid-1980s onwards, a renewed burst of internationalisation extended the reach of capital to new levels. Foreign *direct investment* has multiplied and *portfolio investment and financial flows* have rocketed exponentially. The internationalisation of the world economy now unites trade, production and finance and this enhances enormously the exit options of capital.

This transformation, it is increasingly argued, is eroding the relative structural powers of the state and tipping the balance of power decisively in favour of capital. Mann caricatures the globalisation enthusiasts which this process has spawned: 'Capitalism, now become global, transnational, post-industrial, "informational", consumerist, neoliberal and "restructured", is undermining the nation state – its macroeconomic planning, its collectivist welfare state, its citizens' sense of collective identity, its general caging of social life' (Mann, 1997: 473). These processes, some argue, will also favour the least institutionalised forms of capitalism, i.e. the Anglo-American, which will further undermine the countervailing power of states (Crouch and Streeck, 1997). Thus globalisation emasculates the regulatory power of states and enhances the structural power of capital in general (see the quote from Strange above).

This interpretation has been criticised by Hirst and Thompson (1996), Mann (1997) and others. True globalism or at least extensive transnationalism is contrasted with internationalism and the continuing power of leading states, particularly the US and the other 'triad' members, the EU and Japan. Extensive transnational circuits of capital do exist, but they are intertwined with national economic governance. 'If the commodity rules, it does so entwined with the rule of – especially northern – citizenship' (Mann, 1997: 480). Today's globalism is 'impure'. One cross-national study finds that it has been the *interaction* of international economic tendencies with domestic institutional and partisan forces that explains the secular trend towards more financial openness over the last 50 years (Quinn and Inclan, 1997: 807).

Nevertheless, even these critics accept that a *relative* shift has occurred. By definition, states monopolise the control of territories and populations. They are necessarily rooted in space. The idea of a delimited territory is at the core of all definitions of the state since Weber. Thus, international capital mobility enhances the structural power of capital via its options of 'capital flight' to foreign shores. The same applies within regional trading blocs, such as the European Union. In the British case, competition for capital investment with other EU member states has been a key determinant of policy-making over the last two decades – facilitated by the free movement of capital within the EU but a weak state at the supra-national level.

Given this threat of exit, governments and organisations in civil society must induce private corporations to invest in a wide variety of ways. Governments will aim to ensure positive investment environments for domestic and/or foreign firms. Trade unions will always juggle the demands for immediate improvements in pay and conditions of work with the need not to discourage further investment. Both states and civil society actors will temper preferences for social benefits and provisions with the need to induce capital growth.

Power over labour

The power of capital is enhanced if labourers have no other means of subsistence, such as food allotments, friendly societies or welfare benefits. Workers are dependent on capital for employment and therefore their livelihood. They cannot 'exit' from production in the same way as capital without harming their own livelihoods. This strengthens the relative power of the capitalist class in defining both conditions of production (hours, conditions and flexibility of labour) and rates of pay. Offe and Wiesenthal (1980) further argue that labour is undermined by the contradictory nature of its interests. On the one hand, labour will seek to safeguard and improve wages, jobs and work conditions, but on the other hand, labour must safeguard the competitive position of the capitalist enterprise, since its own interests are dependent on the continued profitability and accumulation of capital by the firm and, therefore, the efficient use of labour. When labour articulates different interpretations of its interests, it can be accused of threatening the future of the business, and hence its own future. Capital, on the other hand, can defend its own interests safe in the knowledge that this will contribute to future competitiveness and prosperity. Its interests equal the national interest and this clearly has electoral implications for governments.

It is true that there is mutual dependence here – capital also needs labour and cannot function without it. However, capital possesses two asymmetrical sources of power. First, it can determine the amount and qualifications of the labour it hires through its control over the capital–labour ratio embodied in new investment. Second, capital has been historically more mobile than labour by many orders of magnitude. This is partly due to immigration laws and other restraints on population mobility, and thus reflects the countervailing power of states. However,

it also reflects the nature of another universal societal activity – reproduction – which requires relatively stable household forms to rear and
socialise children (Doyal and Gough, 1991: ch. 5). As a result of these
two factors, labour is asymmetrically dependent on capital, though the
degree of dependence will vary, as discussed below.

State revenue dependency

Given the dominant role of the capitalist sector in production, investment and accumulation, the state sector necessarily relies on the capitalist sector for its revenues. Whether taxation is levied on incomes
(profits or wages), expenditures or capital values, the amounts raised
will depend on the health and accumulation rate of the capitalist sector.
And if the government chooses instead to borrow to finance its expenditures, it must borrow from the private capital market at rates of interest set by market forces. As Schumpeter (1954) and Offe and Ronge
(1982) have argued, the state is structurally dependent on the capitalist
sector for its revenues: whatever the complexion and programme of the
government in power it cannot pursue policies which undermine capital accumulation. To do so would be to endanger the revenues of the
state and thus, in the broadest terms, the self-interest of state bureaucrats and policy-makers:

> Since the state *depends* on a process of accumulation which is beyond
> its power to *organize*, every occupant of state power is interested in
> promoting those conditions most conducive to accumulation. This
> interest does not result from alliance of a particular government with
> particular classes ... nor does it result from any political power of the
> capitalist class which 'puts pressure' on the incumbents of state
> power to pursue its class interest. Rather, it does result from an
> *institutional self-interest* of the state which is conditioned by the fact
> that the state is *denied* the power to control the flow of those
> resources which are indispensable for the *use* of state power'.
>
> (Offe and Ronge, 1975: 137–47)

Ideological control

For Marxists like Jessop (1982), as well as constrained pluralists like
Lindblom, another power resource of capital lies in the ideological
domain. A group may exercise ideological hegemony if the group's
interests can be legitimised as the 'national interest'. Because of the
foregoing arguments, this is precisely the position that capital is in.
The dependence of society and state on capital profitability and accu-

mulation acts as a gravitational tug on the 'volitions' of the population, according to both Lindblom and the dominant ideology thesis within neo-Marxism. Mann also regards this as an 'obvious' point: since about 1760 in Britain and since about 1860 throughout the West almost all political actors have internalised the logic of capitalism and markets (Mann, 1993: ch. 20). Polanyi (1957) has shown how in early nineteenth-century England the economy became disembedded from society and markets came to dominate society. However he also showed how a counter-movement emerged seeking to re-embed the economy within social relationships. The success of this movement in the twentieth century was witnessed by the regulatory welfare states which have in part decommodified labour and introduced citizenship as an alternative source of identity alongside markets.

Now, theorists inspired by Polanyi contend that a renewed period of disembedding is taking place as market relationships 'colonise' more and more domains of society. For example, according to Mouzelis (1999), the autonomous logic of the higher education system in Britain has been seriously undermined during the 1980s and 1990s by the increased dominance of managerialist and market logics. Cognitive rationality has been weakened and supplanted by the alien rationality of business and markets. In so far as this is true we may speak of the growing ideological power of capital over the state, civil society and everyday life. The real significance of ideology here is that it makes certain policy choices appear normal and others deviant (Block, 1980: 306). This places limits on the choices open to state actors, and also impacts on labour and business actors. Labour is unlikely to pursue what it considers to be unrealistic aims, whilst business has less need to attempt to steer policy in a given direction if it is already skewed in business's favour.

To conclude, the structural power of capital in the present epoch rests on five related but distinguishable foundations: its majority control over investment, its power of exit and international mobility, its asymmetrical power over labour, the dependency of states on economic buoyancy and international financial markets for their revenue, and its ability to colonise sectors of social life through the shaping of underlying preferences.

The contingency of structural power

The section above has stated in the starkest possible way the key sources of capital's structural power, as argued by different advocates of this position. But the very idea of structural power, and each of the specific arguments, have been heavily criticised. We shall concern ourselves with two conceptual-empirical criticisms: the heterogeneity of 'capital' and the issue of variation.

Capital divided

The arguments presented above assume that 'capital' is a homogeneous and unified entity without significant internal divisions. Of course, this is not and cannot be the case. At least three internal cleavages exist: between sectors, notably between manufacturing and finance, between large, medium and small business, and between capitals of different nation states (Mann, 1993). This heterogeneity will qualify, but does not destroy, the case made above. Let us consider here in turn the issues raised by sectoral and national divisions.

The rate of investment, and hence of accumulation, will depend *inter alia* on the cost of capital, notably real interest rates. If financial capital is organisationally distinct from manufacturing capital, as in Britain, then their interests may here conflict: the latter preferring lower interest rates, the former higher (Ingham, 1984). This conflict of interest undermines the first argument: that a single entity called 'capital' controls the accumulation process and that its interests must therefore be acceded to. However, this division is itself variable. If the organisation of finance and industry is intertwined, as in Germany, then potential conflict is reduced. Moreover, if share ownership is relatively widespread among the population, as in the US, the livelihood of the population is increasingly determined by the rate of return on financial assets, as well as by the 'real' investment of industry. In this case, control over investment declines as a source of structural power (but the ideological power of capital probably rises). The structural power of national capitals will positively reflect their homogeneity and institutional integration.

According to Strange, financial investment decisions, including the availability of credit, increasingly hold the key to structural power (Strange, 1988: 30). To some extent credit frees industrial capital, at least in the short term, from its reliance on the accumulation of capital, and facilitates future investments. The decisions of the financial sector, therefore, impact more and more on production and research levels. The result of these moves is the development of a web of reliance between industry, finance and the state.

Second, the intertwining of capitalism and states in the modern era portends real conflicts of interest between national capitals. The resultant combinations, such as mercantilism, economic imperialism and geopolitical imperialism, can hardly be overlooked by any twentieth-

century observer. Now it is one of the arguments of globalisation enthusiasts that these divisions are eroding fast as capital becomes more
international and fungible. Against this, sceptics emphasise the continual embedding of capital in national states, business cultures and emerging regional structures, such as the EU. But either way, there is still a
potential divide between the power of 'capital in general' and that of
particular national capitals. For example, the increased openness of the
British economy to inward investment undermines the control of Brit-
ish-owned capital over investment and accumulation in Britain. The
British state may become simultaneously more vulnerable to the structural power of capital in general, yet less beholden to the power of
British capital. Economic internationalisation does not overcome the
inherent divisions of interest here. The implications for this study are
that any audit of structural power must henceforth distinguish between
the power of specific national capitals and of capital in general.

The variability of structural power
According to Pierson (1995: 9):

> The assertion of business' 'privileged position' has appeared to be ill-
> suited for *comparative* investigations of policy development. Lindblom
> presented his argument as a *general* claim about the nature of private
> power in market economies, but as critics have pointed out, market
> systems are compatible with widely divergent relations between busi-
> ness and the state. Patterns of government intervention vary greatly
> across countries and over time within particular countries.
>
> (emphases added)

This is one important reason for the declining interest in structural
theories and the over-reliance on agency explanations. But this is to
throw out the baby with the bath water. The alternative is to recognise
that *'the structural power of business is a variable, not a constant'* (Pierson,
1995: 10). Before addressing this problem ourselves, let us summarise
the arguments of two others who have followed a similar line: a political
scientist, Marsh (1986), and the political economists, Bowles, Gordon
and Weisskopf (1989).

For Marsh (1986), the views of Lindblom and many Marxist writers
suggest a number of empirically testable hypotheses. The structural
power of capital will vary according to, first, the significance of private
investment in the economy, second, the extent to which governments'
re-election chances are determined by economic performance, and third,

the degree of concentration, internationalisation and flexibility of capital. Marsh concludes that in the post-war period up to the early 1980s, the third aspect of capital's structural power had indeed increased, but that the influence of capital on public policy was more complex than the simple structural position would warrant. Moreover, the extent to which capital used its privileged position to pressurise governments, and governments' policy responses to this pressure, varied. In other words, structural power was itself interdependent with agency power. This undermines the initially clear distinction between the two.

Bowles et al. (1989) wish to study the power of the capitalist class in the United States relative to workers, foreign buyers and sellers, policy-makers and political actors. They ground these power relationships in the institutional environment of the economy-what they call the social structure of accumulation.

The relative power of the capitalist class, according to Bowles et al., depends on four factors:

- The power of capital vis-à-vis labour. Two key factors here are the scarcity of jobs and the cost of job loss (equivalent to the decommodification of labour). They also use a multidimensional index of worker resistance.
- The power of domestic capital vis-à-vis foreign buyers and sellers; measured by the terms of trade and an index of (in their case) US trade power.
- The power of capital vis-à-vis domestic citizens, measured by an index of government deregulation and (the inverse of) capital's tax share.
- The degree of intra-capitalist class cohesion. They focus here on the degree of effective product market competition, measured directly by product market tightness and inversely by the ratio of import penetration.

It is apparent that these factors relate to the components of capital's structural power sketched in section 2 above, yet relativised and operationalised as variables. They apply this model to analyse the conservative economics of 1979–87 in the US. They conclude that the underlying power of the capitalist class rose up to 1965, fell to 1978, and rose again from 1983 onwards.

Assessing the structural power of capital in Britain and the G7

We adopt a country-specific approach here and attempt to measure capital's structural power vis-à-vis the power of nation-states and their governments and civil societies. We shall present some simple quantitative measures of the structural power of capital under four of our five headings plus profitability (the assessment of ideological power raises different research issues and is left aside here). It should be stressed that all our proposed indicators are proxy measures of the underlying concept. Taken together we believe they tell us something about the structural power of capital relative to other institutions in societies, and about its variation over time and across countries. We present information on trends since 1980 in Britain and the other major capitalist powers in the G7 – the US, Japan, Germany, France, Italy and Canada. It should be noted that the trends in smaller OECD countries may not mirror those charted here.

Profitability

We begin with profitability. Profitability serves as an overall outcome index of the power of capital. Profits are also crucial in determining both the ability and the willingness of firms to invest. Profitability can be measured in two basic ways: as the share of profits in total income and as the rate of return on capital advanced. However, both will be affected by both structural and agency power; thus profitability needs complementing by our more specific indices of the structural power of capital.

Concern over the profits squeeze of the 1960s and 1970s eased as the share of profits and income from property once more began to rise in the 1990s. Table 4.1 shows that the net profit rate of all non-financial corporations in Britain tumbled from almost 12 per cent in the early 1960s to 5 per cent in the late 1970s. Since then it has recovered to 10.5 per cent, the level achieved in the late 1960s, and it continues to rise strongly. British profit rates compare most unfavourably with those of its major competitors, but the gap is now narrowing. Table 4.2 presents the gross share of profits (operating surplus) in gross value added, this time for the narrower manufacturing sector. Again a fall up to the late 1970s has been followed by a smaller rise. This pattern is echoed in both Europe and the US, with only Japan among major economies as an exception. One result is shown in Table 4.3: the ratio of stock market

Table 4.1   Net profit rate; business sector, 1960/64–1989/93 (%)

	1960–64	1964–8	1969–73	1974–8	1979–83	1984–8	1989–93	1994
UK	11.7	10.4	8.0	5	6.3	9.1	8.2	10.5
Germany	18.8	15.8	13.5	9.7	8.8	9.5	10.8	
Japan	23.0	25.6	28.3	16.1	16.7	16.9	14.8	10.8
US	25.5	28.7	23.1	19.0	16.2	19.0	19.2	

Source: Glyn (1995), updated from Armstrong et al. (1991).

Table 4.2   Gross profit share in manufacturing, 1960/64–1989/93 (%)

	1960–4	1964–8	1969–73	1974–8	1979–83	1984–8	1989–93	1994
UK	26.3	24.9	23.2	18.2	18.4	22.8	20.9	24.4
France	26.3	27.8	27.9	24.7	21.7	27.3	33.1	
Germany	31.6	31.6	29.3	25.6	21.6	24.2	22.0	
Italy	35.7	34.9	30.6	28.9	31.6	34.9	31.9	33.6
Japan	48.2	47.8	45.3	34.9	34.1	35.7	34.9	27.5
Canada	31.8	32.3	29.2	29.2	28.2	33.3	31.0	
US	25.1	27.3	24.0	24.6	23.4	26.6	28.5	
Europe	29.6	28.4	27.7	24.6	25	29.1	28.6	
OECD	31.2	30.7	29.3	25.9	26.1	30.1	29.6	

Source: Glyn (1995), updated from Armstrong et al. (1991).

Table 4.3   Stock market prices: ratio to wages per head, 1973–95

	1973	1979	1989	1995
UK	100	58	100	103
France	100	42	85	76
Germany	100	66	109	89
Italy	100	17	42	29
Japan	100	60	238	109
Canada	100	59	77	75
USA	100	58	119	175

Source: Glyn (1995).

prices to real wages in Britain has rebounded since 1979 to the levels achieved in 1973 just before the first international oil crisis. Outside the US, this is one of the clearest revivals in property income in the western world.

The overall picture is of a revival of profitability in Britain and much of the western world following two decades of decline. However, this fundamental measure could reflect growing structural or instrumental power of business, or both. To disentangle this we turn to our more specific measures of structural power.

Control over investment

Capital's control over investment is perhaps the most important form of structural power. But private business is not the only agency undertaking fixed capital formation: the state, non-profit agencies and households also do so. One obvious index of capital's control over investment is the share of private investment in total investment and in GDP. Since much household investment is in domestic dwellings with no direct impact on productive capacity, this should be excluded from the total. To take account of possible divisions of interest between British and foreign-owned capital, we shall also need to distinguish home and overseas investment in each national economy.

Table 4.4 shows the shares of total fixed capital formation undertaken by general government, the corporate and quasi-corporate sector and overseas institutions.[4] Since the 1970s public investment has fallen steeply in all countries except France and Italy, where the share of the corporate and quasi-corporate sector has fluctuated erratically. But the most significant change was in the UK where the decline of government investment is clear and sustained.

Table 4.4   Composition of gross fixed capital formation, selected countries (% of total gross fixed capital formation)

	1975	1980	1985	1990	1995
UK					
Government	25.4	14.5	11.2	12.0	12.3
Corporate	62.1	68.0	61.8	63.7	58.3
Foreign			7.6	15.2	10.6
France					
Government	15.8	12.7	16.3	15.1	17.2
Corporate	44.7	43.0	48.8	50.3	49.9
Foreign			2.2	6.0	7.4
*Germany** *(WG before 1995)*					
Government	19.5	14.5	11.5	10.4	11.2
Corporate	83.2	82.0	88.2	85.9	85.3
Foreign			0.4	1.5	0.7
Italy					
Government		11.8	16.6	15.6	12.5
Corporate		29.4	30.8	42.0	36.7
Foreign			1.1	1.7	1.8
Japan					
Govt (+pub ents 1975, 1980)	27.6	29.6	16.9	15.6	22.5
Corporate	51.0	49.1	55.4	58.7	53.4
Foreign			0.2	0.1	0.0
US					
Government	12.5	9.3	8.1	10.8	10.1
Corporate	53.3	54.0	49.4	49.7	55.2
Foreign			2.5	5.0	5.4

* West Germany 1975–90.

Source: OECD, Statistical Compendium (National Accounts) 1997, Table 1; OECD, International Direct Investment Statistics (on diskette), 1996.

Another feature of Table 4.4 is the much greater salience of foreign investment in Britain, expanding to between 10 per cent and 15 per cent of the total in the 1990s. This is a far greater reliance than any other major capitalist power, though the shares in France and the US have grown. Japan and Germany remained significant capital exporters in this period but attract only tiny amounts of inward investment. This suggests that the investment dependency of the British state on foreign capital is high and rising. In so far as overseas capital is less amenable than domestic capital to domestic political pressures, this enhances the vulnerability of the British economy and British citizens. The unwillingness of British capital to invest in Britain has a dual effect on the structural power of capital over the British state, but on balance surely enhances it.

However, the measure presented in Table 4.4 is not ideal. State investment is substantial in many countries but, as O'Connor and others have argued, its role is typically complementary and reactive to private investment (see Chapter 3). If private investment is squeezed to the margins, as in state socialist societies, then indeed capital's structural power is ended. But, within limits, its share may not be a totally valid indicator of variable structural power

Capital mobility and opportunities for exit

Within an increasingly globalised economy, the options for capital exit are more and more important to an understanding of structural power.

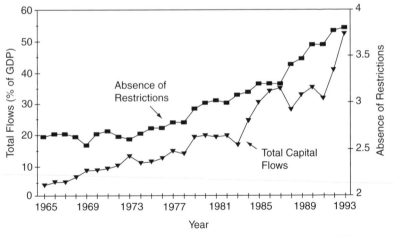

Figure 4.1   International capital mobility: potential and total flows (17-nation annual average of capital mobility)

Source: Swank (1998: 673).

To measure this indicators are needed of the constraints over capital mobility between political jurisdictions and of capital flows in practice. These refer to international and national legislative and other constraints on the payment and receipt of traded goods, invisibles and capital. International codes encouraging liberalisation have been promulgated by the IMF, the WTO and the OECD, and, on a regional scale, the EU.

We look first at outcome measures of capital mobility. Figure 4.1 presents averaged data for 17 advanced capitalist democracies measuring total inflows and outflows of capital as a share of combined GDP, where capital consists of direct, portfolio and short-term and long-term finance of banking and residential sectors (Swank, 1998: 673). It shows a moderate increase up to the early 1980s and a rapid rise thereafter. Figure 4.1 also presents a summary measure of national restrictions on such capital mobility. This codifies the laws governing capital and current account transactions for 21 member states of the OECD. It combines measures of nations' restrictions on exchange payments and exchange receipts (imports, invisibles, capital) with a measure for international legal agreements that constrain nations' abilities to restrict these. The result is a clear deregulation of international financial flows beginning in the mid-1970s and accelerating from 1987 onwards.

Moving to individual countries, the index of 'openness' in Figure 4.2 reveals significant national differences in the timing, speed and scope of financial deregulation. The US has been deregulated since the early post-war period, followed in the 1950s by West Germany. Of the other major countries only Britain in 1979 has moved decisively to deregulate international financial flows. The ability of these three nation-states to control financial capital is thus weaker than others. Nevertheless, familiar and universal feature of the last two decades have been diminishing constraints on international capital mobility, a marked expansion of that mobility, and the enhanced options for exit available to capital everywhere. On this measure, the structural power of capital is resurgent.

Power over workers

We now examine the structural power of capital vis-à-vis labour and other sectors in civil society. This is assessed using two main indices. First, since a surplus of potential workers over jobs will undermine labour and enhance capital, the rate of unemployment is a basic if crude index of capital's power relative to labour. Second, the lower the cost of job loss, *ceteris paribus*, the greater will be labour's ability to stand up to capital over wages and/or conditions of work. This will be affected

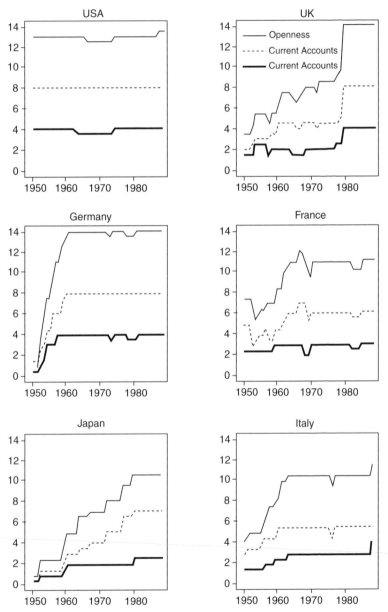

Figure 4.2   Openness, current account, capital account, various countries, 1950–88

Source: Quinn and Inclan 1997.

by the existence of alternatives to wages, notably the generosity, coverage and access to public welfare benefits in cash and in kind. Esping-Andersen's (1990) concept of decommodification is directly relevant here. A low concentration of union membership and fragmented union membership will also, *ceteris paribus*, weaken the bargaining position of labour, and make it less likely that unions will engage in the conflicts which may be necessary in order to win concessions from employers. However, this index would seem to combine the influences of agency with structural power and is therefore not used below.

Beginning with unemployment, Table 4.5 shows a secular rise in rates of unemployment from 1963–73, through 1974–85 to 1986–96 in all major countries; the only exception is a fall in the US level in the late 1980s/early 1990s. The British rate has fluctuated more than most, rising to a sustained high in the 1980s, declining during the Lawson boom, rising again following the Lawson recession and now falling again. On this measure alone, the structural power of European capital over labour has strengthened relative to that in the US and Japan.

Second, however, the opportunity cost to labour of unemployment has also to be taken into account. This will be primarily affected by the extent to which the welfare state enables workers and their families to sustain a socially acceptable standard of living regardless of their ability to participate in the labour market. If social citizenship rights in part supplant market distribution, then the structural dependence of labour on capital is reduced. Esping-Andersen (1990) constructs various indices of 'decommodification' to measure this. The extent to which unemployment benefits decommodify labour, in his study, is a rising function of unemployment benefit replacement rates, the duration of benefits, the proportion of workers covered by the various schemes and some other measures of eligibility. Table 4.6 presents his overall decommodification score for the unemployed in 1980 together with an imitation score

Table 4.5   Unemployment rates

	1963–1973	1974–1985	1986–1996
UK	2.2	6.7	8.5
France	2.3	6.4	10.6
Germany (West)	0.9	4.9	7.3
Italy	4.0	6.1	10.3
Japan	1.3	2.2	2.6
US	4.7	7.5	6.2

Source: OECD, *Employment Outlook*, July 1997, Table 3.2.

Table 4.6   The decommodification potential of
unemployment insurance, 1980 and 1992. Esping-
Andersen index

	De-commodification index	
	1980	1992
UK	7.2	6.8
France	6.3	11.3
Germany	7.9	11.6
Italy	5.1	3

Source: Fawcett and Papadopoulos (1997).

calculated for 1992 by Fawcett and Papadopoulos (1997). Together, they
show that for most EU member states, the decommodification of labour
increased over the period. However, the UK, together with Italy, Netherlands and Ireland, moved in the opposite direction – labour was partially
recommodified in the 1980s.

The 1980s and 1990s witnessed a general resurgence in the structural
power of capital over labour measured by labour surplus and unemployment, with the exception of the US in the 1990s. When the decommod-
ifying effects of state welfare are taken into account, the picture is more
varied and the trends less clear-cut. Unemployment in the 1990s has
been higher and rising in the EU, but is compensated by coordinated
bargaining and better welfare protection. When labour insecurity is also
taken into account the UK and the US do less well. Overall, the structural power of capital over labour has accumulated most noticeably in
Britain to attain almost North American levels.

State revenue dependency

The last measure of structural power presented here relates to the capacity of capital to constrain the revenues of nation states. As regards
taxation, it is frequently argued, by US analysts in particular, that the
share of taxes levied on business will inversely reflect the structural
power of capital. This sentiment has been expressed by the OECD in a
recent report:

'The growing integration of capital markets world-wide has reduced
governments' ability to tax mobile capital. The result is that social
protection expenditure is predominantly financed by taxes on labour.
(OECD, 1997: 10)

Here we concentrate on the share of corporate income taxes.[5] This share fluctuates cyclically in all countries; Table 4.7 shows that it increased in Britain from 1965 to 1985 and has since then begun to decline. In an international context, the corporate share of taxation in Britain is somewhat above average, though far below Japanese levels. The trends too are different. For the OECD as a whole, direct company taxation fell back in the 1970s and has since yielded a rather constant share of total revenue.

The thesis that rising capital mobility will reduce business taxation can be challenged on various grounds. If the *real* or *final* incidence is what matters, then this will be affected by other factors including the very balance of power between business and other groups that we are trying to assess (Gough, 1979: ch. 7). Others have argued that the extent of investment credits is more important in affecting the rate of business investment (Wallerstein and Przeworski, 1995). Still others claim that state expenditure, competitiveness-related programmes and regulation must be considered as a package (Swank, 1998). Thus the formal rate of business taxation alone would be of little or no importance as a measure of the structural power of capital. Swank presents evidence for 17 advanced countries and concludes that there is no evidence to support the case that rising capital mobility has forced down business taxation. According to Swank (1998: 690): 'The evidence is completely in-consistent with the structural power [of internationally mobile capital] thesis.'

However, his analysis does not necessarily undermine the structural power argument since, as discussed above, simple tax rates or tax revenues may be an imperfect measure of business power. Swank himself

Table 4.7 Corporate taxation, % total taxation, 1965–94

	1965	1970	1975	1980	1985	1990	1994
UK	7.1	9.1	6.7	8.3	12.5	10.8	8.0
France	5.3	6.3	5.2	5.1	4.5	5.3	3.7
Germany	7.8	5.7	4.4	5.5	6.1	4.8	2.9
Italy	6.9	6.5	6.3	7.8	9.2	10.0	8.9
Japan	22.2	26.3	20.6	21.8	21.0	21.6	14.8
Canada	14.9	11.3	13.6	11.6	8.2	7.0	6.6
US	16.4	13.2	11.4	10.8	7.5	7.7	8.9
EU 15	6.9	6.8	6.0	5.8	6.4	6.8	6.4
OECD	8.9	8.7	7.5	7.5	7.8	7.6	7.5

Source: *OECD Revenue Statistics 1965–95* (OECD, 1996): Tables 13, 19.

asserts that there has been a common move towards a broadening of the business tax base in recent years across countries, a policy that may be rational given capital mobility, as Slemrod (1990) argues. Steinmo (1993: 175–8) argues that corporate tax reform over the 1980s was intended to do three things: lower overall corporate tax levels, increase investment, and reform the previous system which had tended to favour industrial over financial capital. When considering the broader tax framework confronting capital, there is here a common trend that can be structurally explained by rising capital mobility.

The argument that public borrowing heightens the dependence of states on capitalist financial markets is also ambiguous: the ratio of public borrowing to GDP and the accumulated stock of state debt may both provide useful measures of this further form of revenue dependence. Whereas taxation creates dependency on the domestic economy (including foreign-owned enterprises) borrowing can be interpreted as creating dependency on international financial markets. On the other hand, financial openness permits governments to borrow money from international investors at world competitive prices without crowding out domestic investment, thus reducing their dependence on domestic finance. According to Strange (1998) the finance of governments through issuing bonds has become pervasive in the 1990s, the servicing of the resulting debt now accounting for one quarter of all government spending. Table 4.8 confirms this for all G7 countries except Britain. But the British state has been remarkable successful in reducing dependence on international financial markets during the 1980s. In this respect it is now less beholden to finance capital than at any time since the First World War.

We may conclude that the structural power of capital over the major nation-states of the OECD has grown in the 1980s and 1990s.

Table 4.8   State indebtedness: debt/GDP, 1965–90

	1965	1975	1990	1997
UK	81.7	63.7	34.7	60.8
France	53.1	41.1	46.6	64.3
Germany	17.3	25.1	43.6	65.9
Italy	35.4	60.4	100.5	124.1
Japan	0.1	22.4	69.8	90.8
Canada	58.8	43.1	71.9	
US	52.1	42.7	56.2	63.8

Source   Alesina and Perotti (1995: Table 1); OECD (1997): *Statistical Compendium* (Economic Outlook).

National and international regulation of financial flows has been cut back and state borrowing has risen. The tax rates levied on business have been reduced at the same time that the corporate tax base has been broadened. Britain exhibits the sharpest decline in relative state power, although it alone has sharply cut back government borrowing. However, we may expect more recent figures to show this process underway in the Euro-zone as the conditions of the Maastricht Stability Pact have begun to bite. On some measures the structural power of capital over states is unchanged, but in others it is clearly on the rise. The net effect is a shift in the balance of power from nation-state to capital.

Conclusion

This chapter has attempted to theorise, define, operationalise and measure the structural power of capital. We define it as the ability of capital to pursue its goals without necessary recourse to direct action by its agents. We argue that this power rests on its control over investment coupled with its ability to migrate to other jurisdictions with the growing internationalisation of economic life. This in turn generates structural power over labour, state revenue dependency and the ideological colonisation of social life.

The dominant feature is of eroding national restrictions on the mobility of capital in all its forms coupled with much enhanced transnational mobility in practice. National regulations are least in the US and Germany but Britain stands out for its deregulatory shift in the 1980s. We have found that private capital's weight in investment has changed little, with the significant exception of Britain where it has risen. Power over labour differs between the European, US and Japanese models of capitalism. In Europe, high unemployment weakens worker power, but in other respects (union membership and cohesion and decommodification through welfare benefits) capital has as yet made few inroads. Nation-states' dependency on borrowing through international financial markets has increased (Britain excepted) and capital is taxed at lower rates (though there is no clear trend in revenues from corporate taxes). Overall, the rate and share of profits are beginning to grow again from the nadir of the late 1970s.

However, we firmly resist the structuralist assumption that this structural power is omnipotent and invariant. Rather we seek to assess and measure its variability over the G7 countries across the last two decades. This generates an interesting conclusion. Despite the internationalisation of economic activity and the decontrol of capital mobility, trends in the structural power of capital show marked national variations. The UK stands out in most respects from other major countries in the speed and extent of the resurgence of capital's power. Weak levels of domestic investment have been partly offset by historically high inflows (and outflows) of capital. Public investment has collapsed as the UK becomes more dependent on global footloose capital. Trade unions have been significantly weakened, markets have been deregulated and the cushion of welfare benefits undermined. Though we have not attempted systematically to explain our results, the evidence suggests that the ideological drive of the Thatcher governments has left its legacy in a weakened state and civil society.

Notes

1　Thanks to Paul Pierson, Meir Shabat, Michael Shalev and Guy Standing for helpful comments. Also to all the members of the informal Prior Park discussion group, and to participants in the European Forum at the European University Institute, Florence, where an earlier draft was presented in June 1999.

2　The contrast was overdone. Miliband constantly stressed the importance of the structural constraints of the system (e.g. 1973: 311), whereas Poulantzas recognised the clash between fractions of capital and the strategic role of ruling blocs (see Gough, 1975).

3　Despite the work of, for example, Marsh (1986), Ward (1986, 1989), Jacobs (1988), Przeworski and Wallerstein (1988) and Swank (1992). A more recent, important exception to this neglect is the study by Winters (1996), a book which came to our notice after writing this paper.

4　Most of the last category will be corporate and will thus also figure in the corporate row. In other words there is double-counting in Table 4.4. The undisclosed remainder is accounted for by the household sector. The corporate sector includes investment by public corporations, so exaggerates the role of the private capitalist sector; unfortunately, it was not possible to disaggregate the two on a consistent basis.

5　Direct taxes on profits or corporate income are relatively uncontentious here, but social security contributions (SSCs) paid by firms on behalf of workers are more difficult to interpret, since there is great dispute over the final incidence of the burden of these charges. In some European countries these are very high and will have been taken account of in business strategy and performance.

II

Comparative Social Policies and Welfare Outcomes

5
Why Do Levels of Human Welfare Vary across Nations?[1]

Introduction

This essay reports our attempt to answer a central question in comparative political economy: what are the determinants of national variations in levels of human welfare? It is well established that, on balance, richer countries do better according to certain measures of human welfare than poorer ones, yet some rich nations, such as the US, do relatively badly while some poorer ones, such as Costa Rica, perform relatively well. What explains these discrepancies? Some claim that socialist states do better than capitalist ones, at any given level of economic development, whilst others argue that the communist system hinders both economic and social development. Again, is democracy or a good record in human rights conducive to, or competitive with, social welfare? With the demise of the centrally planned economies and the global dominance of capitalism, these questions do not disappear. Rather, it becomes still more urgent to understand why different capitalist systems vary so much in their impact on the lives and welfare of ordinary people. Many of the dominant international agencies now recognise that levels of welfare ('investment in human capital') can also improve economic performance in a virtuous circle, and for this reason, if no other, are showing a novel interest in the global level and spread in the quality of life.

Research into these questions is long-standing. What, then, do we offer that is new? Two things. First, a theory of universal need that provides a justification for using human need satisfaction as a measure of human welfare, whilst avoiding the criticisms often levelled at past attempts to do this. This theory generates a set of need measures, which avoids the reliance on one crude measure typical of previous studies. Second, we attempt to go beyond simple correlation and multiple regression analyses, which encounter severe problems of multicollinearity, and develop a complex causal model linking our system variables and several indicators of basic and intermediate need satisfaction. The applied model appears robust and generates some interesting results. These show that level of economic development, national dependency and world position, historic paths of societal development, state capacities and dispositions, democracy and human rights, and gender equality all have significant and independent but linked effects on cross-national differences in need satisfaction.

Measures of need satisfaction

Our measures of welfare stem from the Doyal-Gough theory of human need, summarised in Chapters 1 and 2. This generates three sets of indicators: of basic needs, intermediate needs and the societal preconditions for improving levels of welfare. These provide external and independent standards with which to evaluate the performance of very different social, economic and political systems. They thus permit objective human welfare to be assessed independent of the cultural values of any single social grouping. Of course, in practice we must rely on whatever valid and reliable indicators are compiled by international agencies. However the theory of need does contribute something to the exercise by forcing us to select only those which have (some degree of) cross-cultural validity. It enables us to reject some commonly used indicators and to identify the many gaps in present social reporting. Valid and comparative indicators are lacking in many areas; for example, morbidity rates and the prevalence of disability; syndromes of mental illness; the extent of child neglect, abuse and ill-treatment; the presence or absence of primary support groups; and economic insecurity. We must now consider what valid, reliable and universally available indicators exist to map levels of basic and intermediate need satisfactions.

Basic needs

To measure *survival,* we follow common practice and use life expectancy at birth. It applies to mortality throughout the lifespan, and it is more closely correlated than other measure, such as the infant mortality rate, with the 'health intermediate' needs discussed below. However survival chances simply cannot provide a valid measure of *health,* though they are undoubtedly correlated over large populations. Here however the available data, even in high-income countries, falls far short of what is desirable. For example, no reliable information exists on the prevalence of disabilities or of those suffering from severe pain. The only area where some light can be thrown concerns children suffering from developmental deficiencies. The World Health Organisation and United Nations have information on low birthweight babies, underweight babies and infants suffering from 'wasting' and 'stunting'. The data we use is derived from the UN Development Programme's 1992 Human Development Report augmented by Sivard (1989) and UNICEF (1990). The percentage of low birthweight babies (under 2,500 grammes) is a standard index of the risks facing the newborn; the indicators of wasting, stunting and underweight refer to children of under five years, 12–23 months and 24–59 months respectively and so cover different aspects of a child's early development. These indicators face problems of erratic coverage within countries, and of a bias in coverage towards the developing world where the problems are most acute. They exhibit a high degree of multi-collinearity, except for the incidence of wasting, and little can be gained from using the indicators individually. After experimenting with Borda rankings we decided to use low birthweight as a proxy for all these indicators of child health, on the grounds of its greater coverage and reliability.

When we turn to the other basic need of *autonomy*, we encounter more intractable methodological and measurement problems. Ideally we require, as argued earlier, measures of mental disorder, cognitive deprivation and lack of opportunities for participation in socially significant activities. In practice the development of valid and reliable social indicators is sparse in even the most socially aware and resource rich nations; for most of the world there is virtually nothing. The only exceptions are UNESCO indicators of adult literacy, also broken down by sex. Our theory regards literacy as a critical indicator of cross-cultural autonomy, but notes that it taps only one aspect of one component of autonomy of agency (not to speak of critical autonomy). International data on adult literacy are based on UNESCO sources and definitions: the percentage of people 15 years and above who can, with understanding, both read and write a short simple statement on their every day life. These are augmented with the UN Development Programme's own estimates contained in the 1992 Human Development Report (1992, Table 1).

Intermediate needs

It is clear that reliable indicators tapping the eleven groups of intermediate needs shown in Chapter 1, Figure 1.1 are simply not available for all the major nations. The ones we are left with are considered below.

For *nutritional status* we can use the Food and Agriculture Organisation/WHO calculations of daily per capita calorie supply as a percentage of the 'average' requirements of moderately active men and women. There are numerous problems with these figures, both conceptual and practical. It is argued that the calorific requirements of different people vary with their group characteristics and their environment; hence using an average requirement does not accurately measure the welfare, or 'functionings' to use Sen's terminology, generated by the food (Sen, 1984; Doyal and Gough, 1991, pp. 194–5). The FAO's data mainly derive from estimates of food production, imports, storage losses and wastage, and cannot readily be used to identify areas or population groups in special need, except very roughly (UNRISD, 1992). None the less, we must perforce use such data – for 1988 (UNDP, 1992).

Access to *safe water* and *sanitation* is regularly calculated by the WHO on the basis of national survey statistics. 'Access' is defined differently for urban areas (a source of water or sanitation within approximately 200 metres) and rural areas (a reasonable daily time spent fetching and carrying water so that alternative economic activities are not seriously inhibited). 'Safe' is defined to include standardised water purity tests and sanitary means of excreta and waste disposal including latrines, composting and sanitary wells. Interpreting access rights, ownership and distribution entitlements to water and sanitation is complicated, but most social scientists find both measures reliable enough (UNESCO, 1991: 5). These indicators can also be regarded as measuring one aspect of the intermediate need for safe housing.

The next intermediate need for which cross-national data is reasonably abundant is *health care services*, though this area too is fraught with conceptual and methodological problems discussed elsewhere. WHO estimates of the ratios of population to doctors, nurses and hospital beds have been extensively criticised for their implicit bias towards urban and middle-income groups and for ignoring distribution and efficiency concerns especially in many less developed countries (UNRISD, 1992). A second indicator constructed by UNICEF defines 'access to health services' as the percentage of the population that can reach appropriate local health services by local means of transport in less than one hour. It is open to a wide variation in interpretation. Better than measures of medical inputs are direct measures of health care utilisation, such as the numbers immunised against specific diseases. WHO calculates average vaccination coverage for children under one year of age for the four antigens used in the Universal Child Immunisation Programmeme. Its point-of-delivery recording makes it a more reliable statistic than those services which are assessed pre- or post-administration and require more qualitative elements of perception and recall. Faced with such a variety of indicators of access to health services each of which taps something different we calculate a composite indicator using an equally weighted Borda ranking of population per doctor, the percentage of births attended by trained personnel, and the proportion immunised. A Borda ranking simply sums the rank scores of nations on the individual indicators and expresses the result as an aggregate score (Dasgupta, 1990: 8).

One aspect of *economic insecurity* can be crudely approximated by using the UN's calculation of the numbers of people in absolute poverty. This is defined as the percentage of the population who live on an income below a recognised income poverty line below which minimum nutritional and essential non-food requirements are not met. These figures are calculated by the World Bank and are taken from the UN Development Programme (1992). The numerous problems with 'poverty lines' are well known and are discussed at length in the World Bank's 1990 Report (also Kanbur, 1990). The most pressing problem for the purposes of this cross-national study is lack of coverage and comparability. One measure of *physical insecurity* is national homicide rates assembled by both WHO and Interpol. For our purposes, however, their usefulness is limited due to poor coverage and a bias towards developed nations. Another relevant indicator is the incidence of war and war-related deaths throughout the world: Sivard (1989) calculates total military and civilian deaths through war and its related causes for the period 1945–89.

Turning to *education* there is a relative wealth of international data compiled by UNESCO. The problems confronting the user of this material are similar to those discussed for literacy rates (Spearitt, 1990). We shall use the following. To tap the total stock of formal educational experience of a population, we use the mean years of schooling of adults aged 25 and over. This has the problem that it says nothing about the quality and appropriateness of the education received. It has been used because of its superior coverage (all 128 countries in our survey) and because it is separately available for men and women. Second, to tap the flow of children receiving formal education we include the percentage of the population who have successfully completed primary education level. Completion rates are superior to enrolment rates in that they take account of pupil drop-out. Primary education is more appropriate than secondary and tertiary levels which will frequently monitor access to an elitist and technologically inappropriate level of functional education.

Completed primary education taps opportunities to acquire basic functional skills and as such the platform on which an extended basic and critical autonomy can be built.

Our last intermediate need, for *safe birth control and child-rearing*, can draw on some regularly assembled UN data. The first can use indicators of contraceptive use, though these may underestimate total contraceptive practice and will not take into account the relative safety of the techniques available. The second can draw on indicators of births attended by recognised health personnel and, as an indirect measure, the maternal mortality rate. The data are derived from the UN Development Programmeme 1992 Human Development Report.

In Table 5.1 we summarise the range of human need indicators that we consider are reasonably valid and reliable and for which sufficient data exist.

*Table 5.*1   Human need indicators

Basic needs

Survival	LIFEXP	Life expectancy at birth
Health	MATMORT	Maternal mortality rate, per 100,000 live births
	LOWBWB	Low birth weight babies (%)
Cognitive skills	LIT	Adult (15+) literacy rate
	FEMLIT	Female adult literacy rate

Intermediate needs

Nutrition	CAL	Average daily calorie supply as % of requirements
Housing	WATER	Population with access to safe water (%)
	SAN	Population with access to sanitation (%)
Health care	HLTHSERV	Borda ranking of POPDOC, IMMUNI, BIRTHAT and HS
	POPDOC	Population per doctor
	IMMUN	One year olds immunised against UCI diseases (%)
Economic security	POV	Population below poverty line (%)
Physical security	WARVIC	War and war-related deaths 1945–89 (% 1990 population)
Education	PRIMCOM	Primary school completion rate
	YRSED	Mean years of schooling of adults
	FEMED	Mean years of schooling of women
Safe reproduction/	CONCEP	Use of contraception by married women (%)
child-bearing	BIRTHAT	Births attended by health personnel (%)

Cross-national research on welfare outcomes

To date, the most substantial cross-national study, taking into account a full range of theories and hypothesised determinants of basic human need satisfaction, is that by Moon (1991; also Moon and Dixon, 1985). He undertakes a multiple regression analysis of all nations for which there are adequate data – a maximum of 120 countries – including advanced market economies and state socialist economies as well as developing nations. The method is cross-sectional and the bulk of the data refer to the 'early 1970s' (though some hark back to the early 1960s). He uses only one dependent variable – the physical quality of life index (PQLI), which combines life expectancy, infant motality and literacy (Morris, 1979; Rosh, 1988; Moon, 1991).

As Moon points out, cross-sectional designs are dogged by two related problems (Moon, 1991: 31–8). First, the dependent variable may not have fully adjusted to changes in the independent variable, casting doubt on the customary interpretation that the relationships discovered represent a long-term equilibrium condition. Second, cross-section designs cannot of themselves establish the causal direction of the relationship. However he rehearses the argument that these problems are less salient where the theoretical foundations for ascribing causal priority are strong, and/or where the temporal priority of variables is clear and the adjustment times are sufficient to take into account their effects. To cope with multi-collinearity among independent variables he develops a hierarchical design in which variables are introduced in an explicit order. Cross-sectional analysis, he concludes, is most appropriate where both exogenous and dependent variables are relatively stable and slow-changing and where confidence in the causal relationships is high (Moon, 1991: 264–5).

Running a sequence of regressions and then a step-wise regression of the full model, Moon arrives at the following conclusions concerning the determinants of national differences in the level of PQLI:

1 The most powerful predictor is level of economic development, as measured by the inverse of the share of labour in agriculture rather than per capita GNP.
2 Economic structure is important: development centred on the factory and, surprisingly, plantation agriculture produces more effective need satisfaction levels than development centred around mining or subsistence agriculture.

3 State socialist nations exhibit higher PQLI scores than capitalist
  nations, but only at lower levels of development.
4 State capacities, measured by central government expenditure as proportion of GDP and in other ways, are of no importance or have a
  negative impact. On the other hand, military personnel levels have a
  positive effect on PQLI (though when these are included military
  expenditures have a negative effect).
5 Some socio-political factors are significant. Democracy, as measured
  by Bollen's (1980) index, is a significant predictor of enhanced need
  satisfaction, but so is (more weakly) an interactive measure of military
  regimes. Blondel's (1969) classification of regime ideology is not significant (leftwards or rightwards) in isolation. Yet taking state capacities and socio-political factors together as influences on state
  dispositions, Moon finds a significant interlinkage: 'At higher levels
  of state expenditures, the left achieves the best results and the right
  the worst; at very low levels the reverse is true' (Moon, 1991: 142,
  fn.30).
6 A nation's position in the world system is linked in ways that are
  rather variable and weak.
7 A variety of historical and 'distal' influences are significant: PQLI is
  associated positively with a history of plantation agriculture, with
  colonisation by the British, and with Buddhism. It is negatively associated with late national independence (i.e. colonisation), with Islam
  and with an African regional factor.

Overall, Moon's model has an adjusted R^2 of 0.94. The results are
unusually robust over different samples of nations produced by the
addition and deletion of variables where there are missing data. Thus a
variety of politico-economic and historical/world system factors can
explain the bulk of cross-national differences in need satisfaction.
Moon's study is important in the depth and range of the theories that
he explores and then operationalises. However many of his data were 20
years out of date when published. Our first task is thus to update his
analysis.

Research design

We decided broadly to replicate Moon's approach, but with three major
differences. First, of course, we wanted to update the analysis by using
data for 1990 or thereabouts. For the old Soviet Union and Eastern bloc
countries, these data are prior to the economic reforms and the collapse

of some of the constituent nation states. Second, the Doyal–Gough theory of human need dictates that we use a greater variety of more specific measures of need satisfaction than in previous research. Third, it also requires that we consider the interrelation between need indicators, including the possibility that some act as intermediate determinants of others, which leads us to explore alternatives to multivariate regression analysis, including path analysis. The problems of multi-collinearity in global cross-national analysis of basic needs are well known and pose methodological issues which we feel require alternative solutions.

Apart from these differences, the research design is similar to that of Moon. We adopt a quantitative, static approach, looking for associations across a large number of nations at one point in time. Two alternatives were available: a qualitative comparative historical investigation, or a quantitative time-series analysis of trends. A splendid recent example of the former is the study of the development of democracy by Ruesch-meyer, Stephens and Stephens (1992). It exhibits research resources and skills beyond our capacity, though our study has sought to mix a variety of 'qualitative' and 'quantitative' variables to produce insight into the longer-term structural factors that effect need levels. A time-series approach has several merits, but is not appropriate or feasible for our goal, because it taps many more short-term phenomena and can mis-represent longer-lasting, causally lagged structures. The limitations of cross-national analysis have been touched on above but, we believe, are not a threat given the theoretical basis of this work.

Given this basic design we have chosen to investigate all nation states in the world, rather than a selection of them or various subsets of nations. There is a case for and a tradition of investigating welfare out-comes separately within affluent nations of the 'North' and the devel-oping nations of the 'South'. This strategy enables more specific questions to be answered and permits different and more socially relev-ant indicators of welfare outcomes to be used in each country grouping. However, it directly flouts a central tenet of our theory of need that we wish to utilise: that needs are objective and universal, and that indica-tors of need satisfaction should be explicitly cross-cultural.

Our goal of global coverage was tempered in practice by the existence of numerous small countries and micro-states. It is a central tenet of comparative research that each nation is treated equally whatever its population – that Nepal counts for the same as China. However, on the grounds of practicality we follow a common practice and exclude all nations with a population of less than 1 million from our data set. All other countries are included, data permitting, including such 'unusual' countries as oil-rich Middle Eastern states which exhibit high income levels but traditionally rather poor welfare levels. This leaves us with a maximum of 128 countries, and all tables refer to this number unless otherwise stated. Our desire to secure as good a coverage as possible means that in practice good indicators with poor coverage are sometimes rejected in favour of less satisfactory but more available indicators. The individual measures and their sources are discussed in the next two sections.

Determinants of need satisfaction: theories and measures

There is no single accepted explanation of national differences in welfare, so there is nothing for it but to consider all the major theoretical contenders in turn. We shall consider those theories that focus on the following factors:

- economic development
- dependency and position in the international order
- paths of development
- socio-economic system
- state capacities and dispositions
- democracy, human rights and other socio-political factors
- women's status and gender equality

Economic development and income per head

The importance of a nation's level of economic development in explaining its aggregate level of need satisfaction is widely accepted, whether explicitly as in the modernisation and 'stages of growth' theories, or implicitly as a welfare facilitator. It is also widespread in accounts of the development of welfare states and some welfare outcomes within the developed world. For example, industrialisation and modernisation theories regard the general imperatives of economic growth and the varying availability of resources as key determinants of national social policies. Some forms of structural Marxist theories echo this but emphasise the general imperatives of capital accumulation (Evans and Stephens, 1988).

We experiment with several measures and in the end favour GNP per capita at purchasing power parity. National differences in per capita GNP at current exchange rates suffers from well-known conceptual problems. Official exchange rates may be very different from hypothetical market-clearing rates that would prevail in the absence of restrictions, and abrupt devaluations or revaluations shift countries' relative incomes in an unrealistic way. GNP at purchasing power parity is a better indicator of the quantum of productive resources in a society, which is the focus of our attention. We use the log of the World Bank's ICP estimates for 1990 which is highly correlated with both PQLI (0.86) and the Human Development Index (HDI) (0.93).

Of course, income per head ignores the distribution of that income, which will also have an impact on aggregate need satisfaction. To combine the two we propose a new index: the 'real income of the worst off' (Doyal and Gough, 1991: 238). The UNDP now calculate the absolute GNP per capita of the lowest 40 per cent of households in a country, which can serve as a reasonable approximation of this (1992, Table 17). Interestingly, this measure exhibits the highest correlation with PQLI (0.86) and HDI (0.93) of any of our system variables. It suggests that combining the efficiency and equity of an economy in this way provides a most powerful predictor of welfare outcomes. Unfortunately there are data for only 45 countries at present, so we are not able to pursue this line of enquiry here.

Dependency and position in the international order

In opposition to modernisation theories of economic development stand the dependency school (Cardoso and Faletto, 1979; Evans, 1979) and world systems theories (Wallerstein, 1974; Chase-Dunn, 1981). These claim that the interpenetration of poor countries by external actors, whether states or powerful private organisations, generates paths of development which are different in kind from those followed by the advanced western economies (Evans and Stephens, 1988: 785 ff). Generally speaking, it is supposed that welfare is lower (than other factors would warrant) in peripheral nations, is higher in the core nations and is indeterminate in the semi-periphery. The mechanisms by which these dependency relations operate can vary and are disputed. They can embrace economic dependency, such as reliance on single commodities, inward investment by multinationals or trade dependency, geopolitical dependency and combinations of the two. Consequently many different measures have been developed, including trade reliance, export revenue fluctuations, primary product specialisation and penetration by multinational companies. For example London and Williams (1990) use a measure of investment dependency, or the penetration of a nation's economy by multinational corporations around 1967, and find that this is associated with lower PQLI levels, controlling for level of economic development. Moon subjects many of these measures to a typically searching theoretical and empirical analysis. When these factors are entered into his comprehensive model he finds that none of them is powerfully related to welfare outcomes. He concludes: 'While the periphery is not a category of analysis in which we have a great deal of confidence, it does appear to serve us reasonably well as a general summary for a series of attributes that are neither strongly related to one another nor powerfully associated with basic needs levels' (1991: 209).

In the light of this we do not enter any of these single-factor variables into our model. Instead we follow others and use Snyder and Kick's (1979) synthetic index of the structural position of nations in the world economy for the 1960s. This revealed the highest correlation coefficient (0.68) with PQLI and HDI of all the measures we tried.

Paths of development

Both conventional and dependency theories of development imply a temporal aspect that we now need to consider more explicitly. Present geographical differences between world regions cannot be logically separated from different historical paths of development. This insight is a particular feature of world systems theories. The institutional residues of historical experience and their importance in explaining welfare outcomes is also a feature of state-centred theories considered below. One distinction in the modern world to which all such theories accord importance is that between colonised and colonising nations. Hypothesising that nations with a more recent colonial experience should manifest a lower PQLI than other factors would warrant, Moon distinguishes between countries that were and were not independent by 1945; we also use this index, which is significantly associated with PQLI (0.63) and HDI (0.68).

More recently, Therborn (1992) has developed a novel perspective on 'paths to modernity' which, although arising from within the sociological problematic of modernity, provides an alternative way of conceptualising the place of different nation states within the world system. He distinguishes four routes to modernity: (1) the route pioneered in Europe, including, he claims, Russia, East-Central and South-Eastern Europe, (2) the settler societies of the New Worlds including both North and South America, (3) the colonial zone of Africa and much of Asia, and (4) externally-induced modernisation, where nominally independent states, in response to external pressures, undertake autonomous strategies of development (including such nations as Egypt, Turkey, Japan and China). When we allocate each country to one of these four paths, we find that countries in the first two paths have significantly higher levels of welfare, those in the third path have lower levels, and there is no significant association for those in the fourth.

Socio-economic system

The respective contribution of capitalism and socialism to human welfare is the subject of an important debate with a long lineage (Chapter 2). The claims of free-market capitalism are that its efficiency and dynamism create need satisfiers in large quantity and of high quality, sufficient numbers of which trickle down to improve the need satisfactions of the worst-off. Moreover the historically observed development of democratic institutions alongside capitalism ensures that need claims can be voiced and public policies modified. State socialism, on the other hand, is credited with an ability collectively to identify and target the meeting of basic needs as the fundamental goal of national policy, and to plan to produce appropriate need satisfiers and to distribute them equitably. There are also powerful arguments against both systems. Unregulated capitalism suffers from well-established market failures, maldistribution and the threat to democracy posed by economic inequality and the pursuit of individual gain. State socialism suffers from a lack of democratic representation which results in a 'dictatorship over needs' as well as profound information and incentive problems which result in shortages of even basic need satisfiers.

Some studies have tried to test these predictions. Cereseto and Waitzkin (1986) find that at any particular stage of development socialist systems yield higher levels of PQLI than capitalist ones, but they do not take other explanatory variables into account (cf. Lena and London, 1993). Moon (1991: ch. 4) concludes that the 11 countries he identifies as socialist do have higher PQLI levels than would be predicted by GNP per capita, for example, China and Cuba. However, when all other variables are included, the association remains significant only for nations at lower levels of development.

Others have claimed that both systems are fundamentally flawed as socio-economic frameworks within which to improve need satisfaction, and have argued the merits of various forms of mixed economic system. Students of corporatism in Europe and elsewhere have claimed that this represents another variant of modern capitalism, and that a third co-ordination mechanism should be recognised – negotiation between interest groups within a public framework. Gough (1994) has generalised this to generate three variants of contemporary capitalism: neoliberal, statist and corporatist. He hypothesises that corporatist capitalism will do relatively well in meeting human needs, neoliberal relatively poorly and that statist capitalism is indeterminate in the absence of information about the goals that state economic and social intervention will pursue. Thus a variety of theories exist predicting different linkages between economic system and human welfare.

Unfortunately, there is no widely acceptable index available which identifies such differences in socio-economic systems. We have had recourse to Gastil's (1989) categorisation of countries into five groups: capitalist, state capitalist, mixed capitalist, mixed socialist and state socialist. However, the derivation of his categories is unclear and an inspection suggests that not all of his allocations are plausible; for example, Germany is characterised as a 'pure' capitalist system. None of the systems has any significant association with good or poor levels of PQLI or HDI except for (weakly) the mixed capitalist group. This finding supports the mixed economy theories and questions the role of both pure capitalism and pure state socialism as frameworks for human welfare. But to get at more subtle measures of differences in economic systems we must consider the role of the state.

State capacities and dispositions

A broad range of neo-institutional theories regard the capacities and dispositions of different states as crucial in determining economic and social outcomes (Moon and Dixon, 1985; UNDP, 1991: ch. 3). For our purposes, two features are of major importance (Rueschemeyer and Evans, 1992). The first comprises the resources available to a state to pursue its goals. Skocpol (1985: 17) persuasively argues that 'a state's means of raising and deploying financial resources tell us more than could any other single factor about its existing (and immediate potential) capacities to create or strengthen state organisations, to employ personnel, to coopt political support, to subsidise economic enterprises and to fund social systems'. An effective tax state is the most general precondition for an effective welfare state, and when we calculate the share of taxation in GDP we find a significant association with both PQLI (0.56) and HDI (0.52).

Government expenditures, on the other hand, are better regarded as indicators of state dispositions. The most useful here is the 'social priority ratio' constructed by the UNDP (1991: ch. 3) which calculates the share of social expenditure allocated to priority concerns, such as primary education and health care. Unfortunately, this is only available for a minority of nations at present. Using instead the share of total health and social expenditure in GNP (Sivard, 1989) we find it to be significantly correlated with PQLI (0.58) and HDI (0.59). Unlike Moon, we do not find military expenditures to be significantly associated either way.

Democracy, rights and other socio-political factors

Two socio-political factors are frequently regarded as significant predictors of welfare outcomes. The first is the existence and extent of democracy in a country. What Hewitt (1977) calls the 'simple democratic hypothesis' contends that the degree and extent of democratic institutions generates egalitarian policies, since the equal distribution of the vote countervails the unequal distribution of property. However, this can be criticised on the grounds that it does not predict what particular political coalitions will be formed to press what interests. More general is the argument advanced above that extensive civil and political liberties and the broadest range of democratic decision-making in a society are a necessary pre-requisite for rational programmes to improve collective human welfare (Doyal and Gough, 1991: ch. 11).

To take these theories into account requires indices of both civil and political rights. The former have been expertly and comprehensively monitored by Humana (1986, 1992), who has devised an index based on various international Human Rights treaties, which is now recognised by the latest UNDP Report. The cross-national operationalisation of democracy has improved greatly in recent years (Bollen, 1991) and provides us with several alternative measures which we have subjected to scrutiny and statistical testing. Of the up-to-date indices perhaps the most sophisticated is by Hadenius (1992); unfortunately, however, he calculates it only for Third World countries. In the end, we have had recourse to Gastil's frequently cited and annually updated index of political liberties, using his 1989 index (1989). It is closely correlated with PQLI (0.60) and HDI (0.61). The use of the 1989 index may, however, overestimate the impact of democracy on need satisfaction given the wave of democratisation which swept the world in the 1980s (UNDP, 1992: 28).

The second socio-political factor hypothesised to affect the disposition of state policy-making and thus welfare outcomes is the class balance of forces in society. This theory has both a social democratic and neo-Marxist provenance and has been advocated for both the First and Third Worlds. Korpi (1983) and others argue that collective action in trades unions and/or left political parties enables the working class to exert leverage on both state policies and private institutions in advanced capitalist societies. They are likely to use that leverage to pursue welfare-related policies of various kinds. Moon and Dixon (1985) and Evans and

Stephens (1988) argue that in developing nations too, relative class power is a crucial variable intermediate between democracy and socio-economic development. There is, however, disagreement over the respective roles of the working class, agrarian classes and the middle classes in pressing for welfare reforms. Unfortunately, despite the theoretical case for its inclusion, we know of no conceptually sound and up-to-date data on regime ideology or the class balance of forces in societies, and must therefore omit this factor from our analysis.

Gender differences and households

The above theories all tend to 'stop at the front door' and to be gender-blind (Elson, 1991). They assume that the family or household is the basic unit of society and do not enquire about the distribution of income and welfare within the family, between women and men, adults and children, and between other household members. A growing body of theory and evidence has revealed the importance of intra-household power, wealth and status for welfare outcomes. In particular, the position of women and gender inequalities are very relevant to the need transformation process identified above (Stewart, 1985: ch. 5; World Bank, 1990). This has been recognised in the 1992 UNDP report in the form of a 'gender-sensitive HDI' which measures the gender ratios of its constituents, although it is presently available for only 33 (mainly developed) countries. After experimenting with a variety of available measures to tap gender inequalities and the status of women, we use the composite index of the 'status of women' calculated for 127 of the countries in a study by the Population Crisis Committee (1988). More especially we favour their separate sub-index of women's social equality, which combines measures of women's political and legal equality, gender differences in economic equality and equality in marriage and the family. This records very high rank correlation coefficients with both PQLI (0.72) and HDI (0.66).

Summary

We find that almost all these factors exhibit a significant association with PQLI and HDI in the late 1980s. Only types of economic system appear not to be linked to welfare outcomes: socialist societies are not more likely to exhibit higher levels of basic need satisfaction than capitalist ones, and only the mixed capitalist systems show any significant positive correlation. Of the remaining system variables we attach especial importance to those listed in Table 5.2. These constitute our independent system variables in the following analysis.

Correlates of basic and intermediate need satisfaction

We are now in a position to enquire about simple associations between our more sophisticated measures of need satisfaction and our basic independent variables. Table 5.3 shows the correlation coefficients with five basic need indicators, and Table 5.4 with six intermediate need indicators.

Table 5.2 Independent system indicators

Economic development	GDP	GDP per head (ICP estimates)
	LOWINC	Real income of the poorest 40%
Dependency and world position	DEPEND	Dependency index (Snyder and Kick) (-ve)
Paths of development	DEBTEX	Debt-export ratio, 1990 (-ve)
	INDEP	Independence by 1945
	PATH1	European
	PATH2	Settler societies
	PATH3	Colonial zone (-ve)
Economic system	MIXEDCAP	Mixed capitalist system
State capacities/dispositions	TAX	Tax/GDP
	SOCEXP	Social expenditure/GDP
Socio-political factors	RIGHTS	Human rights index
	POLLIB	Political liberties (Gastil)
Status of women	GENDEQ	Women's social equality index

Table 5.3 Spearman correlation coefficients between basic need indicators and independent variables

	LIFEXP	MATMORT	LOWBWT	LIT	FEMLIT
GDP	0.83**	−0.82	−0.73**	0.75**	0.59**
	(N=128)	(N=128)	(N=119)	(N=128)	(N=82)
DEPEND	−0.64**	0.62**	0.51**	−0.63**	−0.31
	(N=104)	(N=104)	(N=98)	(N=104)	(N=65)
INDEP	0.49**	−0.48**	−0.44**	0.54**	0.42**
	(N=128)	(N=128)	(N=119)	(N=128)	(N=82)
MIXEDCAP	0.27**	−0.27**	−0.20	0.2	0.02
	(N=128)	(N=128)	(N=119)	(N=128)	(N=82)
TAX	0.50**	−0.54**	−0.40**	0.58**	0.27
	(N=103)	(N=103)	(N=98)	(N=103)	(N=61)
SOCEXP	0.58**	−0.59**	−0.54**	0.52**	0.19
	(N=117)	(N=117)	(N=111)	(N=117)	(N=75)
RIGHTS	0.53**	−0.52**	−0.39**	0.52**	0.42**
	(N=127)	(N=127)	(N=119)	(N=127)	(N=82)
GENDEQ	0.64**	−0.62**	−0.41**	0.74**	0.54**
	(N=95)	(N=95)	(N=91)	(N=95)	(N=56)

N= number of countries for which data
1-tailed signif: * = 0.01, ** = 0.001

Table 5.4 Spearman correlation coefficients between selected intermediate need indicators and independent variables

	CAL	WATER	HLTHSERV	YRSED	FEMED	CONCEP
GDP	0.74**	0.74**	0.87**	0.77**	0.76**	0.87**
	(N=94)	(N=126)	(N=101)	(N=128)	(N=128)	(N=101)
DEPEND	−0.22	−0.55**	−0.70**	−0.62**	−0.61**	−0.64**
	(N=73)	(N=103)	(N=83)	(N=104)	(N=104)	(N=82)
INDEP	0.25	0.45**	0.48**	0.55**	0.56**	0.55**
	(N=94)	(N=126)	(N=101)	(N=128)	(N=128)	(N=101)
MIXED	0.01	0.25*	0.27*	0.19	0.20	0.20
CAP	(N=94)	(N=126)	(N=101)	(N=128)	(N=128)	(N=101)
TAX	0.22	0.46**	0.60**	0.49**	0.50**	0.54**
	(N=72)	(N=102)	(N=84)	(N=103)	(N=103)	(N=88)
SOCEXP	0.34**	0.53**	0.64**	0.50**	0.50**	0.51**
	(N=85)	(N=115)	(N=95)	(N=117)	(N=117)	(N=97)
RIGHTS	0.01	0.42**	0.50**	0.50**	0.53**	0.56**
	(N=94)	(N=126)	(N=101)	(N=127)	(N=127)	(N=101)
GENDEQ	0.16	0.41**	0.65**	0.67**	0.69**	0.67**
	(N=65)	(N=94)	(N=78)	(N=95)	(N=95)	(N=83)

N= number of countries for which data.
1-tailed signif: $*$ = 0.01, $**$ = 0.001

These tables suggest the following conclusions. First, GDP per capita at purchasing power parities continues to prove a powerful predictor of cross-national variations in need satisfaction. Second, national economic dependency, as measured by the Snyder index, is significantly associated with poorer need satisfaction levels, except for nutrition where the association is not significant. Third, political independence by 1945 is positively linked to all the dimensions of welfare covered in these tables. Fourth, of the types of economic system only the mixed capitalist system reveals any association with need satisfaction, and this is erratic and weak, though positive. Fifth, the level of government taxation, a measure of state capacity, is a significant predictor of health status and of most measures of intermediate need satisfaction. However it is not significantly associated with literacy levels or nutrition. Social expenditure, a measure of state dispositions, on the other hand, is strongly linked to all the indicators covered in these tables. Sixth, human rights (and political liberties, not shown) are strong predictors of high levels of need satisfaction in all dimensions. Seventh, gender equality is positively associated with all need indicators except for nutrition.

Of the dependent variables, the least supported by our explanatory hypotheses are literacy and nutrition. Our indicators of physical and economic insecurity – 'war victims' and 'poverty' (not shown in the tables) – also do not reveal significant associations. These aberrant findings warrant further investigation, but they may be due to the relatively small number of countries for which we have data on these dimensions of need satisfaction.

Nevertheless, there is *prima facie* evidence supporting six of the seven theories we are seeking to test. However the overwhelming problem remains that the degree of inter-correlation between many of these independent variables (not to speak of the dependent variables) is so high that few firm conclusions can be drawn from simple correlation analysis.

A path analysis of the determinants of need satisfaction

One of the main problems with global cross-national data of this kind is multi-collinearity: the high linear correlation between the regressor variables which can lead to serious problems in identifying the underlying causal linkages. For example, Gastil's political liberties index (POL-LIB) is highly correlated to the status of women (WOMSTAT) and logged GDP (LOGGDP) and more loosely to most of the other explanatory variables. Indeed almost every independent variable is closely correlated with almost every other. Many previous studies have relied on traditional methods of multivariate regression analysis to overcome this. For example, Moon develops a 'hierarchical' design whereby additional regressor variables are added stage by stage using Ordinary Least Squares principles. He points out that he chose this method in order to highlight rather than deemphasise this causal complexity. We too experimented with multiple regression analysis but found that it is unable to overcome the problems associated with multicollinearity between the regressor variables. We next turned to Principal Components Analysis to attempt to group the system variables into a smaller number of related categories which could be justifiably used in a fuller regression analysis. However, once again we encountered problems since only two principal components were identified between which there was a substantial overlap (Gough and Thomas, 1993).

What we require is a method of statistical analysis that can (a) cope with several inter-correlated independent variables, (b) handle more than one dependent variable (in order to take account of the range of indicators of basic and intermediate needs) and (c) test simultaneously for direct and indirect causation. This last prerequisite is necessary to handle more complex transmission mechanisms from system variables to both basic and intermediate need variables, and to allow for other causal relations between our dimensions of welfare discovered in past analysis – for example, the impact of literacy on health. Path analysis meets all these conditions.

Path analysis is a method for testing a postulated linear causal model for internal consistency and can display the results in the form of path diagrams. It enables complex systems of direct and indirect causation to be tested simultaneously in a recursive system. Simple regression and interdependent system techniques are normally nonrecursive. Path analysis entails ordering a set of jointly dependent or effect variables regressed on the independent or cause variables. We use a single causal model using covariance structure analysis in the LISREL computer programme. (For further details of the methods used together with diagnostic tests for our final model, see Gough and Thomas, 1993, Appendix 3.)

The first task is to specify the hypothesised causal linkages between our variables, and these are shown in Figure 5.1. We begin by commenting

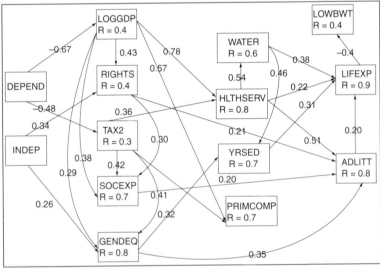

Figure 5.1   Path Diagram of the Determinants of Need Satisfaction
Maximum likelihood estimates
Diagnostics:
Total Coefficient of Determination for structural equations is 0.652
Chi-square with 36 degrees of freedom = 70.95 (P = .000)
Goodness of fit index = 0.860
Adjusted goodness of fit index = 0.590
Root mean square residual = 0.053

on each of the causal arrows shown, and leave discussion of the results till later. In the interests of clarity we have had to omit several system and need variables; even so the final model is rather complex. It is divided into four stages, shown as columns in Figure 5.1. These are, from left to right: first, temporally-prior system variables; second, the remaining system variables; third, four indicators of intermediate needs; and fourth, three basic need indicators. All the linkages are hypothesised to be positive, except for those from DEPEND to all other variables and those from other variables to LOWBWT. In the remainder of this section we justify the causal assumptions of this model.

A major reason for singling out Snyder and Kick's measure of economic dependency in the 1960s and Moon's measure of political independence by 1945 as causally prior is that they are temporally prior to all the other variables. However, there is also theoretical argument and statistical evidence for this. Several studies find that dependency partly determines level of economic development, whether using a broad-based measure of economic dependency such as we do or a more specific measure of penetration by multinational corporations (Chase-Dunn, 1975; Bornschier et al., 1978). Bollen (1983), using a modified version of the Snyder and Kick index, finds that both peripheral and semi-peripheral countries are less democratic than core countries, holding level of economic development constant. Dependency also impacts on both our measures of state strength, according to Rubinson (1977) and Delacroix and Ragin (1981). There is also evidence linking economic dependency to at least one of our measures of gender equality: gender differences in labour force participation (Marshall, 1985; Clark, 1992).

Hard evidence linking political independence by 1945 to the other system variables is less systematic. Moon (1991: 234–9) presents an argument why former colonies have a poorer level of economic development than nations with a longer history of statehood. Therborn's (1992) analysis of the effects of different paths to modernity on the development of universal suffrage clearly demonstrates the relative backwardness of the colonial zone. The association between his 'path 3' and independence by 1945 is highly significant and negative. Besides with long temporal priority, we feel confident in defining political independence along with economic independence as a causally prior explanatory variable.

Next we turn to the causal relationships between the variables in the second column of Figure 5.1. From the remaining system variables we select five, representing per capita income, democracy and human rights (for which, taken together, we prefer the more systematic Humana index as a measure), state capacities and dispositions, and gender equality. First, our model hypothesises that per capita GDP affects positively all the remaining components. The impact of economic development on democracy has been the subject of numerous studies which posit different and conflicting mechanisms to explain the link (Lipset, 1960; Rueschemeyer et al., 1992). But whatever the mechanism, the link is well established in cross-national research (Bollen, 1983). Comparative analysis shows that economic development affects the share of state expenditure in GNP in a curvilinear way, increasing from low to middle per capita incomes and then declining (Chenery and Syrquin, 1975), although the association is rather weak. If state revenues and expenditures are assumed to covary, then a similar impact of GNP per capita on state capacity as measured by share of tax revenue may be assumed. Comparative research has also consistently demonstrated that per capita income partially determines social expenditures on health, education and social security (Pryor, 1968: chs. 4–5; Wilensky, 1975; Schmidt, 1989). A link between democratic pressures and state social expenditure is implied by Hewitt's (1977) 'simple democratic hypothesis' and is demonstrated in the case of social security programmes by Cutright (1965).

In the third column of Figure 5.1 we introduce four indicators, representing just three of our intermediate needs, for which reasonably reliable and comprehensive data exist: access to water supplies, access to health services, primary school completion rates and mean years of schooling of adults. We assume that per capita incomes, level of political and human rights, state capacities and state social expenditure will all act positively on all four intermediate need variables. This is a commonplace of much cross-national research and will not be separately argued here. Gender equality is assumed to impact on the education variables but not on access to water and health services. More extensive rights for women are likely to enhance the schooling of girls and thus the aggregate schooling ratio and the mean years of education of women and the whole population.

In the fourth column of Figure 5.1 we introduce three indicators for our basic needs: low birth weight, life expectancy and literacy. The first is used by default as the only proxy indicator of infant health available for a sufficient number of countries. These three indicators are hypothesised as lying at the end of our causal tree – they are the final variables which we wish to explain. In specifying their determinants we begin by assuming, following the Doyal–Gough theory, that they are affected by the level of satisfaction of our four intermediate need variables. However, we also assume that literacy is directly determined by level of democracy, state social expenditure and gender equality. Lastly, we allow for causal relations between basic needs; notably the evidence from many studies that literacy (and in particular female literacy) impacts upon health standards (World Bank, 1991: ch. 3; King and Hill, 1993).

Results: explaining cross-national variations in need satisfaction

Figure 5.1 also presents the results of our analysis (see Gough and Thomas, 1993, for further details). Let us summarise the results of the model from right to left starting at the top of our causal hierarchy with *survival/health*, as measured by life expectancy and low birth weight. The low birthweight measure performs poorly and appears to be unrelated to other variables, except life expectancy, casting doubt upon the validity and/or the reliability of this indicator. However inter-country variations in life expectancy are significantly affected by the extent of adult literacy, confirming findings of other studies. It also shows that three of our intermediate needs – access to safe water, the utilisation of health services and mean years of schooling of adults – all significantly affect final health status as measured by life expectancy. Overall these factors contribute to a high R^2 of 0.9.

The extent of adult *literacy* plays an important role in our model. It is influenced significantly by only one of the intermediate need indicators – our composite measure of health services. The absence of a significant linkage running from mean years of schooling to literacy rates may reflect the fact that the former only relates to 1980, or to differences in the groups included (those over 25 years and 15 years respectively). On the other hand, this absence may be because years of schooling is really another and broader measure of educational outcomes. Literacy *is* directly and positively affected by the respect a country accords to civil and political rights, by the share of government social expenditure in GNP, and by the degree of gender equality. Here there is direct support for theories linking democracy, state welfare effort and women's rights to levels of human welfare.

Turning to our intermediate need indicators we find that both *health services* and *primary school completion* rates are influenced by national income per head and tax shares. The extent of *adult education* is influenced by gender equality and by access to safe water, which may serve as an indicator of housing conditions. The R^2 for these three intermediate needs are reasonably high, but the model offers no significant explanations of access to water. By this stage we find evidence linking all five of our system variables with welfare outcomes, both intermediate and final.

When we consider the system variables themselves, the most striking aspect is perhaps the relatively small part played independently by GDP per head in the direct explanation of welfare outcomes. It does, however, indirectly promote welfare via its influence on the rights accorded to women, human and political rights, and a state's social expenditure share in GDP. These findings replicate those of previous studies but they elaborate on their interconnections. Lastly, the temporally prior system variables capturing national economic and political dependence/independence are both found to be significant. The former is negatively associated with contemporary income per head, as would be predicted, and with low tax shares. Political independence by 1945 is positively associated with human rights levels and gender equality, supporting the independent importance of paths of development for universal citizenship rights.

Taken as a whole the model provides striking confirmation for six of the seven theories with which we began. Aggregate levels of need satisfaction are explained by a range of interdependent factors and not simply by income per head as the outcome of a unilinear process of development. Paths of politico-economic development, position in the world economy, state capacities and dispositions, political and civil liberties, and gender equality all play a role. The influence of these other factors is often disguised when simple regression techniques are used.

Disaggregating measures of need satisfaction, as we have done, also reveals the interconnections between different dimensions of welfare. In particular the role of literacy is revealed as crucial in influencing health status. Human needs are not passive 'requirements'; they indicate the capacities people have to act – and to act critically to change their environment. No doubt further feedback loops could and should be introduced into our model to reflect this, for example between literacy and income per head and human rights.

Conclusion

This project is premised on the theory of need developed by Doyal and Gough and has two goals. The first is to evaluate, as far as is possible in a study such as this, the validity of our general model of human need. The second aim is to test various theories advanced to explain cross-national differences in need satisfaction in the contemporary world.

The first task is most closely approximated in the final model shown in Figure 5.1. It tentatively confirms two of the linkages advanced by the Doyal–Gough theory. Variations in levels of intermediate need satisfaction impact upon variations in levels of basic need satisfaction in significant ways. The concept of universal satisfier characteristics which in all cultures and social settings contribute to final levels of welfare is supported, in so far as we can model these relations with the data at our disposal. The system variables in the second column of Figure 5.1 can stand as proxy measures for some of the procedural and material preconditions in the Doyal–Gough theory: production of satisfiers (LOGGDP), the prioritisation of need satisfiers together with their production and distribution (SOCEXP), the need transformation process (GENDEQ), respect for civil and political rights and political participation (RIGHTS). The model shows that all of these preconditions are significantly and positively associated with levels of satisfaction of at least one of our intermediate needs. There is support in all this for the concept of universal, cross-cultural societal preconditions for enhanced need satisfaction.

The results of the second task are also best illustrated in Figure 5.1. Of the seven theories we tested for, six receive support from our analysis. *We may conclude that level of economic development, (lower levels of) national economic dependency, early political independence, state capacity, democracy and human rights, and relative gender equality all contribute positively to need satisfaction and human welfare.* And since state capacity captures some of the aspects of different socio-economic system discussed above, our model does not necessarily rule out support for this seventh theory. These effects are both direct and, in the case of income per head and human rights, indirect. Put another way, income per head and more generally level of economic development does not by any means explain all cross-national variation in need satisfaction. The form of economic development, the extent of political dependence and the presence or absence of our procedural preconditions (civil, democratic and women's rights) all play an independent causal role.

These are encouraging findings. They suggest that social rights and levels of human welfare are best guaranteed by forms of economic development guided by an effective public authority which guarantees civil and political rights to all and is thus open to pressure by effective political mobilisation in civil society.

Note

1   Co-authored with Theo Thomas, and first published in *International Journal of Health Services*, 24(4) (1994) pp. 715–48. This is an abbreviated version.

6
Social Safety Nets in Southern Europe[1]

Introduction

In the last few years serious research into the social welfare systems of
southern Europe has taken off. Descriptive and historical studies have
been complemented by analyses which seek to explain their particular
patterns of welfare development in terms of the categories and concepts
developed to understand the welfare states of northern Europe and
other regions of the OECD. Others have argued that the southern countries of Western Europe constitute a distinct welfare regime (Leibfried,
1993) comprising extravagant constitutional promises alongside rudi-
mentary social rights and weak public implementation, superimposed
on a greater role of church, family and hidden economy than in the
North. Membership of this group always includes Spain, Portugal and
Greece; they are normally joined by southern Italy or all Italy, and
sometimes by France. In this chapter I shall consider all these countries
except France, but I shall also include Turkey. Though the major part of
Turkey is strictly speaking not in Europe I shall use the term 'southern
Europe' to describe this set of five countries.

The most sophisticated attempt to discern their common social
policy features has been made by Ferrera (1996). He identifies the following:

1 A dualistic income maintenance system in which very high benefits
  are provided for privileged groups with strong attachment to the
  formal labour force alongside zero or low and discretionary benefits
  for the rest of the population. It is also inegalitarian in that pensions
  tend to be generous whereas unemployment and other benefits for
  individuals and families of working age are weak.

2 By contrast, health care systems are universalistic. Yet here, and in other social services in kind, practice falls far short of promises: the private sector, markets and privileges are integrated into the public health services. Waste is endemic and efficiency is low.

3 The planning and delivery of certain public welfare services is characterised by particularism, clientelism and even corruption. In contrast to the Weberian model of bureaucracy, it is political parties which dominate, exchanging favours and benefits for political support.

4 The combination of dynamic transfer expenditures and inefficient tax collection has generated a 'fiscal crisis of the state' worthy of the term. Government net borrowing as a share of GNP is higher than in all EU member states except the UK, and the gap is projected to increase.

These features are systematically linked and, short of political crises, are self-reinforcing. Thus clientelism impedes bureaucratic and rights-based reform, high benefits reinforce a dual labour market, and both exhaust public finances making the development of a safety net and adequate services for all harder to attain. At the same time the social pressures which these problems throw up have been sufficiently absorbed by the family, community and informal economy to undermine campaigns for reform.

My purpose in this chapter is to investigate one fiscally minor but socially important aspect of social policy in southern Europe: the provision of a national income 'safety net' via social assistance programmes. Pressures to improve on current provision have come from the European Union, for example the Observatory on National Policies to Combat Social Exclusion and the 1992 Council Recommendation on Sufficient Resources. In northern Europe the need for social security reform grows as labour markets diverge more and more from the ideal assumed in classic social insurance programmes, as changing patterns of behaviour undermine assumptions about family obligations and as 'the new poverty' creates novel risks and insecurities (Room, 1990). Yet very little is known about the nature and extent of social assistance in southern Europe, its goals and administration or its effectiveness in reducing poverty or achieving other aims.

This chapter aims to fill that gap drawing on a recently completed study of social assistance in the OECD conducted by colleagues at the Social Policy Research Unit at the University of York and myself. This studied the full range of assistance programmes in all 24 OECD countries in and around 1992. The data on social assistance arrangements were collected using two questionnaires: one sent to officials in the appropriate government departments and the other to academic informants with a knowledge of social assistance. The replies to the questionnaires were collated into a single national report, which was sent back to the informants for validation, and a volume has been produced (Eardley et al., 1996b) comparing the systems country by country. This volume provided the raw data for the other more analytical report in which arrangements are compared and contrasted across countries (Eardley et al., 1996a). Except where stated, the material below is drawn from these two volumes.

Social assistance and safety nets – preliminary definitions

The term 'social assistance' does not have a fixed or universal meaning. In discussing southern Europe this is important because 'social assistance' in these countries embraces a wide range of non-resource-tested but categorically targeted social aid for such groups as orphans, immigrants, victims of natural disasters, homeless people, and so on. On the other hand, the term usually excludes means-tested or income-related benefits which are administered as part of social insurance, for example means-tested 'social pensions'.

There are three, and only three, basic mechanisms by which the state can directly[2] allocate income or services to individuals or households (see, for example, Atkinson, 1989). The first mechanism is the 'universal' or contingency benefit allocated to all citizens within a certain social category. These benefits are not related to income or employment status. Secondly, there is social insurance, where the benefit is related to (a) employment status; and (b) contributions paid in to the scheme. Both these conditions can be interpreted more or less stringently. The third comprises means-tested or income-related benefits where eligibility is dependent upon the current or capital resources of the beneficiary, though other categorical conditions may also apply. Our study focuses principally on the third category which I shall refer to as means-tested or resource-tested benefits.

Resource-tested benefits are sometimes referred to as 'targeted' benefits, but this is not always a helpful term. Both contingency and social insurance programmes can be directed at low income groups or at those in other categories of acute need. Contingency benefits and services can be aimed at groups highly correlated with poverty or extreme need, such as homeless children or long-term unemployed people. Social insurance programmes can build in minimum pensions and other benefits to provide an income floor below which no members of the scheme will fall (such as the Italian *integrazione al minimo*). The present study addresses these schemes only in so far as they involve resource-testing.

Within resource tested benefits we can distinguish three main groups:

1 *General assistance:* makes available cash benefits for all or almost all people below a specified minimum income standard, for example Income Support in the UK or the Belgian Minimex. This comes closest to what most would think of as a guaranteed national safety net.
2 *Categorical assistance:* provides cash benefits for specific groups, such as the elderly or unemployed
3 *Tied assistance:* provides access to specific goods or services in kind or in cash, such as housing or medical care.

I shall refer to all three in what follows. Table 6.1 uses this classification to list the present range of assistance schemes in the five countries.

Table 6.1   A taxonomy of national means- and income-tested programmes

Country	General assistance	Group assistance	Tied assistance
Greece	No general assistance	Scheme for Unprotected Children; Scheme for the Protection of Maternity; Scheme for non-insured elderly	Housing benefit for non-insured elderly
Italy	Local cash assistance (*minimo vitale*)	*Pensione sociale; Pensione di inabilita*; Veteran's Pension	Local assistance services
Portugal		Family Allowance; Supplementary Allowance; Nursing Allowance; Orphan's pension; Social Invalidity Pension; Social Old Age Pension; Young people's integration benefit; Survivors Grant	Housing benefit
Spain	*Ingreso minimo de insercion*	Means-tested Aged pension; Means-tested Disability Pension; Unemployment Assistance	
Turkey	Social assistance and solidarity scheme	Old age and disability assistance	Green card medical assistance

Source: Eardlery et al (1996a), Table 2.1.

Social assistance in southern Europe: national profiles

Italy

In the nineteenth century religious charities (*opere pie*) provided the dominant form of poor relief, though in the cities municipal poor relief also has a long history. The development of social insurance institutions in the 1930s initially left the assistance programmes undisturbed. According to the post-war Constitution, Article 38, 'every citizen unable to work and lacking the necessary means to live is entitled to sustenance and social assistance', but this was given no legislative expression in the post-war period.

Indeed there is no national system of social assistance in Italy. In the 1960s national categorical schemes were set up for low-income pensioners (*pensione sociali*) and disabled people (*pensione di inabilitá*). These provide guaranteed benefits considerably lower than most social insurance benefits. The rest of the population relies on local assistance schemes and church and voluntary relief agencies. Jurisdiction for this assistance was transferred downwards to the regions in 1972 and to municipalities in 1977 and the power of communes was further strengthened in the Local Autonomies Act 1990. The regions are permitted but not required to establish general frameworks for social assistance. By 1990, eleven had established specific guidelines or had tied benefits to social or supplementary pension levels; the remaining nine provided no guidelines or delegated the task to communes or local health authorities. The *minimo vitale* has not yet established itself as a right of citizens. At the same time church agencies like *Caritas* play a considerable role and other non-governmental organisations flourished in the 1970s and 1980s. Their role in social policy was further promoted in the Voluntary Associations Act 1991.

Italy thus relies on local authorities, the Church, voluntary bodies and the family to substitute (imperfectly) for an official safety net. Lødemel and Schulte (1992) label it an 'incomplete differentiated poverty regime' where the absence of general assistance forces large groups to rely on the family and voluntary organisations for aid. A recent attempt to introduce a national framework law (*Leggo-quadro sull'assistenza*) has failed (Ferrera, 1987; Ministry of Internal Affairs, n.d.; Cerami, 1979: ch. 3; Saraceno, 1992; Negri and Saraceno, 1996).

Spain

Until recently poor relief in Spain was the responsibility of local communes and the Church. The national government only intruded in 1933 when the Vagabonds Act introduced harsh controls. The origins of modern minimum income provision date from 1960 when the Franco regime enacted a law establishing the National Fund for Social Assistance (FONAS). This administers Minimum Pensions and Invalidity Pensions, means-tested benefits for elderly and disabled people who lack contributory insurance coverage.

In 1978 the newly democratic Spain established a new Constitution pledging economic security and a guaranteed minimum income (Article 41). In the face of high and rising unemployment, the socialist government introduced in 1984 an unemployment assistance scheme which now accounts for the bulk of assistance expenditure. The FONAS benefits were unified and codified as rights in the 1990 Law of Non-Insurance Pensions (Cabrero, 1992). It was not until 1988 that the Basque authorities pioneered a general minimum income scheme (*Ingreso Minimo de Insercion* or *Renta Minima*). Variations of this scheme are now in place in 16 of the 17 Autonomous Communities of Spain (all except the Balearic Islands) but there is no national framework and the programmes vary considerably.

Portugal

In Portugal, the post-Salazar Constitution promises 'to create and update a national minimum income' (Art. 59, quoted in Pereirinha, 1992). Following the revolution against the Salazar dictatorship the first categorical assistance benefits – again for old age and invalidity – were introduced in 1974. Since then, however, Portugal has gone further in accruing a range of specific non-contributory assistance schemes, including nursing allowance, orphan's pension, family allowance and Young People's Integration Benefit. These are administered by a range of ministries and agencies and are uncoordinated. Portugal has made few moves towards a general safety net scheme.

Greece

In Greece, too, social assistance is limited and of minor importance within the social security system as a whole. Until recently the term 'social assistance' referred to emergency lump-sum protection for such groups as earthquake victims and refugees. In response to immediate crises some more permanent categorical schemes have evolved, but not all of these are means-tested. The first was the scheme for unprotected children, legislated in 1960 to provide for orphans, children with one parent, children with disabilities, children at risk or in poverty. The programme mainly benefits those in poverty resulting from agricultural decline and victims of the Civil War and now aids the repatriation of Greek citizens from Eastern Europe and other areas of the Mediterranean. Following Legislative Decree 57 in 1973 people on low incomes are eligible for free cover for medical expenses. Unlike all other southern European countries, the elderly and disabled were not the first to be covered by categorical scheme, though this was legislated in 1982. There is no general safety net programme (Karantinos et al., 1992).

Turkey

Despite the programme of westernisation and modernisation initiated by the Republic of Turkey since 1923, poor relief has remained the province of localities and Islamic foundations. The first break was not until 1976 when the Old Age and Disability Assistance Scheme was established for penniless elderly people or disabled people. However in 1986 Turkey established the Social Assistance and Solidarity Scheme for people in need or who could become independent with minimal education and training assistance – a general assistance scheme of sorts, though with vestigial benefits. In 1992 the Green Card scheme was set up to provide basic health care for those with low incomes and without social security coverage. The extent and role of local general assistance is unknown.

Assistance in southern Europe: a common pattern

Despite different historical trajectories and socio-economic and cultural features, social assistance in these five countries exhibits many common features.

There is no national income safety net

The most distinctive feature is the absence of a national assistance programme providing benefits for all people who lack sufficient resources despite quite grand constitutional commitments. There is no codification of social welfare law and no agreed standards for defining a statutory minimum subsistence level.

Yet national group-specific assistance schemes do exist

Apart from Turkey, there is a plethora of group-specific or categorical schemes. All five countries now have social pensions attached to the national social insurance programmes for the aged and disabled. Most have programmes for orphans or unprotected children, though these are not necessarily means-tested. Other categorical assistance schemes vary across the region; for instance, Spain has a large Unemployment Assistance Programme. The different schemes are usually administered by different government departments or agencies, resulting in fragmentation and lack of coordination. The upshot is that the aged and disabled have some form of national protection in all countries (how effective remains to be seen) whereas other groups must mostly rely on whatever local assistance is available.

The basic schemes are decentralised and discretionary

What general assistance schemes there are regional (Spain) or local (Italy, Turkey) and are of recent origin. Local social welfare officials have a good deal of discretion in awarding benefits, especially in the case of one-off emergency payments which are common across southern Europe, and they can be tied to the receipt of social work services or advice.

Residential conditions are common

In all five countries few groups are excluded from benefits for reasons of citizenship, ethnic or linguistic group or immigrant status. For example, Kurds fleeing the Gulf War were eligible for and some received the SASS benefits. The main group excluded from benefits are illegal immigrants, of whom there are now substantial numbers. However, as a result of the decentralisation residential requirements are common: residence in the municipal territory in Italy, one year's residence in the region in Spain (and ten years residence in Spain for the means-tested pension), two year's residence in Greece.[3]

The means test is both stringent and informal

In one sense the means test is stringent: there are no or few exemptions for any item of income or property, and benefits are reduced *pari passu* as income increases. Moreover, in Greece and Turkey the resources of the household are assessed when determining entitlement as opposed to those of the nuclear family. On the other hand, procedures of assessment and means testing are normally informal, requiring no more than a signed statement of income and assets.

Social assistance has low salience within social security

Table 6.2 presents three measures of salience. First, the numbers of persons in households receiving social assistance is low in all our countries: Italy apart, less than half the proportion in the EU. These figures hide inequalities in terms of region and population group. In all countries except Spain it is the elderly and disabled who comprise the majority of

Table 6.2 Social assistance: numbers receiving and expenditure

Country	SA recipients as % of population	SA exp. as % GDP	SA as a % soc. sec. exp.	Change in % SA recipients 1980–92	Change in % SA expend/ GNP 1980–92	Change in % SA expend/ soc. sec. 1980–92
Greece	0.7	0.1	n/a	n/a	0.0	−0.4
Italy	4.6	3.3	9.1	+1.2	+0.4	0.0
Portugal	2.1	0.4	3.8	+1.2	+0.2	+1.5
Spain	2.7	1.2	8.4	n/a	+1.0	+6.3
Turkey	n/a	0.5	n/a	n/a	n/a	n/a
EC 12 mean	6.3	1.9	11.5	+2.5	+0.8	+4.2

Cols. 3 and 6: Social security denominators from OECD Household Transfer Data Base, except for Portugal, where government calculations of social security used.

assistance beneficiaries. In Spain the combination of a unique unemployment assistance programme and unemployment rates averaging over 20 per cent concentrated on the young and long-term unemployed has meant that this benefit dominates among assistance households. The numbers receiving unemployment assistance grew from 106,000 in 1982 to 937,000 in 1992. In all countries the share of expenditure on social assistance is below the EU average, though not by much in the case of Spain and Italy.

Assistance benefits are low

These features of social assistance in southern Europe compound the problems in estimating and comparing benefit levels. EU data on social minima regularly show the four south European members at the bottom of their league tables for social protection in old age, invalidity (except Italy) and especially unemployment, where no formal level of support is guaranteed (CEC, 1993: 62). However these data cannot take account of the package of benefits and costs affecting different family types.

To take account of this our study has undertaken simulation exercises using model families, described in the Appendix. Using this approach there are then two ways of comparing average assistance benefit levels across countries: absolutely, by comparing payment levels in terms of a common currency, and relatively, by comparing benefits with average wage or income levels within the country. Table 6.3 adopts the first method and compares the total disposable incomes of six different family types on social assistance in terms of a common currency. Each family type was assumed to be ineligible for social insurance benefits but

Table 6.3   Net monthly disposable incomes of families on social assistance ($ at purchasing power parity), 1992

	Single age 35	Couple age 35	Couple + 1 child age 7	Single + 1 child age 7	Single age 68
Greece	48	48	52	60	60
Italy	(388)	(705)	(833)	(666)	388
Portugal	251	251	270	270	124
Spain	312	358	417	377	208
EC 12 mean	368	531	627	524	378

See Appendix for methods.
The figures for Italy make optimistic assumptions about the likelihood and level of awards to all except the pensioner household. They should be treated with great caution.

Table 6.4   Social assistance benefit levels in 1992 and extent of poverty, 1987–90

Country	Absolute benefit levels: before housing costs	Absolute benefit levels: after housing costs	Relative benefit levels: after housing costs	% poor persons 1987–90
Greece	−91	−119	−16	18.7
Italy	(0)	(28)	(60)	21.1
Portugal	−63	−90	19	24.5
Spain	−45	−41	25	16.9

Col. 1:   Disposable income of social assistance recipients (before housing costs) in purchasing power parities expressed as a proportion of the mean for all OECD countries: average for nine household types.

Col. 2:   As for column 1, but calculated after taking housing costs and any housing assistance into account.

Col. 3:   Disposable incomes of social assistance recipients as percentage of disposable incomes of the same household types where the head is earning average male earnings: average of six household types (as above but excluding single pensioner, pensioner couple, and couple with one child aged 3) after housing costs.

Cols. 1–3: See Appendix for methods.
The figures for Italy make optimistic assumptions about the likelihood and level of awards to all except the pensioner household. They should be treated with great caution.

Col. 4:   Persons in households with incomes less than 50 per cent of national average equivalent expenditure.

Source: Ramprakash (1994: 120).

the table takes into account any other benefits to which they would be entitled as well as assistance. The table shows that benefits for all family types are much lower in the south of Europe.

Table 6.4 presents aggregate estimates for all family types using both methods. A further distinction is made between benefit levels before and after taking housing costs into account. The table makes clear that benefit levels are low in southern Europe on all measures. The simulation method assumes that all those entitled to benefits actually claim and receive them; this is even less likely than normal in the largely fragmented, localised and discretionary systems of southern Europe, so that benefit levels in reality are likely to fall still further behind the rest of the OECD and the EU. Within southern Europe Italy provides the highest benefits and Greece (and Turkey, not shown) the lowest.

And poverty is extensive

Table 6.4 also presents estimates of relative poverty in 1985, defined as household expenditure below 50 per cent of each nation's mean equivalent expenditure, for the four southern EC member states (Ramprakesh, 1994). The estimates should be treated with caution, but in all four countries the incidence of poverty is higher than in all other member states. Regional inequalities compound this, notably in Spain, Italy and Turkey. Thus the south of Italy has a poverty rate (defined as above) about twice that of Italy as a whole (Saraceno, 1992).

The southern social assistance regime in a European context

We can summarise the material presented above by identifying a south European *social assistance regime* and comparing it with those elsewhere in the OECD world. In a pioneering study Lodemel (1992) and Lodemel and Schulte (1992) distinguished four 'poverty regimes' using two criteria – whether or not social work/treatment measures are attached to the receipt of assistance, and the degree of centralisation of programmes. One of these, which they label the 'incomplete differentiated' regime, characterises France and the Latin countries of southern Europe. We agree with the relevance of their two criteria but wish to take into account the other factors noted above. On this basis we arrive at eight distinct social assistance regimes across the OECD. The US, Japan and Australasia each have a distinct system but Europe has five. These are:

1. Welfare states with integrated safety nets: *Britain, Ireland and Germany*

This is a varied group of countries but with sufficient common factors to place them together. British Income Support is a large, national, general programme providing an extensive safety net at or below social insurance levels. When housing benefit is included, benefit levels are above the OECD average. Rights to benefit are relatively well entrenched and the means test contains important disregards, with some work incentives for people with children through Family Credit. Ireland is at first sight different: there are numerous categorical assistance schemes covering a high proportion of the population with means tests and entitlements on a par with those in Britain. However it is moving towards a more integrated system. Germany, from different historical antecedents, has also developed in a similar way: *Sozialhilfe* is, despite its federal–*Land* structure, geographically equitable, codified, rights-based, extensive and of average generosity.[4]

2. Dual social assistance: *France and the Benelux countries*

These countries provide categorical assistance schemes for specific groups, but have supplemented these with newer programmes providing a general basic safety net. Local discretion remains, but is now firmly placed within a national regulatory framework. Assets tests are moderately flexible as are earnings disregards. But benefit levels vary considerably between generous Netherlands and Luxembourg and below-average Belgium. All countries also use 'insertion agreements' requiring some form of work experience or training as an aid, it is argued, to social integration.

3. *Residual social assistance*: the Nordic countries

A tradition of full employment and universal welfare provision has relegated social assistance to the margins of social programmes in these countries – or rather did so until sharp rises in unemployment hit Denmark in the later 1980s and Finland, Iceland and Sweden in the 1990s. Each country has a single general scheme with generous benefits. Though there are national regulatory frameworks, the role of local authorities is substantial and links with social work and social care persist. Strict means tests combine with a view of family financial responsibilities which place more emphasis than in most countries on the individual, particularly in relation to cohabitation. General citizenship-based appeals procedures modify this situation in all countries except Norway.

4. Generous but local and discretionary relief: *Austria and Switzerland*

These countries contain elements of both the Nordic and southern European models. Assistance consists of localised, discretionary relief, linked to social work and with wider kin obligations. However benefit levels are above average – in Switzerland, the most generous in the OECD (according to the cantons and communes selected). Yet relatively small numbers claim social assistance. This is due partly to a record of full male employment and partly to the substantial powers of intervention of local social welfare workers

5. Rudimentary assistance: *Southern Europe and Turkey*

National categorical assistance schemes cover certain specific groups, mainly elderly and disabled people. Otherwise there is local, discretionary relief provided by municipalities or religious charitable bodies (nationally regulated in Greece and Turkey). Means testing is not especially stringent and (apart from in Turkey) obligations do not extend beyond the nuclear family. Money assistance tends to be integrated with social work and other services. Benefits are very low or, for some groups and areas, non-existent.

It will be evident that the five southern countries are not alone in lacking an integrated, national income safety net. The same is true in the Nordic and the Alpine nations. However, in all these countries full employment has been an integral feature of their welfare states, in marked contrast to the southern group (Therborn, 1986). In the Nordic countries, except for Norway, unemployment rates have climbed in the 1990s, but the provision of comprehensive, citizenship-based welfare has broadly been sustained. The southern five are unique in their lack of either an integrated social assistance programme, or an institutionalised commitment in the recent past to full employment, or a comprehensive social security system.

Towards an explanation of social assistance regimes

Social-structural factors

Both social-structural factors and political-institutional factors offer several candidates to explain the backwardness of social assistance in southern Europe (Ferrera, 1996). Let me consider each in turn, beginning with four social-structural factors: level of economic development, family-household structures, features of the labour market and migration.

One explanation of south European backwardness is economic. Industrialisation and, in significant respects, modernisation are relatively recent developments in southern Europe. Their assistance schemes therefore also lag behind, exhibiting pre-modern features that have been swept away by the processes of collectivisation over the past two centuries in north-western Europe (de Swann, 1988: ch. 2). While this account would suffice to explain Portugal, Greece or Turkey, it cannot cope with Spain and above all Italy. Italy has 8 per cent of its workforce in agriculture compared with 44 per cent in Turkey and 22 per cent in Greece. Italy's national income per head is more than three times greater than that of Turkey. The very distance between these countries in terms of development undermines a simple 'stages of development' explanation.

The next two factors refer to the other of the state–work–family nexus and suggest that there is less need for a public safety net in southern Europe than might otherwise be suspected and greater obstacles in the way of establishing one.

The first of these is the nature and role of the 'southern family'. As Table 6.5 shows for the four EU member states, demographic and family structures remain remarkably distinct from those in northern Europe. Divorce, births outside marriage and single parenthood are all rarer (except for Portugal as regards births outside marriage). Moreover, a far higher proportion of elderly people live with their children: 37 per cent in Spain in 1985 and 39 per cent in Italy in 1990 (OECD, 1994b: 105). According to the Commission of the European Communities (1995a: 19): 'Events which have become commonplace in the north are still peripheral in the south: cohabitation prior to marriage, births outside marriage, frequency of divorce, proportions of single-parent families and reconstituted families.'

These features and others enhance the solidarity of families and enable more of them to provide material and social support to those who would otherwise be excluded. So long as one family member can maintain a link with the primary sector of employment and its associated social benefits, then a family safety net of sorts can substitute for a

Table 6.5 Selected demographic, social and economic indicators

	Fertility rate, 1992	% births outside marriage, 1992	% single parent families, 1990–91	Female employment /pop., 1980–91	% young people employed by family
Greece	1.4	3	6	36	69
Italy	1.3	7	–	34	65
Portugal	1.6	16	9	55	58
Spain	1.2	10	6	29	61
EC12	1.5	18	12	44	39

Sources: Cols 1–3, 5: CEC (1995a: 18, 19, 49); Col. 4: OECD (1994b: 115).

public one. Furthermore, social assistance typically presumes a nuclear family unit and requires small and stable households to undertake means testing (Goodin, 1992). The southern European pattern thus poses organisational problems for the extension of means testing.

Working against this is the rapid and unprecedented decline in fertility rates in all southern countries except Turkey. As well as engendering a fast increase in the ratio of aged in the population over the coming decades, this will undermine the ability of future families to care for their members. The generational shift – as the existing grandmother generation is replaced by the 1960s generation grown old – may also bring about a rapid change in family solidarity.

The third aspect of social-structural distinctiveness is the employment structure. In terms of unemployment there is no uniform pattern: the more developed economies of Italy and Spain have above-average unemployment, but the other three are below average. However, when we turn to employment, all the southern countries exhibit low participation rates, especially for women (except Portugal), and high underemployment coupled with extensive self-employment an large informal economy. Hard information on the latter is lacking but one indication is shown in the table – between 58 per cent and 69 per cent of young people are employed by their family members in the four EU countries.[5] These features of the labour market may reduce the need for, and increase the difficulties in, means testing. It has been recognised that the existence of extensive informal sources of income invalidates the use of income earned in the formal economy as a measure of overall resources (Gough, 1994; Goodin, 1992).

Fourth and last there is migration. The southern countries have in recent years switched from being net exporters to net importers of population. This is due to the return of some guest workers in northern countries and to exceptional waves of new immigrants. The latter include the return of Greeks from the Balkans and the former Soviet Union plus Albanian legal and illegal migrants into Greece, the return of Portuguese from the ex-colonial territories in Africa, and refugees and illegal immigrants to Spain, Italy and Greece from the Mashrek and Mahgreb. These movements have posed new demands on state or voluntary agencies. However, their potential to fuel demands for more systematic state support is minimal; rather they have focused public debate on the issues of race and immigration.

There remain many respects in which the four EU members differ sharply; for instance, Portugal has a distinctly superior unemployment record than the other three. But in the three areas of family, work and migration there are important parallels which can help understand why all five lack a state safety net.

Political-institutional factors

In addition there are three political-institutional features common to the southern European states which can explain the absence of an institutionalised regime of social assistance: the interest groups fostered by their regime type, their distinctive political processes and their historical pattern of development of categorical assistance.

First, all five countries have inherited a 'conservative-corporatist' welfare regime as delineated by Esping-Andersen (1990). These are characterised by segmented social insurance structures which generate segmented interest groups to protect and extend the benefits of their members. These interest groups may be expected to oppose universalistic reforms, including the provision of a state-financed safety net. The high cost of pensions and other benefits for the *garantismo* further blocks radical reform of social security. Yet this feature alone will not suffice to account for southern exceptionalism, for how then can we explain the establishment and expansion of *Sozialhilfe* in West Germany?

At the second level focuses more on the distinctive political processes of the southern states. Ferrera (1996: 29) summarises these as follows:

> Welfare rights are not embedded in an open, universalistic political culture and a solid, Weberian state impartial in the administration of its own rules. Rather they rest on a closed, particularistic culture and on a 'soft' state apparatus, both still highly imbued with the logic of patron-client relationships which has been a historical constant in this area of Europe.

He identifies a 'soft' state, strong parties and ideological polarisation as three elements in this matrix which shape the 'power games' around social policy issues.[6] Though Left parties have been successful in introducing universal health services in the four southern member states of the EU, they have failed to repeat this in the sphere of social security. As well as the opposition from the extreme Left they had open to them an alternative route open to them to aid and attract more marginal workers: patronage. Thus in southern Italy invalidity assistance benefits mushroomed alongside invalidity pensions in the 1980s – and continued to expand in the early 1990s. These provide an alternative benefit for unemployed in the south of Italy. In other words, the clientelist system enables political parties to adapt the present categorical assistance schemes to serve other needs. Patronage acts to redefine the present system and to block reform.

The third explanation focuses on the distinctive historical antecedents and development of categorical assistance schemes in southern countries. In all of them, the national state played only a little role in nineteenth-century poor relief, either through direct provision of indoor or outdoor relief, or through the regulation of charities, communes or other relief agencies. Apart from the state control of charities introduced by the Italian government in 1890 and the Vagabonds Act passed in Spain in 1930, poor relief has remained the responsibility of local government and mainly religious charities. These countries did not move to collectivise and nationalise parish poor relief (de Swann, 1988: ch. 2). As in almost all Western countries the final break with the poor law came via the provision of separate assistance schemes for deserving groups, in almost every case the elderly. Outside Britain, Ireland and all the Nordic countries except Finland, this did not occur until after the Second World War: in Greece and Spain in 1960, Italy in 1969, Portugal in 1974 and Turkey in 1976.

However, unlike in other countries such as the Netherlands and France, this has not led to a third wave of reform creating an integrated, national income safety net. To explain this, Lodemel (1992) analyses the effects of categorical assistance for the 'deserving' (the aged and disabled) on the development of assistance for the 'undeserving', able-bodied poor of working age. The provision of means-tested assistance for pensioners provides an alternative to the reform of contributory social insurance. Thus categorical assistance schemes continued to flourish and new ones were established where a politically salient group could establish the need. But by separating off the deserving from undeserving groups this discouraged the establishment of a general programme which could benefit the able-bodied poor.[7]

In this way social structures and political processes can, separately and together, provide an explanation of the lack of a safety net in southern Europe. Of course as adumbrated above this account suffers from 'overdetermination' with more explanations than cases (Castles, 1989). More historically grounded research is necessary to isolate the weight of these factors, and others, in influencing policy development in these five countries.

Current issues and future scenarios

Though there are disagreements, international bodies, national governments and students of social policy agree that a range of economic, social and demographic changes are transforming the environment of modern welfare states (e.g. OECD 1988, 1994b; Commission of the European Communities, 1995b: ch. 2; Pfaller et al., 1991; Esping-Andersen, 1996). These include the following:

- the present and prospective ageing of the population and rise in dependency ratios
- the growth of unemployment and irregular patterns of work
- changes in the roles of women and the increase in non-traditional family forms
- yet pressures to contain public expenditure, and
- to adapt social policy to the requirements of economic competitiveness.

According to a study of EU members these pressures are generating some common policy responses. One of these is increased 'targeting' of benefits, by greater use of means testing but also by linking benefits received to income in other ways and by taxing benefits (Commission of the European Communities, 1995b: 37–48). Thus we may expect to see a growing reliance on social assistance in the southern member states as much as in the north. Table 6.2 shows some increase in the extent of assistance benefits since 1980. However outside Spain the rise in the numbers of recipients and the cost of the programmes has been small – and less than in other member states and in the OECD as a whole. There is little sign of convergence according to these figures, contrary to the view expressed in the EC Report.[8] Is this likely to change in the near future?

We may answer this question using the same two-part framework developed in the previous section, by asking, first, whether there are systemic pressures heralding a crisis in the southern social assistance programmes; and second, whether there are groups of actors with the desire and the means to achieve fundamental reform.

Systemic pressures from above

My answer to the first question is 'no': none of the systemic changes listed above has much salience for the future of social assistance in southern Europe.

The ageing of the population will make little difference to the costs of assistance programmes for the elderly, in sharp contrast to the problems they will engender for insurance-based pension programmes. This follows precisely from a dominant feature noted earlier – the combination of generous pension benefits for core workers alongside smaller pensions for those outside the *garantismo*. Even in Italy, where social pensions for the aged and disabled are widespread, their cost amounts to just 7 per cent of the total pension bill.

Similarly, the inexorable rise in EU unemployment levels, which has proved costly for northern welfare systems, has had and will have little impact on those in the south for the simple reason that assistance provision for the unemployed (as opposed to social insurance benefits for certain groups) is negligible or non-existent. Those with marginal attachments to the labour market are the very groups excluded from both insurance and assistance benefits in all countries except for Spain. There has been some experimentation with work and integration schemes in Spain, Portugal and Italy, but their implementation has been patchy. In Spain we may expect to see further measures to shift the growing numbers receiving unemployment assistance towards active programmes of work and training.

The increasing payment of assistance benefits to lone parents, which is a distinctive feature of the English-speaking countries (except for the US, where benefits have been cut) is likewise unlikely to occur in southern Europe. First, we have noted that moves towards single parenting are small and that the wider family retains a greater role. Second, single parents are not one of the groups favoured by a separate, nationally regulated and more generous categorical assistance scheme in any of the five countries.

Finally, neither pressures to cut public spending nor to align social programmes with economic goals pose problems for these programmes in southern Europe. Both the costs of assistance and the disincentive effects of benefits on labour market behaviour are marginal, except in Spain.

Political mobilisation from below

If the fiscal crisis of the state, which for some will force a restructuring of the southern model of welfare, will leave the assistance element largely unaffected, what are the prospects for a transformation from below?

Popular dissatisfaction with the degree of social protection for vulnerable groups in the four EU member states is higher than in any others

(Robbins, 1993: 45), which suggests that there is a political constituency favouring reform waiting to be tapped. Yet in none of the five countries has a broad political mobilisation developed around these issues. This is the conclusion of the Second and Third Reports of the EC Observatory on National Policies to Combat Social Exclusion (Room, 1992; Robbins, 1993) as well as of our own research. For example, writing about Italy, the Second Report identifies the elderly and disabled (the deserving poor) and drug addicts and Third World immigrants (the threatening poor) as priority groups. 'Children living in stressful situations, multi-problem families, and even more "ordinary poor" families and adults, school drop-outs and inadequately educated and skilled young people with no behavioural "problems", are much less visible' (Room, 1993, Supplement: 20).

There remain two further possibilities. The first is pressure form the European Union. The European Council Recommendation on Sufficient Resources of 1992 (92/441/EEC) is fostering a discussion in Spain and Portugal about how to implement it, though this is conspicuously lacking in Italy and Greece. The second would be a change of strategy among Left and Centre parties to prioritise the issues of social citizenship and the right to a statutory minimum income. This is not inconceivable in the context of a general political realignment, of the sort now taking place in Italy. For example, the *Commissione di Indagine sulla Poverta e sull'Emarginazione* (1995) recommended the establishment of a state-financed and rights-based minimum income scheme but so far the Centre–Left parties have not included this demand in their policy platform.

However, this would require a more general and more radical reform of the welfare system. The poverty lobby in Italy, for example, has to work against a public distrust of the perceived corruption, waste and ineffectiveness of social welfare programmes. In addition, the cost of a minimum income guarantee is not inconsiderable. According to Carbonaro (1994) it would have cost 15,400 billion lire in 1992 to bring all Italian citizens merely up to the level of the social pension plus allowances (using the official equivalence scale to calculate benefits for larger households). This is an amount four times the outlay on the social pension in that year and would add another 1 per cent of GDP to the social budget. It will prove politically difficult to achieve this in Italy (as elsewhere in the south) in the absence of a more radical restructuring of the entire welfare system.

Appendix to Tables 6.3 and 6.4

To compare average benefit levels we have adopted the model families simulation method – asking national informants to simulate the impact of social assistance benefits on a selection of model families (Eardley et al., 1996b: ch. 6). The method involves calculating, at a given point in time (May 1992), what would be the net disposable resources of variety of family types in three situations: receiving social assistance, receiving social insurance and working for national average earnings. We have calculated both absolute and relative benefit levels using this method. The former uses purchasing power parities (PPPs) to convert national currency amounts into a common monetary denominator. Table 6.3 shows the results for six family types.

Table 6.4 produces two overall indices of absolute values by taking the mean of the amounts in purchasing power parity £ sterling paid to nine family types (single persons age 35, couple age 35, single person age 68, couple age 68, couple with one child age 3, couple with one child age 7, couple with two children age 7 and 14 years, lone parent with one child age 3, lone parent with one child age 7), and then expressing that total as a proportion of the mean for all OECD countries. The first two columns of Table 6.4 show the results of these calculations both before and after taking housing costs into account. Housing costs are a particularly difficult element to take into account in comparative research yet they are too important to be ignored.

The third column in Table 6.4 shows estimates of relative benefit levels based on replacement rates of social assistance (before housing costs) for a range of family types. These replacement rates are calculated by comparing the level of disposable income of persons receiving social assistance with the disposable incomes of the same household type where the head is earning average male earnings. They will probably understate the real replacement rates of individuals in each country who are actually receiving social assistance, since it could be expected that such individuals would be earning less – perhaps substantially less – than average male earnings if they gained a job.

Notes

1 First published as 'Social Assistance in Southern Europe', in the inaugural issue of *South European Society & Politics* 1(1) (Summer 1996), pp. 1–23. I am grateful to the Nuffield Foundation for supporting the research described here through a Social Science Research Fellowship in 1993–94. The end-result reflects my collaboration with Jonathan Bradshaw, John Ditch, Tony Eardley and Peter

Whiteford at SPRU, University of York, who were funded by the Department of
Social Security and the OECD. Many thanks to Martin Baldwin-Edwards,
Maurizio Ferrera and Graham Room for helpful comments on a first draft.

2 'Directly' restricts this to the provision of cash or non-cash benefits by state
agencies. Other indirect methods include tax allowances and mandated private benefits or services. 'Individual and households' means that services
targeted on specific spatial locations are excluded, though geography may
enter into the definition of the contingency which the benefit or service is
designed to meet.

3 However such restrictions are common in the 'continental' EU: the extreme
case is France, where foreigners need ten years' residence to qualify for RMI
(*Revenu Minimum d'Insertion*).

4 The argument of Lødemel and Schulte (1992) for putting Germany in a separate
category turns on the existence of a separate programme for the unemployed,
which is in practice a peculiar hybrid of social insurance and assistance, and the
existence of wider family obligations. This last is a distinguishing feature of the
German-speaking countries in Europe, but appears to be of limited significance.
Yet in other respects Germany can also be viewed as a bridge to the second
group of countries below.

5 The labour market in Turkey is different in several respects, notably the higher
share of employment in agriculture and the continuing high rate of births and
population. Nevertheless, the 1993 OECD report identifies several features
which apply across southern Europe:

   'Another key feature of the Turkish labour market is the extremely low level
   of female participation rates in urban areas.... The resort to child labour in
   both agriculture and the informal sector, sharp differences in the regional
   distribution of income, and the existence of seasonal migration in agriculture on a significant scale are further factors.... The fact that many members of the urban labour force in some form still retain their economic as
   well as social links with agriculture as their sector of origin also warrants
   attention. Another salient feature is the big share of the public sector in total
   urban employment'   (OECD, 1993: 36–7).

6 The third is not applicable in the case of Turkey, with which Ferrera was not
concerned.

7 The one exception to this was the introduction of unemployment assistance
in Spain in 1984. We should also note that, by the time these nations had
achieved the second wave, recession and restructuring had begun to take
effect and many guestworkers were beginning to return home thus com-
pounding the difficulties of economic adjustment.

8 Nor, in my view, is there evidence of the southern countries of Europe making
'progress towards the establishment of systems comparable in their coverage
and levels of support to those in other Member States' (Commission of the
European Communities, 1995b: 57).

7
Enterprise Welfare and Economic Transition in Russia[1]

Introduction

This chapter looks at the traditional system of *sotskultbyt*, the enterprise-based social welfare typical of state socialist economies and of Russia in particular, and the changes brought about by the economic transformation of recent years. The range of services and benefits provided under this system is very wide and can cover health care, housing, kindergartens, subsidised food and transport, and tickets to sanatoria, tourist resorts and pioneer camps. It is thus a major feature of the overall welfare system in Russia – some claim that it is the one that marks it off most distinctively from western welfare states. The fate of enterprise welfare in the transition to the market economy is thus of great importance to many millions of Russians. We report the results of research conducted in 1993–94 on enterprises in two Russian city-regions: Samara, a major military-industrial centre on the Volga, and the Kuzbass, a huge coalfield in western Siberia with mining townships and two industrial cities – Novokuznetsk and Kemerovo. These case studies enable us to chart in some detail what happened to enterprise welfare during this crucial period and to begin to explain why.

The fate of enterprise welfare in the pioneer country of state socialism is of intrinsic interest and importance in its own right. It also raises wider questions and can contribute to a broader debate. The official agenda of the present Russian government and of western advisers is to effect a complete transition from a command economy to a free market economy as rapidly as prudence, that is, political stability, will allow. Yet, Polanyi's insight that market economies are, of necessity, more or less embedded in a set of social relations, suggests that such radical surgery runs a grave risk of system disintegration. The coincidence of the collapse of communism and the renaissance of pure, free market models of capitalism has encouraged a premature conceptualisation of markets and social reform. A detailed study of enterprise welfare in Russia can cast light on these broader issues.

The remainder of the chapter is in seven sections. The first presents an account of the traditional system of *sotskultbyt* and its place in the Russian enterprise under state socialism and the second summarises recent studies of its extent and restructuring. The third section outlines our research project, its organisation, sources and methods. Then, in the fourth section, we chart the provision of enterprise welfare before and after the significant changes of 1993 and 1994, clarifying the extent of continuity and change. Section five interprets some of these findings in terms of issues of distribution and control within the enterprise. A crucial factor affecting the future of enterprise welfare is the willingness and capacity of local authorities to take on these responsibilities, and this is the subject of section six. The conclusion summarises our findings and relates them to Polanyi's concept of embeddedness.

Social welfare, *sotskultbyt* and the Russian enterprise

In classic centralised socialist economies, enterprises played a central role in delivering many aspects of social welfare which, in capitalist societies, are usually the responsibility of the state or parastate bodies. Apart from financing most income maintenance benefits and directly paying some of these, such as sickness benefit, enterprises provided a range of other in-kind services. These included the construction and management of two-fifths of Russian housing, the provision of a majority of kindergartens, numerous polyclinics and many hospitals, and subsidised access to rest centres, sanatoria, pioneer summer camps, holiday centres, foodstuffs and specific consumer goods.

> Ministries and their enterprises operated over a sweeping range of functions which made a huge difference to the daily life of Soviet citizens: they had wide powers in housing and town planning, in transport and social infrastructure from sewers to roads, and in supplying medical and recreational facilities, foodstuffs and scarce consumer goods.   (Whitefield, 1993: ch. 4)

This whole unique system of occupationally-based social welfare is one important example of the domination of the economy and of elite institutions of party and state by the ministries. Access to rewards became 'verticalised' and the role of 'horizontal' bodies, the local Soviets and administrations, were weakened as a result.

Sotskultbyt benefits can be divided into three categories (Commander and Jackman, 1993). First are services for current workers provided as part of their work conditions. Such things as canteen meals, sports facilities and vacations are similar to those provided in capitalist enterprises. Second are services for current workers and their families (and, we would add, for past workers), including housing, kindergartens, health clinics, cheap goods and the availability of meals, etc. to family members and retirees. These are a much more distinctive feature of socialist enterprises. Lastly, there are collective services provided by some enterprises for the local community, including hospitals, transport services, infrastructure such as road-building and repairs, gas, water, sewage and waste disposal, area heating and hotels. These functions are quite unique to the Russian enterprise, though they are not universal; they are more a feature of the provinces, in particular of 'company towns' where a single firm dominates the local community. Though we are concerned with all three groups of activities, it is the second on which we focus.

What has been the effect on this whole system of enterprise welfare of the economic restructuring of the Russian economy? We shall argue that the form of privatisation has affected the development and fate of enterprise welfare, so we must say a few words here about the different stages and forms. '*Nomenklatura* privatisation' began in the Gorbachev era with the Law on State Enterprises of 1987. These early reforms created two new forms of company. First, 'closed joint-stock companies', where insider managers and/or closely affiliated public officials and agencies were transformed into major shareholders; and second, 'concerns' – new corporate complexes of related state enterprises formed out of branches of ministries controlled by former ministry bureaucrats and enterprise managers.

From 1991 more radical privatisation schemes were undertaken under President Yeltsin. Medium to large-scale enterprises (with from 1,000 to 10,000 employees) were to be privatised through conversion into 'open joint-stock companies'. Members of the workers' collectives could choose between three options, of which the first two are most important.[2] Option 1 – the 'open' form of privatisation – provides minority ownership for insiders (workers and managers) with the majority of shares sold through public auctions. Under Option 2, the 'closed' form, insiders have a controlling share – they can buy up to 51 per cent of the total authorised capital at a somewhat concessionary rate.

Medium-small enterprises with between 200 and 1,000 employees could choose between the above methods or privatisation through open competitive auction. However, strategic enterprises were excluded from this legislation. They include very large firms with more than 10,000 employees as well as those in strategic industries such as energy, communications and the military sector. In most of these the state was to retain a controlling packet of shares, though some may be permitted to privatise using the above options. About two-thirds of medium-to-large enterprises had elected for option 2 and most of the remainder for option 1 (Bim et al., 1993).

However, Presidential Decree 168 of January 1993 limits the privatisation of social welfare agencies (OECD, 1996: 147–8). Firms are expected to go private but their *sotskultbyt* activities must remain in public hands. The most common solution advocated to deal with this dilemma has been to transfer juridical ownership of these facilities to municipal administrations. However this need not, and in the case of housing usually has not, entailed transfer of their finance or even their management. Nor are municipalities necessarily able or willing to take on these functions. It is the present balance between *de jure* transfer and *de facto* enterprise responsibility which forms an important subject of our research.

Previous studies of enterprise welfare in Russia

A collection of studies published by the OECD (1996) uses a variety of research methods to study the impact of transition on enterprise welfare in Russia. Broadly speaking there are three research techniques. The first, by Rose (1996), uses data from his Fourth New Russia Barometer, a nationwide household survey of 2,000 adult Russians in April 1995. This finds that 28 per cent of Russians received no enterprise benefits, 35 per cent received one or two different benefits and 37 per cent received three or more. The most common benefits were medical care (44 per cent), kindergartens (33 per cent), holidays (33 per cent) and meals (21 per cent). Only 11 per cent received housing benefits in 1995. Compared with the results of the first survey in 1992 there had been a rapid decline in the receipt of benefits, notably holidays (a decline of 31 per cent of the sample population), housing (−29 per cent), kindergartens (−19 per cent) and food (−20 per cent) and shortage goods (−24 per cent). The benefits were unevenly distributed across the population, being more extensive in large firms and in the energy and military sectors. Enterprise welfare is portrayed as of declining significance and of surprisingly little importance in the total 'welfare mix' or sources of households' livelihoods.

Household surveys of this type are valuable in providing an overall audit which can be related to other sources of income and in-kind benefits received. However, the immense size of the Russian Federation, together with wide regional variations, undermines the validity of results based on such a relatively small sample. For example, the marginal role of enterprise housing in this survey conflicts with other findings below.

The second approach is to undertake large-scale surveys of enterprises using postal questionnaires backed up with selective interviews with managers. This approach was pioneered by Commander and Jackman (1993) and has been repeated by Tratch et al. (1996) to survey 97 enterprises across 13 *oblasts* in 1995. They deliberately over-represented Siberian *oblasts* and excluded firms founded since 1989, which will tend to exaggerate the extent of enterprise welfare. They find that, between 1989 and 1995, about 80 per cent of former state enterprises in the sample were privatised and there had been considerable divestiture of social assets. The numbers of kindergartens had fallen by 66 per cent by 1995 and there had been significant falls too in sports and cultural establishments of about one-fifth, subsidiary farms (−24 per cent), apartment blocks (−18 per cent) and medical and recreation facilities (−17 per cent). The majority of these facilities were transferred to municipalities. Yet, the picture was qualified in four ways. First, enterprises continued to provide an extensive array of welfare services in 1995. Second, one-fifth were continuing to invest in new housing. Third, firms were also developing novel social establishments to meet new needs. Fourth, in European Russia the decline in enterprise social facilities had levelled out by the end of 1993. The picture which results is a more qualified one, with significant obstacles to the continuing divestiture of social facilities by privatised firms.

Enterprise-based surveys can tap the full range of services provided and situate them within the overall pattern of *sotskultbyt* within individual firms. They can also chart the extent and patterns of divestiture over time. However, the definition of enterprise welfare in Russia is fluid and its extent uncertain. For example, new apartment blocks can be built by production-line workers and their costs hidden from view. Standardised questionnaires often cannot probe beneath official statistics and explanations to discover the real nature of enterprise welfare and its transformation.

The Research Project

To tackle these problems, we have adopted a third technique using direct field research in a sample of enterprises.[3] Our study investigated a sample of enterprises in two city-regions outside the Moscow/St Petersburg metropoles which are atypical for many reasons. We employed two teams of researchers all of whom were native Russian speakers with strong and established links with the enterprises and good access to personnel at all levels (Gough and McMylor, 1995: appendix). Three sources of information were gathered. First, official documents, including firm statistics, internal papers, factory newspapers, etc. Such documents are notoriously unreliable in Russian enterprises for well-known reasons, so these were augmented by, second, an extensive range of interviews with managers, social welfare department managers, workers in accounting departments, trade union officials, and rank-and-file workers. Third, there was direct observation by the researchers of 'their' enterprises over a lengthy period. This threefold research strategy enabled us to uncover informal relations and practices within *sotskultbyt* hidden from the other research techniques discussed above.

The two sites differ considerably. Samara, a city of 1.25 million people, was a former 'closed city', one of the foremost military-industrial centres in the USSR. Its industrial development took off during the Second World War when major weapons plants were moved to escape the German advance. In the post-war period it developed the production of weapons, aircraft, aluminium and engineering and has been heavily reliant on the defence industry. These giant strategic enterprises have provided a great part of the city's social infrastructure. They owned 69 per cent of all kindergartens, 65 per cent of housing in the city, all bar one of the palaces of culture, and most of the sanatoria and sports complexes. Samara is not a company city but it approximates to a 'ministry city'.

The firms in Samara selected for the research are shown in Table 7.1. They comprise three very large military/engineering firms, and four medium-small enterprises – two in engineering, one in food processing and one garments. All but one have been privatised by creating a joint-stock company in which the labour collective (managers, workers and past workers) hold the majority of shares – the 'closed' option. The one exception is 'Zim' which, at the time of our research, was regarded as a strategic enterprise to remain in federal ownership.

Table 7.1 Social welfare employment at enterprises in Samara, 1993

Enterprise	Zim	Shar	Sameko	Russia	Sokol	TranspEng	Vlada
Sector	Military/Engineering; once secret	Bearings	Aluminium; guns	Chocolate	Lifting mechanisms	Buses and repairs	Garments
Form of privatisation	State-owned, not to be privatised	Option 2	Option 2	Option 2	Option 2	Option 2	Option 2
Employment 1993	17,000	22,136	19,412	1,590	612	555	709
Total social welfare employment	1,315	1,482	3,175	61	76	25	66
Social welfare as % of total employment	7.7	6.7	16.4	3.8	12.4	4.5	9.3
Housing	3.0	2.5	2.6	0.1	4.6	1.4	1.7
Kindergarten	0.0	1.8	3.5	0	5.4	0.0	3.9
Medical	0.0	0.1	1.2	0.6	0.0	0.2	0.0
Refectory	1.7	1.5	4.2	2.4	1.6	1.8	1.0
Leisure	2.2	0.7	2.2	0.4	0.8	1.1	0.3
Subsidiary	0.8	0.1	2.3	0.0	0.0	0.0	0.0
Other	0.1	0	0.4	0.3	0.0	0.0	2.4

The Kuzbass is a vast region in western Siberia developed around coal-mining. The mines dominate several of the smaller cities – Belovo, Leninsk-Kuznetsk, Kiselevsk and Prokopievsk. We studied Leninsk-Kuznetsk as an example of a 'company town'. Other cities in the Kuzbass contain industry alongside mining. In this category we looked at the mines in Angero-Sudgenskaya and Novokuznetsk. Kemerovo, the regional centre, is an industrial city of 520,000 population with chemical and engineering enterprises alongside mining. Here we studied four large chemicals-based enterprises. The cities and enterprises surveyed in the Kuzbass are listed in Table 7.2. Three of the four large chemical companies in Kemerovo have been privatised with a minority shareholding for the labour collective. 'Progress' was once a military firm and could not, in 1993–94, be privatised.

In the coalfields, all six mines in Novokuznetsk and Ossiniki were, by the time of our study, incorporated into large coal associations or 'concerns'. In the mining towns the concerns ran not only social services but vital collective services for the community, including boiler houses, the heating system and the sewerage system. In the mixed towns and cities individual enterprises were more significant and their range of functions was not quite so broad. Nevertheless, in all the coal mines the central body of the coal industry – formerly the ministry 'Minugolprom', now 'Rusogol' – financed their social welfare budgets. Every mine presented estimates for their welfare services to the concerns which processed them and sent them to Moscow, which distributed funds down the chain to the mines. Thus the industry exhibited a continuation of the old ministry role in a new guise. As result there were practically no claims on profits to finance enterprise welfare. Of the six mines, two had been converted into closed joint-stock companies under the earlier '*nomenklatura* privatisation' noted above, two pursued an open privatisation and two remained is state hands because they were scheduled for closure.

Developments in enterprise welfare, 1992–94

The lower halves of Tables 7.1 and 7.2 present a simplified summary of the extent of enterprise welfare in Samara and the Kuzbass in 1992. They present employment statistics for our sample of enterprises and thus provides an estimate of the relative size of the 'unproductive' social welfare workforce in the total. The research teams believe that these statistics are more reliable than the expenditure figures frequently used in other studies. Our figures show that the traditional *sotskultbyt*

Table 7.2 Social welfare employment at enterprises in the Kuzbass, 1993

	Leninsk-K	Angero-S	Novokuz				Kemerovo			
Enterprise	Oktyarbs-kaya	Angerskaya	Abashevs-kaya	Alarda	Dimitrov	Shushtalep-skaya	Azot	Khimprom	Progress	Khimvol-okno
Sector	Coal mine	Coal mine	Coal mine	Coal mine	Coal mine	Coal mine	Chemicals, fertilisers	Fertilisers, chemicals	Chemicals, technical equipment	Chemical fibres
Form of privatisation	Option 2	State (to be closed)	Option 1	Option 2	State (to be closed)	Option 1	Option 1	Option 1	State	Option 1
Employ-ment 1993	2,500	n/a	3,356	n/a	2,074	1,661	10,500	4,227	6,000	6,200
Social welfare employment	329	251	271		304		2,736	860	1,013	685
Social welfare as % of total employment	13.2		8.1		14.7		26.1	20.3	16.9	11.0
Housing	4.0						6.6	7.6	7.3	2.0
Kinderg	6.4		6.1		5.8		7.7	4.8	3.2	5.3
Medical	0.8				1.4		2.4	1.4	0.5	0.4
Refectory							3.6	2.0	1.2	
Leisure	0.6		2.0		3.2		1.4	0.8	0.6	0.5
Subsidiary	1.4				2.8		2.6	0.1	0.4	2.2
Other								3.4	3.5	0.7

activities engaged between 8 per cent and 26 per cent of firms' work-forces, with the share in most enterprises lying between 10 per cent and 20 per cent. This provides striking confirmation of the social importance of the Russian enterprise as late as 1993.

Of this total, kindergarten staff were consistently the most numerous, accounting for around 6 per cent of the total labour force. In those enterprises with a housing programme up to 7 per cent of the workforce were engaged on administration, building and maintenance, but this may have been an underestimate. The other 'mainstream' social policy area – health care – was less widespread at enterprise level and typically accounted for about 1 per cent of total employment. But considerable numbers were employed in leisure facilities, canteens and food shops and subsidiary activities.

As previous studies found, the extent of enterprise welfare varies roughly with firm size. 'Azot', the largest firm in the Kemerovo sample, employed no fewer than one quarter of its workforce on a wide array of social and cultural activities. The smaller mining enterprises typically employed about one-eighth. Kindergartens were almost ubiquitous irre-spective of firm size, whereas housing, refectory and food programmes showed the greatest variation. There did not appear to be any systematic variation by industrial sector, despite the subsidies provided by the coal mining concerns to member firms for *sotskultbyt*. Khimvolokno, the one large enterprise in Kemerovo with relatively few social welfare staff, was a relatively new firm, supporting the finding that the age of enterprises is a relevant factor.

The range of services provided at this time was extremely wide. For example, Khimprom in Kemerovo possessed 10 kindergarten, 111 blocks of flats comprising 300,000 m^2 of floor space, two hostels for young families, a polyclinic, a medical post and sanatorium with 100 beds, a museum and library, a sports complex comprising ski centre, sauna and swimming pool, two canteens, a department of trade and shop to supply cheap goods and goods in scarce supply, plus land lots for vegetable gardens for pensioners and much else besides.

What then was the effect of the privatisation of these firms between 1992 and the end of 1993 on their welfare facilities and activities? By late 1993 the situation could be summarised as follows.

Housing

Of those enterprises which formerly owned apartments, five had trans-ferred juridical ownership (in whole or in part) to the cities. In two other large enterprises (Zim and Azot) there was a stand-off with Samara and

Kemerovo municipal administrations respectively. Yet there was no agreement in any case over the finance and management of the housing stock. The pattern of new building also varied, with two firms in Samara (Sameko and Russia) continuing to undertake new building for their workers.

Kindergartens

Here the findings are relatively consistent – in all enterprises which previously owned kindergartens, juridical and in most cases financial ownership had been transferred to city authorities. The only exception was Sameko where there was a stalemate in negotiations with Samara.

Medical facilities

The picture here was variable. Substantial medical facilities and services continued to be provided in two coal mines and at Azot and Shar. In another three enterprises they had either been transferred to the cities or were negotiating to. Khimprom and Zim retained ownership but faced growing financial problems and a gradual deterioration of service.

Canteens

The general pattern was for enterprises to retain their canteen facilities and the access of non-workers, such as pensioners, to them, despite rising financial costs. In at least one mine in the Kuzbass and at Khimprom in Kemerovo additional developments to supply subsidised foodstuffs through the firm were underway.

Leisure

The provision of leisure and rest facilities was planned to continue at every enterprise which had them, except for two in Kemerovo which transferred ownership to the city, despite frequently mentioned financial difficulties. In only one mine and one factory was commercialisation being considered as a solution.

Subsidiary enterprises

All three of the large enterprises which ran 'social' side businesses faced growing losses but wanted to retain and even develop them, as did the Oktyabrskaya mine. Only 'Russia' seemed actively to be contemplating commercialisation of these operations.

In conclusion, the fate of *sotskultbyt* activities in industrial enterprises divided into three at this stage. First, canteen, leisure and subsidiary facilities were in general retained by firms, despite considerable losses in some cases. Second, in the more traditional 'social policy' areas, notably education/child care and health, ownership had been transferred to local administrations or negotiation about transfer was underway. There were exceptions such as Sameko in Samara which managed to retain their kindergartens. Third, in the financially critical area of housing, formal transfers were agreed in most cases (not at Zim or Azot) but there was in general no agreement on the transfer of housing 'balances' to municipal administrations. At a time when most enterprises did not face a hard budget constraint many enterprises wanted to continue with the bulk of their *sotskultbyt* activities. In the mines, where the majority of social welfare facilities belonged to the local coal concerns and there were healthy prospects for coal production, there was still more continuity with the past.

In late 1993 the economic situation of many enterprises deteriorated sharply. In Samara, Zim cut its workforce to 15,000, Shar and Transpeng shut down for one month each in spring 1994, Sameko dismissed 2,300 employees in May 1994. Similar problems affected Progress in Kemerovo. This led to a change in the attitudes of many enterprise managements and they began to press for a rapid transfer of the costs of *sotskultbyt*, and especially of their housing balances, to municipalities. The extent of these more recent changes in selected enterprises are documented in Tables 7.3 and 7.4, mainly for housing and kindergartens.

Enterprises owned 277 of the 400 kindergartens in Samara in 1992–3. Of these 57 were transferred in 1993–4 taking the numbers of municipal kindergartens to 180. In Kemerovo, 95 were transferred raising the municipal numbers from 22 to 117, out of 209 in the city. Some in Samara were subsequently 'reprofiled', that is, changed to other uses, such as health centre or social assistance centre. At the same time the city decided to raise parental fees. This supports the more recent study of Tratch et al. (1996) which identified 1993 as the peak year for reprofiling enterprise social assets; the rate of restructuring tailed off quickly thereafter.

Sotskultbyt: Issues of distribution and control

So much for basic measures of the extent of enterprise welfare. We now augment these with some more qualitative findings. In the old system the specific form, content and quality of social welfare could vary between enterprises. For example, our research team in Samara found

Table 7.3 Changes in Enterprise Welfare: Samara, 1993–94

	Zim	Shar	Sameko	TranspEng	Vlada
Housing	Programme continues; new building frozen, but began again in 1994. Stalemate with LA over transfers. Growing debts.	1994 – nearing agreement with LA on transfer. Problem of 'marginal people' occupying appartments.	Seeking transfer to LA – no agreement in face of harsh conditions from *oblast*. But tax privileges from LA. Building continues; some flat sales	Transferred to LA balance. New house building.	None
Kindergartens	All formally transferred to LA balances. 40 per cent places retained for employees' children.	All transferred to LA. No agreement on employees' children. Cuts in allied staff.	Managed to retain under earlier legislation.	None	Transferred to LA, but want back. *Oblast* requisitioned one for military use.
Other *Sotskultbyt* (SKB)	Considerable continuity despite growing financial problems.	Considerable continuity despite growing financial problems.	Continuity. Transfer back from LA of medical facilities.		
Background notes	Dire economic situation 1994. Much SKB managed by Oblast committee.	Near collapse in 1994. Falling standards in SKB.		Falling production 1994.	

Table 7.4 Changes in Enterprise Welfare: Kuzbass, 1993–94

	Ossiniki			Kemerovo	
Firm	Kapitalnaya mine	Alarda mine	Shushtalepskaya mine	'Azot'	Khimvolokno
Housing	Owned by Kuznetskogol concern. No transfer.	Owned by Kuznetskogol concern. Substantial new house building	Owned by Kuznetskogol concern.	Stand-off in transfer to LA; no new building.	No agreement on transfer.
Kindergartens	One half transferred to LA.	Retained, but one to be closed.	Both transferred; new one built.	Ten transferred by 1993.	All transferred; six leased back. Growing debts.
Other *sotskultbyt* (SKB)		Mostly retained	All SKB now to be liquidated.	Substantial continuity.	
Background notes					Decline in economic production in 1994.

some evidence of a gender effect when they analysed 'Russia' – a quite successful factory making chocolate. Its welfare system included such items as sewing and shoemaking enterprises, a manicure and beauty parlour, and green houses. The former director of the enterprise before privatisation was a women and two-thirds of the staff were female. The field researchers suggest in their report that such a large-scale female presence shaped some elements of its welfare system.

Following privatisation most of these items, which were located on the territory of the factory, were included in the assets of the company. But some were not allowed by law to be privatised, including the enterprises pioneer camp, kindergarten and tourist base. The basic strategy followed by 'Russia' was to maintain those services that existed on the site of the enterprise and to provide subsidies to employees using a wider range of social services such as medical facilities. The enterprise provided other basic necessities of life through bartering with other enterprises – for example, free milk and sweets – and also provided regular hot food in the canteen. Former workers and pensioners also received subsidised products such as milk, vegetables, sugar, potatoes and chocolate as well as hostel accommodation and rest provision. There was much continuity here.

The distribution of these goods and services among the employees is arrived at by a mixture of formal and informal rules. The formal rules have traditionally followed criteria common in the old Soviet Union, such as labour contribution, number of children, age of worker and length of service. Formally this distribution depended on the officially sanctioned influence of the line manager and the president of the official trade union committee. However, in practice, workers depended upon their personal connections with the people who undertook the distribution. Bribery and other forms of corruption were not uncommon. The leader of an independent trade union who had been a leading official in the official trade union described it thus:

> You know that the basic function of the trade union was distribution. And they always stole everything, that is to say they shared everything for their own benefit, people sat there for decades. And by the way, nothing has really changed. I also had to carry out distribution, and it was difficult not to compromise myself in front of the workers because distribution is connected with theft.

This same man went on to point out how these channels of distribution were then used in a changed political environment to discipline and control the workforce, especially those who joined the independent union:

> It is like a gradual strangulation, because they remember that I know the law. If they did this officially, for example through a declaration or an order to cut us off, I would be very pleased because I would take it up to court. For example, literally yesterday they handed out cigarettes. But they gave four packs to members of the official union and only two packs to us. This may seem trifling, but it is strangulation. At any moment they can say that there are no more *putyovki* (tickets to rest homes and tourist hostels). Well, I cannot get hold of their documents to find out whether or not they have really run out.

This reveals how embedded the social welfare system was – and still is – in the social relations of production in Russia. Both research teams characterised this as a system of paternalism. Given the administrative latitude inherent in a system controlled and distributed via the enterprise itself rather than a separate welfare bureaucracy, the possibilities of subtle and divisive control were extensive.

In the mining area of the Kuzbass the system of distribution in some mines became more complex and refined after privatisation. For example, special nominal dollar accounts were created for each worker which can be used only for buying goods within the enterprise. This system allowed a much more precise and individualised assessement of the contribution of the individual worker, closer to a real wages system. It involved the creation of a whole new administrative structure for maintaining special accounts, running mine shops, etc. The administration controlled this system as they decided which goods entered the distribution network. Between 5 per cent and 15 per cent of such goods were diverted into the 'Director's Fund'. Such access to resources allowed management to buy off or punish key individuals and groups via the distribution of goods and service.

Yet in another respect – the role of official trade unions – the old order was changing. These bodies, which were of course quite incapable of independent political action, nevertheless had an officially sanctioned role in all enterprises and the administration had to work closely with them in relation to welfare. We can see from the independent union officials' comments that in some respects this role was waning.

For example, before 1993 the trade union committee at the Sokol Engineering Plant in Samara controlled the social insurance fund and had considerable influence in the enterprise. After 1993 the trade union was confined to an advisory role on a number of commissions which supervised particular social welfare services but which could no longer take important decisions. In many respects the trade union had been demoted to the role of bookkeeper. Economic reform has here strengthened the hand of management at the expense of those who at least nominally represented workers.

Transfers to Local Authorities

We must now introduce another set of actors into the analysis – the regional and local authorities of the Russian Federation. These comprise 91 *oblasts*, the regional authorities, and around 2,000 *raions* and municipalities. Both have played a role in the transfer of enterprise social facilities following privatisation. The *municipalities* were to receive those social welfare facilities excluded from the privatisation process by the 1991 Federal Law on Property and the 1993 Presidential Decree. To study this the research teams looked in particular at the transfer of kindergartens and housing to the municipalities of Samara and, in the Kuzbass, to Kemerovo and Osinniki.

The *oblasts*, through their Committees of Property Management, are meant both to manage federal property in their region and to oversee the process of privatisation. Thus the transfer of enterprise welfare becomes subject to a three-way set of forces. The *oblasts*, more powerful than the municipalities and with close ties to the old ministry structures, introduced new conflicts into the process of transferring enterprise *sotskultbyt*. For example, the Samara *oblast* committee decided to take one of the Vlada enterprise kindergartens and transfer it to a military division of the city of Samara. The municipal authority, the formal owner of the kindergarten, was not consulted and did not participate in the decision-making process.

In general the local authorities were prepared to accept the formal transfer of assets but wanted to maintain them on the 'balances' of their old enterprise owners. As an interim measure in 1993–4, contracts for up to ten years were negotiated between the local authorities and the enterprises for the latter to maintain financial responsibility. However, this process of contract-making was becoming harder and at times impossible as two essentially insolvent institutions each tried to minimise their financial liabilities.

For example, the ZIM enterprise in Samara continued to pay the wages of the 500 people administering its works housing but refused to pay the costs of maintenance or to pay the local authority for gas, water, electricity or central heating. At the end of 1993 the city authorised the housing transfer on condition that all necessary repairs were carried out at the enterprise's expense beforehand. This made the transfer impossible as ZIM's housing stock was old and in need of substantial work. A stalemate emerged between the impoverished bodies of the enterprise and the authority.

The problems surrounding the transfer of social welfare will not be resolved until coherent mechanisms for funding the newly expanded welfare role of local authorities are in place. Given the scale of past enterprise subsidies this will not be easy to achieve. But even if achieved, services will not necessarily improve. Both research teams found that local authority transfer usually entailed a decline in standards for kindergartens. Staff wages were lower in the municipal sector, though more certain of being paid, and the quality of the food provided for children and of building repairs deteriorated.

Conclusions

Generalisations are dangerous in periods of uncertainty such as still obtain in Russia but some general conclusions can be drawn from our study.

Russian enterprises did not face a hard budget constraint until 1994, at the end of our study period. Before then, credits were made available to large enterprises and substantial amounts of inter-enterprise and municipal debt were tolerated. From spring 1994 onwards, crisis increasingly forced the hands of many enterprises. The majority wished to transfer their most expensive social welfare asset, their housing stock, to local authorities or appealed for tax concessions or subsidies from local authorities. According to Tratch et al., (1990) divestitures peaked in 1993 and 1994.

Yet, this is by no means the whole story. There has been considerable resistance to divesting social welfare assets by many privatised firms. What can explain this apparent disregard of company economics? We consider the following factors to be important.[4] The closed form of privatisation entrenches the power of managers and workers who may have an interest in retaining these facilities, because of:

- the value of goods and services in kind during a period of high inflation
- perceived opportunities for profitable exploitation of the facilities

- the continued adherence of some managers and workers to a collective service ethic
- the ability of enterprises to exert patronage over other enterprises and the municipality who use their welfare facilities
- the lack of public sector alternatives and the lack of development of 'horizontal' municipal alternatives to the 'vertical' enterprise.

For some or all of these reasons, many Russian enterprises may continue to fight to retain their *sotskultbyt*. There is no inevitable pressure towards total divestiture.

The work of the Hungarian historian and economic anthropologist Karl Polanyi (1944/1957) helps us to interpret these findings. Polanyi viewed the transition of British society in the 'long nineteenth century' from traditional society, though a 'pure market society' to a regulated market society as a move between *embedded, dis-embedded* and *re-embedded* economies (Olofsson, 1999). The separating-out of the market with *laissez-faire* policies generated contradictions and conflicts which in turn led to policies and practices to restrict the regulate and constrain the market mechanisms. In the twentieth century the predominant forms of re-embedding have been the welfare state, Keynesian economic management and corporatist policy-making.

Polanyi appears to have regarded the rise of both Fascism and Bolshevism as the result of the *failure* of the nineteenth century to re-embed market societies. These were not viable or desirable new forms of economy–society relations, a theme echoed by Glassman in his analysis of contemporary Poland (Glassman, 1994). The Speenhamland system in England between 1795 and the 1830s was a flawed attempt to resist the claims of developing market relations like that of Bolshevik rule in Poland. Similarly, the New Poor Law was reflected in the mass marketisation of the 1990s. He quotes Polanyi: 'if Speenhamland meant the rot of immobility, now the peril was death through exposure' (Polanyi, 1957: 183). The crash marketisation of Polish society was a predictable, yet equally dire, consequence of Communism.

Russia today is undergoing extensive marketisation but perhaps institutional continuities are more securely entrenched than in Poland. Enterprise welfare was an integral part of the ministerial organisation of the economy and of the provision of welfare in state socialism. It was securely embedded in an economic system which in turn was embedded in a cohesive set of social relations. But the result was paternalism, democratic suffocation and an ineffective welfare system. Fundamental economic reform cannot leave the system of *sotskultbyt* untouched, but there is a choice – between marketisation and re-embedding. The former is leading, just as in nineteenth-century England, to Beveridge's Five Giants: of Want, Disease, Idleness, Ignorance and Squalor. The latter requires that intervening institutions be nourished to take over responsibility from enterprise welfare. The most salient are local authorities and voluntary associations. However, both were emasculated under Russian state socialism and now need resuscitating. The problem is that there is not much time left in which to do so.

Appendix: Funding enterprise welfare

There are seven possible sources of funds for sotskultbyt activities:

1 *Grants from ministries*. This was a major source of finance until 1990, and continues in the energy and military sectors. In our sample this is now the case only for the coal mines in the Kuzbass who all receive grants from 'Rosugol'.
2 *'The Social Fund'*. Sometimes called the 'Consumption Fund' this is a special fund set aside to finance *sotskultbyt* activities. It is usually, but not always, financed from enterprise profits; at Sokol in 1993 it claimed 60 per cent of the total profits. Sometimes it is augmented by further *ad hoc* grants from profits.
3 *Material or prime costs*. In several firms, some social welfare departments are regarded as production departments or workshops so their expenses are hidden as part of overall production costs. This is the case at Zim and at Transport Engineering in Samara. Again, production workers may be used on occasion to build or repair apartments or stadia, so that costs are merged into general production.
4 *The Social Insurance Fund*. Under official and then independent trade union control, this is primarily used to pay social insurance benefits to workers. However, it can and has been used in the past to fund *sotskultbyt* activities. For example, some of the fund at 'Russia' in Samara was spent on maintaining the tourist base and firm dispensary.
5 *Trade union budgets*.
6 *The municipal government*. Samara is continuing tax privileges to firms which retain social welfare facilities and/or invest in new ones. More directly local administrations can pay firms for the use of their facilities, either in cash or via subsidised use of other facilities in return.
7 *Payments by users*. This is a source of finance planned to increase in the future, and some examples are appearing. At Khimprom in Kemerovo

payments by parents accounted for 20 per cent of kindergarten costs in 1993.

In general the first source was prevalent until 1990, since when enterprises have had to bridge the gap from other sources, notably 2–5. The intention is that the last two – local government money and user charges – will grow in the future, but they remain insignificant at present.

Notes

1   Co-authored with Peter McMylor and published in *Journal of Area Studies*, no.11, Summer 1997. An earlier and fuller version was published as *Enterprise Welfare in Russia and the Transition to the Market Economy* in CID Studies No. 8, CID, Copenhagen Business School, Copenhagen, 1995.
2   The collective actually includes, besides managers and current employees, pensioners, former employees and persons discharged from the firm as a result of staff cuts after January 1992.
3   Another example of this approach is Mikhalev (1996) – a study of three enterprises in two Russian cities, Krasnoyarsk and Kaluga. His study provides much in-depth information, but is unfortunately limited to health care and recreational facilities.
4   See le Cacheux (1996) for a similar analysis.

III

Social Policy, the Economy and Alternative Futures

8
Social Welfare and Competitiveness[1]

Introduction

The relationship between social welfare and competitiveness is a perennially topical issue in both political and academic debate. From the mid-1970s it was increasingly asserted that welfare states undermine the competitiveness of advanced economies. This view was developed by a variety of schools of thought including supply-siders, monetarists, theorists of institutional sclerosis, quasi-moral critics of welfare dependency, and so on. In these and other ways the welfare state was implicated in the allegedly deteriorating performance of certain, usually European, nations.

Yet in the earlier post-war years the opposite view was commonplace: that the welfare state was a necessary element in an efficient and competitive capitalist economy. In the 1990s this older view has gained new adherents, as indicated by the following quotations from across the political spectrum.

> A strong welfare state can complement, not hinder, more flexible markets by reducing the fear of change.
>
> (Kenneth Clarke, Mais lecture, May 1994)

> Economic and social policy are inextricably linked; they are two sides of the same coin ... A new sort of welfare state is required to match an investment-led economic strategy.
>
> (Commission on Social Justice, 1994: 97, 103)

> While wealth creation is essential for social progress, the social environment is also an essential factor in determining economic growth.
>
> (EU White Paper on Social Policy: CEC, 1994a: 12)

Yet this coexists alongside a renewed concern about the competitive handicaps of an unreformed welfare system:

> Unemployment insurance and related benefit systems . . . have drifted towards quasi-permanent income support in many countries, lowering work incentives.   (OECD, 1994a: 48)

> The high level of non-wage labour costs [in the EU] is prejudicial to employment, exerting a dissuasive influence.
> (EU White Paper on Growth, Competitiveness, Employment: CEC, 1994b: 154).

Perhaps the consensus today can be summed up as a recognition that both positive and negative effects can coexist.[2] The goal is to design a welfare system that at least does not damage economic competitiveness and that at best enhances it.

In all that follows I shall be concerned with only one direction of causality – the effect of social policy on competitiveness. There are five possible relationships between the two variables:

1 incompatibility: more extensive social policy undermines national competitiveness
2 compatibility:[3] more extensive social policy enhances national competitiveness
3 neither: social policy has little impact on national competitiveness
4 both: different aspects of social policy have different and opposite effects
5 contingency: the relationship between the two is contingent on one or other or both of (at least) the following:
    (a) other national economic, social and political institutions
    (b) the position of the nation state in the world economy.

(4) may be regarded as a form of (5), while (3) is best regarded as a residual relationship if all else fails. This leaves me with three theses to consider and evaluate: compatibility, incompatibility and contingency. My goal is simply to survey the major theories and the attempts of others to evaluate them. This chapter does not present any new empirical work; nor does it attempt any theoretical synthesis; nor does it consider the historical development of the relationship between social and economic policy.[4]

It will be apparent that different theoretical perspectives are juxtaposed here which any research must recognise. First, we can distinguish between theorising at the *micro* level, concerning the effect of social policies on individuals' behaviour, and at the *macro* level, concerning the effect of social policies on national economic performance. A frequent criticism levelled at the economic literature is that hypotheses concerning micro-level relationships are used to make sweeping generalisations about relationships between macro-level variables (Esping-Andersen, 1994; Rubinson and Browne, 1994). I attempt to avoid this snare by treating these arguments separately.

Second, we confront here both *economic* and *sociological* theories. Apropos incentive behaviour, Esping-Andersen (1994: 721) distinguishes them as follows:

> Sociologists and economists disagree fundamentally on incentive behaviour. The former see incentives embedded in social relations, identities and cultural values ... while the latter, uninterested in their origins, relate incentives to individual marginal utilities.

In general, the discipline of economics has inspired and informed incompatibility theory whereas sociology has generated the contingency approach discussed below. Both have contributed to the compatibility thesis.

Lastly, though I will refer to 'evidence' for and against different theories, it should not be forgotten that the three main theses offer quite different frameworks for understanding the question before us and that they in one sense 'construct' the evidence chosen to evaluate them. I shall try to evaluate and use the available evidence as objectively as possible.

Another issue concerns the period of time to be investigated. It is most unlikely that the relationship between social welfare and economic competitiveness has been invariant to the profound transformations in the economic organisation of capitalism. One school of thought in particular highlights the shift from 'Fordism' to 'post-Fordism' as of epochal importance for the development of the welfare state.

> Crudely, it has been suggested that if Fordism is represented by a homology between mass production, mass consumption, modernist cultural forms and the mass public provision of welfare then post-Fordism is characterised by an emerging coalition between flexible production, differentiated and segmented consumption patterns, pots-modernist cultural forms and a restructured welfare state.
>
> (Burrows and Loader, 1994: 1)

According to Jessop (1994) Fordism was characterised by the Keynesian welfare state pursuing full employment and redistributive welfare rights in order to generalise mass consumption, whereas Post-Fordism is witnessing the emergence of the 'Schumpeterian workfare state' subordinating social policy to the needs of labour market flexibility. One reason for this shift is precisely the new imperatives of international competition on more open national economies. Traditional social policy has become an increasing fetter on capital accumulation, so much so that social policy is presently being transformed to conform more closely to the requirements of the new economic order.

This is one form of a more general argument concerning globalisation. All agree that the global economy is transforming rapidly. The EU (1994b) cites, *inter alia*, the following changes:

- the new industrial revolution and accompanying changes in technologies, jobs and skills
- the growing interdependence of markets and in particular the freedom of capital movements
- the emergence of new competitors notably in the Asian-Pacific region.

However, the extent, causes and implications of such trends are disputed. Some claim that globalisation, in the sense of market, productive and financial integration across the world, is at hand. Others contend that this is closest to being realised in financial services, but that in manufactured goods the pattern is one of regional blocs, notably those in and around the US, Europe and Japan. Some argue that accompanying trends include a demassification of the working-class and a declining collective working-class interest, an erosion of the corporatist institutions of capital and labour, and a weakening of the authority and capacity of interventionist states – all of which undermine the traditional bases of the western welfare state. Others argue that the authority of states is enhanced by such shifts and that significant national differences persist in the face of such globalising trends.

Yet there is widespread agreement now that the welfare state was built on, and constituted a key element in, an economic model which is fast disappearing. Reality has transformed while the welfare state has not (Commission on Social Justice, 1994). This chapter takes on board these arguments to the extent that it focuses on the relationship between social policy and competitiveness during the last 20 years or so – roughly from 1980 onwards.

The rest of the chapter is organised in three sections. First, the meanings of 'social welfare' and 'competitiveness', are clarified. The second and longest section considers the compatibility and incompatibility theories and summarises some of the evidence. In the third section I adumbrate one form that a contingent relationship between social welfare and competitiveness could take, based on the work of Esping-Andersen (1990).

Definitions

Social policy, social welfare, welfare state

Much confusion can stem from a failure to distinguish between these related concepts. The following is my attempt to draw some usable definitions which are not too far removed from the current consensus in social policy studies. It is a commonplace in policy analysis to distinguish between the inputs, outputs and outcomes of the policy process, and my definitions draw on this distinction.

Social policies are specific policy outputs of government or government-mandated bodies. These outputs can be specified empirically, by reference to a list which usually includes income maintenance, health care and social services, and sometimes includes education, housing and employment policies. Frequently, however, social policies are defined, and contrasted with economic policy, according to their distinctive goals or the values embedded in these goals, such as integration or the enhancement of individual or collective welfare. This, I think, is misleading, since a broad range of policies, including economic policies, can be directed to these goals, and since social policies can pursue quite other goals (for example, the extensive social policies of Nazism). I have proposed an alternative unifying theme: social policies are forms of state intervention in the sphere of reproduction of the labour force and the household, whereas economic policy is state intervention in the sphere of production. Economic policy is directed at economic enterprises; social policies are directed at agents of reproduction, namely families and households. Piachaud (1989) has claimed that this is ambiguous, and at the borders between the two (as, for example, with self-employed households) no doubt this is true. But some such distinction must be made if we are to distinguish state social interventions from social welfare and the welfare state according to criteria other than the values they embody.

Social welfare refers to final outcome states of individuals or groups. The most common desirable measure of welfare in the literature is equality. However there are conceptual and normative problems associated with equality as a goal of social policy (LeGrand, 1992). Esping-Andersen (1990) proposes the concept of decommodification as a synthetic measure of welfare outcome, but this too has been criticised. In my view welfare is best captured by Sen's (1992) concept of capabilities and by our own concept of human need satisfaction (Doyal and Gough, 1991). Whatever the exact specification, welfare refers to some morally justifiable notion of well-being.

A *welfare state* is then a set of state policy outputs which pursue the goal of enhancing human welfare, thus defined. This is close to the idea of the 'People's Home' developed by Moller in inter-war Sweden and to T.H. Marshall's view of the welfare state developed in post-war Britain. For both, the welfare state entailed a double commitment: 'granting citizens social rights and claims on government, and guaranteeing that it would uphold the welfare of the entire social community' (Esping-Andersen, 1994: 712). This still leaves open the institutional forms by which these rights and guarantees are met. In an earlier work we use the term 'welfare statism' to keep in mind the fact that states differ in the degree that they guarantee the welfare of all, and I shall continue with that usage at times below (Pfaller, Gough and Therborn, 1991).

It thus makes a difference whether we consider the relationship between competitiveness and (a) social policy, (b) social welfare, or (c) the welfare state. To chart variations in each of these terms, a variety of measures are available. Social policy *inputs* are usually charted by levels of state social expenditure or the taxation required to finance them. Social policy *outputs* can be measured at the programme level via indicators of programme coverage, benefit replacement rates, etc.; at the societal level the concept of *welfare regimes* offers an overall summary of the patterns of policy outputs. Welfare *outcomes* can be assessed in a variety of ways, such as degree of redistribution, decommodification, level of equality and approximation to full employment. Thus there are a variety of concepts and measures relating to social policy inputs, outputs and outcomes. The choice between these variables will affect hypotheses and findings concerning their relationship with economic competitiveness. I shall consider all three below.

Competitiveness and economic performance

Competitiveness is normally a characteristic associated with economic enterprises. According to Porter, a firm attains competitive advantage by adding value:

The ultimate value a firm creates is measured by the amount buyers are willing to pay for its product or service. A firm is profitable if this value exceeds the collective cost of performing all the required activities {to produce this output}. To gain competitive advantage over its rivals, a firm must either provide comparable buyer value but perform activities more efficiently than its competitors (lower cost), or perform activities in a unique way that creates greater buyer value and commands a premium price (differentiation).   (Porter, 1990: 40)

But no nation can be competitive in, and a net exporter of, everything, so what does it mean to speak of national competitiveness? Welfare states are by definition national in scope and so are most social programmes. If we are to study their impact on competitiveness we need some way of aggregating firm competitiveness into national competitiveness.

In an earlier work (Pfaller, Gough and Therborn, 1991) we distinguish two levels of competitiveness:

(a) *performing* competitiveness, which refers to the ability of national enterprises to sell abroad in contested markets, and
(b) *structural* or *underlying* competitiveness, which refers to the ability of nations to provide high and growing per capita incomes whilst being exposed to foreign competition.

It is the second type – underlying competitiveness – which is most relevant to societal level studies, though the former has a role at the sectoral level.

Performance competitiveness can be assessed in a variety of ways, but several of these conflict with measures of structural competitiveness. Two measures of success are a positive trade balance and a rising share of world exports – either in the aggregate or decomposed by trade region or product. However, these results can be achieved by lowering wages and/or continually devaluing the currency, which will harm real incomes. Moreover strong firms might devolve the production of part of their output abroad rather than export from home whilst retaining overall control of the process. Porter (1990) uses as his measure 'a significant and sustained share of world exports [in a given industry or segment] to a wide array of nations and/or foreign direct investment reflecting skills and strengths created in the home nation' (1990: 283).

The main indicator of structural competitiveness is growth in productivity (Pfaller et al., 1991; Porter, 1990: 6). If the principal economic goal of a nation is to produce a high and rising real income for its citizens, then the ability to do so depends on the productivity with which the nation's resources (labour and capital) are employed. Since there is a close link between growth in aggregate productivity and growth in aggregate output, to study the impact of social policy on national competitiveness is not a million miles away from studying its impact on economic growth. This is useful because there has been considerably more work on this second question.

Nevertheless, a variety of concepts and measures of competitiveness are on offer, and which is chosen may well affect hypotheses and findings about the effect of social policies. In what follows I use 'social policies' and 'competitiveness' as shorthand terms which can embrace the above range of particular interpretations.

Why bother?

It may be asked why we should concern ourselves with this whole issue. On the one hand, Krugman (1994) contends that competitiveness is a meaningless word when applied to national economies. Even today much of US production, is for domestic use, and the same applies to the European Union (though not to individual member states), so a deterioration in the terms of trade has only a marginal effect on the growth of real incomes. On the other hand, a moral criticism can be made. If the ultimate goal of all economic activity is to enhance the level of social well-being, and if this is also the goal of the welfare state, as I have argued above, is not the question redundant? And if this is not the goal of economic activity, then should not the goal of social welfare trump that of competitiveness?

Both these critiques are misplaced, in my view. Nation states in an increasingly competitive global economy must accept performance competitiveness as a constraint on the pursuit of other goals. For example, a persistent current account deficit leads to vulnerability in the international credit market and to the danger of firm buy-outs by rivals backed by stronger currencies. Yet to seek to overcome this by forcing labour costs down, either directly (via lower wages) or indirectly (via lower social charges), is to risk incurring losses in underlying competitiveness. It is also politically difficult in a democracy. Thus, outside exceptional circumstances, it is reasonable to assume that the maintenance of reasonable levels of structural competitiveness is a pervasive constraint on national economic and social policy. It is therefore important to study the countervailing effect of national social policies on the competitive advantage of nations.

Incompatibility and compatibility: a selective survey of theories and evidence

The fundamental neoclassical case against the welfare state is that deliberate alteration of market prices and wages – with a view to redistributing income or achieving some other social goal – weakens or perverts both the signalling and incentive functions which prices perform in market economies. This reduces efficiency in the allocation of resources and the supply of savings and labour. In Okun's phrase, there is a trade-off between equality and efficiency. Redistribution takes place in a 'leaky bucket': the poor will not receive all the money that is taken from the rich (Okun, 1975). This line of argument has a long history in economic thought (e.g. Fisher, 1935; Gilder, 1981).

Leading exponents of the compatibility thesis include Polanyi (1944), Myrdal (1960), Barr (1987) and human capital theorists. It is apparent that this group varies between institutional-historical sociologists at one extreme to economists working within the neoclassical paradigm at the other extreme.[5]

Figure 8.1 displays a matrix of links between social welfare and competitiveness. Vertically, it distinguishes between three dimensions of 'social welfare': as input (levels of social expenditure and taxation), as policy output (sets of social programmes) and as outcome (final states of welfare). Horizontally, it distinguishes the three mediating variables through which they can influence structural or underlying competitiveness: the supply of capital, the supply of labour, and the productivity of capital and labour. Of course, each, particularly the second and third, can be disaggregated in turn. The supply of labour will be affected by changes in both the quantity and quality of labour. Productivity will be affected by either or both of (a) the internal efficiency of firms, and (b) the efficiency by which resources are allocated between firms and sectors.

Thus there are nine basic ways in which our independent variable, social welfare, can influence our dependent variable, national competitiveness. Each of these can, in principle, be positive or negative in direction: in Figure 8.1 negative or incompatibility effects are shown in normal type and positive or compatibility effects are shown in italics. Let me now comment briefly on those relationships listed in Figure 8.1 in three stages, beginning at the top. To save space I shall not cite the large number of primary studies, but only selected secondary or tertiary surveys.

Figure 8.1.   Compatibility and Incompatibility – a selective summary

	Supply of capital	Supply of labour	Productivity of capital and labour
Expenditure/ taxation	1.1 Borrowing crowds out investment. 1.2 Social security charges encourage export of capital. *1.4 Macro-economic stabilisation effects*	1.3 Direct taxes reduce labour supply.	
Social Programmes	2.1 Pay-as-you-go pensions reduce savings.	2.2 Pensions reduce labour supply 2.3 Unemployment and/or sickness benefit reduces labour supply. 2.4 Minimum wages, employment protection pose barriers to hiring	2.5 Public sector social services have lower internal efficiency.
		2.8 Support for women's employment.	*2.6 Market failures, e.g. unemployment insurance, chronic health services.* *2.9 Human capital improvements via education and training.*
	2.7 Deregulation of housing leads to equity withdrawal and rising consumption		
Welfare outcomes			Redistribution undermines price mechanism.
	3.3.Crime deters investment.	*3.2 Reduced costs of ill health* *3.3 Crime harms child education*	*3.1 Welfare enhances flexibility via greater trust and reduced transaction costs.* *3.4 Enforcement costs of inequality.*

1.   The impact of state welfare effort

1.1 One effect on the supply of capital arises if rapidly growing social expenditures are financed by government borrowing which then 'crowd out' private capital investment. Bacon and Eltis (1976) hypothesised a direct crowding-out effect, when expansionary government activity are offset, wholly or partially, by reductions in private sector spending.

However this is generally discredited and attention now focuses on financial crowding-out when governments run deficits financed by bond sales. A thorough survey by Klau and Saunders (OECD, 1985) concluded that the effect of fiscal stimulus on long-term interest rates is mediated by monetary policy. If this accommodates to the stimulus then crowding-out is weak, but if it remains unchanged, then the threat is real. Again, according to a McKinsey Group Report, global capital markets are becoming more sensitive to the risks of highly indebted governments which are being forced to pay bigger risk premiums (*The Economist*, 1994). Thus government borrowing could indirectly raise the costs of capital and reduce its supply. However, these factors need not necessarily reduce aggregate investment – if the increment in government spending is on capital goods and the decrement of private spending is on consumption.

1.2 Capital supply could also be undermined, it is argued, by high social charges on enterprises as a consequence of an extensive and expensive welfare state. For example, tax and social security charges account for more than 40 per cent of overall labour costs in the EU, much higher than in the US (30 per cent) and Japan (20 per cent) (CEC, 1994b). As well as exacerbating unemployment, these levels could encourage firms to locate production activity outside the EU where labour costs are lower with adverse effects on both performing and underlying competitiveness. However, cutting back on social programmes and expenditure is only one of five policies which can correct for this and improve performance competitiveness. The others are: reducing direct labour costs, reducing other costs, redistributing the costs of welfare statism from enterprises to households, and devaluing the currency (Pfaller et al., 1991: 7). The choice between these is basically a matter of societal preference though each will have other economic consequences.

1.3 High taxation and social security contributions could also react adversely on the supply of labour.[6] All direct and indirect taxes insert a wedge between the cost of labour to an employer and the value of the goods workers can buy with their wages. However the effect of this on the supply of labour depends on other considerations. The fact that the substitution and income effects offset each other makes the overall outcome theoretically indeterminate, but this does not stop many commentators from asserting that taxes, specifically direct taxes, dampen labour supply, motivation and effort. An OECD survey showed that income taxation has no significant effect on the labour supply of men but some negative effect on women. However, this is swamped by the impact of other government programmes and the system of taxation of couples (OECD, 1985). A recent compilation study of the effects in high-tax European countries came to similar conclusions: small negative effects of tax levels on aggregate labour supply, except for married women and lone parents in certain countries and circumstances, which are outweighed by tax structure factors. For example, if the German system of income-splitting for married couples were to be changed to the Swedish system of separate taxation, it is estimated that this would raise the labour force participation rate of German women by 8–10 percentage points – an effect which dwarfs the impact of other features of their respective tax systems (Atkinson and Mogensen, 1993: ch. 8).

1.4 Against these macro-economic dangers must be set the Keynesian, demand-side argument for the efficiency effects of extensive and redistributive welfare systems. This contends that high and redistributive social spending will contribute to economic stability because social programmes such as unemployment benefit are countercyclical in their effects; because poorer people will spend money on consumption more steadily than richer people; and because the balance of payments constraint on macro-economic policy is relaxed if, as is usually the case, the consumption basket of poorer people and public infrastructure spending have a lower import content than the private consumption expenditure of the better-off (Corry and Glyn, 1994).

Cross-national evidence

Respectable theoretical arguments can thus be advanced for both the compatibility and the incompatibility theories and isolated pieces of evidence can be cited in support of both. I consider here some aggregate-level research which tries to test the overall effect of 'welfare state effort' on economic performance. This can take the form of time-series studies of one country or cross-national studies or both. The most common measures of welfare state effort are the shares in GDP of taxation, social security spending and total social expenditure. The only study to try to directly measure competitiveness, to my knowledge, is our own, which included measures of performance and underlying competitiveness for OECD countries for the 1970s and early 1980s (Pfaller and Gough, 1991). However, we ran only correlation tests and did not use regression or other sophisticated modelling techniques.

Taking the growth rate of manufactured exports 1980–6 as our measure of performance competitiveness, we found no significant correlation with the share of social spending in 1979 or with the change in this share 1973–9. However, we found that the change in export shares in the earlier period 1973–9 did exhibit a significant negative relationship with social spending in 1973 ($R^2 = -0.54$). A synthetic measure of welfare statism combining social spending and full employment revealed no significant correlation. Turning to structural competitiveness we used growth of manufacturing productivity (real value added per employed person in manufacturing) as our main measure. This revealed a series of weak negative correlations with the above measures of welfare statism. These were stronger (and still negative) when countries were ranked according to the 'competitiveness scoreboard' established by the European Management Forum (1986). Lastly, we correlated our social measures against economic growth and found a series of rather high negative associations between social spending levels in 1979 and economic growth rates 1980–7 ($R^2 = -0.63$).

This suggests that state welfare was becoming more incompatible with competitiveness in the 1980s. However, like other studies, we found that the inclusion or exclusion of specific countries makes a big difference to the association. In particular the presence or absence of Japan has a profound effect in so many of these exercises (Saunders, 1986). So too can the time period selected, particularly with economic variables affected by the trade cycle. Lastly, correlation exercises cannot take account of the host of other variables which may reasonably affect national competitiveness. More complex modelling is required to take these on board.

Atkinson (1995) has reviewed the major empirical studies which have regressed social security transfer spending as a share of GDP, on economic growth rates.[7] Of the nine studies, four find a negative (incompatibility) relationship, three a positive relationship and two an insignificant relationship. Another survey of studies is undertaken by Esping-Andersen (1994), this time those using a broader definition of welfare state effort – total levels of social spending as a share of GDP. Again the studies reveal a mix of positive, negative and insignificant effects on national output. The conclusion of a wide range of macro-level regressions is that there is no consistent support for *either* compatibility *or* incompatibility perspectives. But given the widespread assertion that the modern welfare state undermines growth and competitiveness, these agnostic findings deserve wider dissemination.

2. Specific social programmes

Such indeterminate findings are not really surprising, given the number of problems facing aggregate empirical evidence of this kind (Atkinson,

1995). In particular, many of the incompatibility arguments rest on micro-economic foundations which cannot be easily aggregated into macro-level variables. Moreover, so many of the arguments depend on what Atkinson calls the 'fine structure' of particular social programmes. It is time to turn to some of these.

2.1 Pay-as-you-go state pension schemes, some economists argue, weaken investment, capital supply and thus structural competitiveness (e.g. Saint-Paul, 1992). Assuming a neoclassical growth model with endogenous technical progress and a model of life-time savings with a finite lifetime and no bequests, then it can be shown that a state pension scheme financed by a payroll tax will displace all or a large part of private savings. Assuming further that changes in savings translate automatically into changes in investment then it can be demonstrated that a major feature of all western welfare states has an adverse impact on the long-run growth rate.

However, several of the assumptions in this model can be questioned (Atkinson, 1995). If state pay-as-you-go pensions are replaced by private funded pensions, the institutional structure of capital markets is profoundly affected by the rise of large-scale occupational or private pension funds. These may intensify the takeover constraint facing firms thus reducing their investments and firm growth rates despite the higher aggregate levels of savings in the economy. The effects of pension schemes on savings, investment and growth cannot be conceptualised independent of institutional structures and their alternatives. There is little empirical support either: an OECD survey of cross-national research found no evidence that state pension schemes reduced household savings (OECD, 1985: 143–6).

2.2 State pensions can be indicted for their adverse effects on the supply of labour as well as the supply of capital since the enhancement of state pension levels might be expected to reduce the retirement age of workers. Time series studies, mainly in the US, do indeed show an inverse relationship between pension levels and the labour supply of older men, but cross-national studies reveal no such relationship. Here, much more depends on the availability of work for older men and the effects of other features of national welfare systems (Esping-Andersen, 1994).

2.3 Unemployment and sickness benefits may adversely affect labour market behaviour if they provide a high replacement rate. A rise in the benefit replacement rate will reduce the cost of being without a job and thus, it is argued, induce some individuals to quit their jobs and/or prolong periods of unemployment. It could also raise the reservation wage which the unemployed will accept and in this way increase long-term unemployment. An OECD survey of empirical studies suggested that the effect of replacement rates is modest but that the duration of benefit does adversely affect employment rates. (OECD, 1985). The recent compilation study of Atkinson and Mogensen of selected European countries found that both unemployment and sickness benefits in Germany and the UK do not discourage return to work, while those in Denmark and Sweden do generate longer periods of unemployment or work absence. However, the Swedish schemes are found to have positive effects: unemployment insurance results in a higher propensity to stay in the labour market and parental benefits encourage women to participate. Much more consistent is the finding that income-tested benefits discourage entry into the labour force or extra hours of work by imposing high marginal rates of taxation, especially in combination with direct taxation (Atkinson and Mogensen, 1993).

McLaughlin (1994) argues that the assumptions on which the theory is built are flawed. In particular, women do not face a straight choice between work and leisure but a three-way choice between paid work, unpaid work and leisure, and this will be affected by the conditions attached to the receipt of their partner's and their own benefit. In other words, the relationship between unemployment benefit and labour supply is mediated by the detailed regulations of national schemes. However, Atkinson (1993: 31) argues that the incorporation of household production into models of decision-making does not necessarily affect predictions concerning labour supply.

2.4 More generally, minimum wage legislation, employment protection laws and product market barriers can create barriers to firms hiring extra workers. The OECD (1994) claims that there is powerful evidence for this. Others argue that the effects of benefit generosity are swamped by the commitment of different welfare states to full employment (Esping-Andersen, 1994). Gregg et al. (1994) have developed a specific criticism of these disincentive arguments. They claim that monopsony power exists in many low pay labour markets enabling employers to pay wages below the marginal product of labour. This means that there are some workers who do not find it worthwhile to work at the going wage and have little incentive to improve their skills since this too would not attract a commensurate improvement in wages. Thus both employment and skills levels in the economy are inefficiently low. Minimum wages and labour market regulation, along the lines of the Equal Pay Act, racial discrimination legislation and the EU Social Chapter, may in certain circumstances enhance, not diminish, labour market performance and competitiveness.

2.5 It is also alleged that state welfare impacts directly on productivity levels because public sector social services exhibit lower internal efficiency than their private sector counterparts. This arises from their frequent monopoly position in supplying the service and/or from the politicisation of the decision-making process in the public sector. Reviewing the evidence, Ringen (1987: ch. 5) concluded that there is considerable support for this view. However there are clear exceptions. The excessive costs of privately mediated health care in the US and their effects on industrial relations may constitute a competitive disadvantage avoided by those countries relying on lower-cost public provision (Brailer and Van Horn, 1993). Nor is monopoly provision a necessary feature of social policy or of the welfare state; quasi-markets and other forms of welfare pluralism can be designed to obviate these drawbacks.

2.6 Turning now to compatibility arguments, there are a range of market failures to take into account alongside state failures. Unregulated markets will fail to provide certain benefits, such as unemployment insurance, and certain services, such as health care for uninsurable risks due to well-established market failures including information failure, adverse selection in insurance schemes, moral hazard and uncertainty. The implication of this argument is that the internal inefficiency of public provision must be offset against the external inefficiency – due to sub-optimal levels – of private provision (Barr, 1992).

2.7 State policies affecting the production, finance and regulation of housing may affect the supply of capital and labour in ways which strengthen the compatibility case. According to Muellbauer (1990), the converse deregulation of the British housing market in the 1980s caused sharper fluctuations in house prices, the phenomenon of negative equity and greater regional inequalities in housing markets. These effects may have exacerbated inflation and inhibited labour mobility between buoyant and depressed areas, though hard evidence is lacking.

2.8 Further criticisms of the labour disincentive case against social transfers and support services have been advanced once gender effects and the special labour market position of women (especially women with partners) are recognised. The provision of nursery education and pre-school care together with supportive leave and other social policies enables women (and men) to juggle more effectively the competing claims of paid and unpaid work (Commission on Social Justice, 1994). By enhancing access to the labour market for all groups, such social programmes may increase overall productivity, even those with clear local costs such as generous sickness benefit schemes. 'What at first glance appears as a work disincentive emerges in the larger picture as a precondition for labour supply. Sickness benefit programs may be costly and high rates of absenteeism may generate production problems for firms; yet they are also a means for (gender) equalisation and for greater national economic output' (Esping-Andersen, 1994: 722; Atkinson and Mogensen, 1993).

2.9 Most contemporary restatements of the compatibility theory focus on the supply side of the economy. Of these, *human capital theory* has the longest pedigree since it is related to (is an economics-based variant of) technical-functional or modernisation theories of social development. These argue that modern state education systems contribute to economic development, first, by socialising students to modern values and attitudes, and second, by teaching job-related competencies and skills (Rubinson and Browne, 1994). Human capital theory relates this to individual efficiency in production by applying the marginal productivity theory of wages to assess the rates of return to different levels of education. The social rate of return typically relates the gross earnings of people with different educational qualifications to the total societal costs of their education, while the private rate compares net, post-tax differences in earnings with the private costs of acquiring that education. A World Bank survey of national studies shows that rates of return to formal education vary considerably across countries from 4 per cent to 24 per cent and that the social rate of return is somewhat lower than private rates, though still positive and rather high (ranging from 5 per cent to 15 per cent in the majority of cases). Evidence from the US and UK shows that this declined somewhat in the 1970s and early 1980s (OECD, 1985: 124–8).[8]

More recent research in this area has focused on training for specific skills and other delimited aspects of the education system. Britain performs relatively poorly in educating the lower half of the ability range at school, in persuading them to stay on after school-leaving age, and in providing comprehensive vocational training either in college or with employers. The researches of Prais and other suggest that resulting skill shortages have hindered the expansion of several growth sectors of the economy, including engineering and information technology (Prais and Wagner, 1987; Worswick, 1985). Finegold and Soskice see Britain as trapped in a 'low-skills equilibrium, in which the majority of enterprises staffed by poorly trained managers and workers produce low-quality goods and services' (1988: 22). What we have called performance competitiveness in this situation will derive from low productivity and pay and may make further training irrational for individual workers and enterprises. Yet this undermines productivity growth and structural

competitiveness which requires a more extensive education and training policy and one, moreover, which is more closely integrated with
other social programmes.[9]

Welfare outcomes: equality and competitiveness

Mention has already been made of the alleged conflict between efficiency and equality, with its corollary that state redistribution harms
those groups it is designed to help. The opposite view has been recently
put by the Commission on Social Justice (1994: 97).

> Social inequality – low educational levels, unemployment, poor
> health, high crime – holds back economic growth. It does so directly
> through the costs to government (higher spending on benefits, low
> revenue from taxes) and also to business (higher spending on security
> and on training workers in basic English and arithmetic). It does so
> indirectly by deterring investors from whole parts of our cities and
> regions, depressing the demand for goods and services.

Other goals of the welfare state are distinguished by Barr (1992);
they include income security or the protection of one's accustomed
standard of living, equity and social solidarity. Welfare policies – in
so far as they contribute to these goals – may have a competitive pay-
off. Let me consider some of the specific ways in which they may be
related.

3.1 From an institutional economics paradigm, the most general argument concerns the way inequality 'obstructs the evolution of productiv-
ity-enhancing structures for the governance of transactions' (Bowles and
Gintis, 1994). More equal societies may be capable of supporting levels of
co-operation and trust unavailable in more economically divided societies; they thus assist the development of co-operative or negotiated
forms of co-ordination alongside competition and command forms (see
Chapter 2). This in turn can reduce transaction costs and improve incentive structures. Some sociologists also argue that the move towards a post-
Fordist quality-based production system requires greater social solidarity
and integration, which in turn requires a social infrastructure of collective goods (e.g., Rogers and Streeck, 1994).

Katzenstein (1985) has contributed to this thesis from within a political science perspective. He shows how the small open European states
have developed democratic corporatist structures as an alternative to
protectionism and extensive economic interventions. An important
feature of the bargained consensus which results, especially in the 'social

corporatist' countries, is advanced welfare policies. Building on this, and Rieger Leibfried (1998) contend that, since in the face of globalising pressures even the biggest states wield a diminished range of economic policy instruments, a near-universal welfare state is now more relevant to economic performance. Acting as a 'filter and buffer' the security which it provides reduces opposition to change and flexibilisation among workers and other groups and staves off social disintegration and political upheaval. This is a return to Bismarck's case for the legitimising role of the welfare state and to the productivist arguments for the Swedish welfare model, both adjusted to the new situation of globalisation (Stephens, 1996). It is a theme of the recent EU Green and White Papers on European Social Policy: 'Many believe that productivity is the key to competitiveness and that high labour standards have always been an integral part of the {European} competitive formula' (CEC, 1994a: 31; 1993).

Let me turn to specific mechanisms by which these effects may be transmitted.

3.2 Poor health can indirectly disrupt economic production through sickness absence as well as impose direct costs on the health services. Wilkinson (1994) makes a case for a strong form of compatibility here – arguing that absolute levels of health are influenced by relative, not absolute, relative standards of living. If so, then a redistributive welfare state would help reduce such costs.

3.3 Welfare states may have both direct and indirect effects on crime. Econometric studies have identified various forms of relationship between economic indicators, including unemployment and inequality, and crime rates (council of Europe, 1995). Income support, training and employment provision can play a direct role in mediating the link between economic conditions and crime levels, particularly among young people. Welfare systems may also have strong indirect effects on crime rates through their mediation of processes of individual and community marginalisation – by reducing the segregation and concentration of vulnerable people and families.

This still leaves open the links between crime and economic performance where, outside the US, less research has been conducted (Hagan, 1994). Businesses operating in high crime areas must pay excessive insurance costs or may be refused cover altogether: more than 20 years ago 'insurance red-lining', whereby firms in zip-code areas regarded as high risk are refused insurance cover, was recognised as a significant disincentive to investment in deprived areas of US cities (US Department of Housing and Urban Development, 1978). More generally, crime, poverty and social dislocation may stunt children's cognitive and emotional development with long-term harmful consequences for their education and acquisition of skills. This could be the most important cost of inequality to competitiveness in the long term.

3.4 Lastly, there is the diversion of resources towards enforcing law and order and away from more productive uses. One estimate of the more general 'enforcement costs of inequality' made by Bowles and Gintis (1994) calculates expenditures on work supervision, security personnel, police, prison guards, and so on. They estimate that in the US, a highly inegalitarian society, these categories of 'guard labour' constituted over one quarter of the labour force in 1987. If high crime and low trust are correlated with inequality, a redistributive welfare state can reduce these costs.

Cross-national evidence

Some comparative investigations have been carried out on the relationship between levels of inequality and economic performance. All of these show a positive link between degree of equality and economic growth rates across nations (Persson and Tabellini, 1994; Glyn and Miliband, 1994; also Esping-Andersen, 1994). Kenworthy (1995) also finds a positive link between egalitarian income distributions and healthy trade balances, one measure of performance competitiveness. What comparative evidence there is supports the compatibility theory.

Conclusion

It is striking that incompatibility arguments predominate where the concern is with aggregate levels of government spending and taxation. Despite the micro-economic foundations on which many of these arguments rest, they have frequently and promiscuously been generalised to aggregate relationships at the level of the economy. Partly for this reason, there is no empirical consensus on the direction of the relationship between welfare state effort and economic competitiveness. Yet when we look at the imputed outcomes of welfare statism much theory and some aggregate evidence can be adduced to support the compatibility case. These findings suggest that cost-effective welfare programmes directed at improving the supply of capital and labour and at egalitarian redistribution are an essential component of a policy for national competitiveness. On the other hand, expensive programmes focused on non-egalitarian transfers and non-productive expenditures are likely to burden the national economy, especially in the current epoch of globalisation.

However, the bulk of research concerns the effects of specific national programmes, and here no such general conclusions can be drawn. When our attention is turned to the 'fine structures' of individual social programmes, it is the contingency of these relationships which is most noticeable. Does this mean that no more general conclusions can be drawn about the relationship between welfare systems and competitiveness? I now consider whether the concept of welfare regimes provides a more systematic framework to investigate my third conceptual position – that the effect of social welfare systems on competitiveness is contingent on other national institutions and practices.

Contingency theories

At the end of his survey of the economic impact of welfare states, Esping-Andersen concludes (1994: 725) :

> the effects of a welfare state cannot be understood in isolation from the political-institutional framework in which it is embedded ... there may exist a trade-off between equality and efficiency in countries where the welfare state is large and very redistributive but in which the collective bargaining system is incapable of assuring wage moderation and stable, nonconflictual industrial relations. Thus, in concrete terms, a Swedish, Norwegian or Austrian welfare state will not harm growth, while a British one will (even if it is smaller).

This is related to a second conclusion: that the economic impact will differ according to the type of welfare state and, more broadly, welfare regime. In other words the effect of social policy on competitiveness is *contingent* on the institutions of the nation state and its place in the global economy. Following Esping-Andersen's book (1990) the notion of 'welfare state regimes' has become commonplace. 'To talk of a regime is to denote the fact that in the relation between state and economy a complex of legal and organisational features are systematically interwoven' (1990: 2). According to Kolberg and Uusitalo (1992) modern capitalism is characterised by increasing functional integration; the goal now is to study national 'institutional complexes' relating together the family, welfare state and labour market.

Esping-Andersen's (1990) model of the three worlds of welfare capitalism is too well known to require much elaboration. He distinguishes three welfare regimes according to their policy outputs, their welfare

effects on 'decommodification' (the extent to which a person can maintain a livelihood without reliance on the market), and their feedback
effects on systems of stratification. The *liberal* regime, whose exemplar is
the United States, places greater reliance on social assistance and residual state welfare alongside private provision; it exhibits low decommodification; and it fosters a dualistic class system in which the better-
off have an incentive to exit from the state welfare system. The *social
democratic* regime (exemplar: Sweden) provides generous, universal state
benefits in cash and in kind; generates high redistribution and decommodification; and fosters solidaristic class relations. His innovative third
regime type, the *conservative*, or *corporativist* or *Christian democratic*,
whose exemplar country is Germany, is characterised by classic social
insurance schemes which tie benefits to labour market performance;
achieves moderate levels of decommodification; and reinforces both
existing status differences in society and middle-class support for state
welfare.[10]

A body of comparative research suggests that the three regime types
are broadly linked to various welfare outcomes, including employment/
labour market participation, gender relations and equality. For example,
welfare state strategies for managing deindustrialisation can be grouped
into three: cheapen labour (the US, UK, New Zealand), reduce labour
supply (the EU countries) and expand employment through combined
demand and supply side policies (Scandinavia, Japan) (Esping-Andersen,
1995). Studies of gender relations distinguish between (the majority of)
'strong male breadwinner states' and moderate and weak male breadwinner states (Lewis, 1993; Lewis and Ostner, 1994). Though the link
with welfare regimes is not perfect – France and Germany are similar
regimes with different gender outcomes – many are agreed that the
change in gender relations and life cycle has progressed farthest in
Scandinavia and that this is linked to the form of welfare state. Studies
of income distribution find growing divergence between countries since
the 1970s between liberal and corporatist economies (the latter en-
compassing conservative-corporatist and social-democratic regimes).
Inequality rose rapidly in the US and Britain but changed little in the
other countries (the only exception to this pattern was Canada which
showed no change) (Green et al., 1994). There is thus considerable
support for the idea that national welfare regimes have a salient effect
on a wide range of *welfare* outcomes.

Do they affect *economic* outcomes and in particular competitiveness?
Evidence is beginning to accumulate that these regime differences
impact on some aspects of economic performance. Calmfors and Driffill

(1988) rated OECD countries according to the degree of centralisation of wage bargaining structures and discovered a U-shaped relationship between this and employment growth. Both liberal, unregulated labour markets, such as that in the US, and highly centralised systems like the Scandinavian performed well in creating jobs, but the in-between nations, notably the EU member states, performed poorly. Rowthorn (1992) takes this further and relates it to wage dispersion and the welfare system. The US expansion of jobs occurred alongside growing wage inequality whereas that in Scandinavia and Japan combined with much narrower inequality.

I conclude by outlining a comparative framework for a contingent analysis, one which is heavily indebted to the recent writings of Esping-Andersen (1995, 1996). This develops the insights of his original analysis of welfare regimes, by relating state welfare systems to labour market systems and family/household structures to show how they interrelate and reinforce each other within distinct regimes. I shall build on the survey of research findings above to suggest links between these regime types and issues surrounding competitiveness. In particular I speculate that each regime type generates a different set of *problems* for or *threats* to national competitiveness, that these generate different recommended *policy solutions*, but that these in turn may generate further *dilemmas* or *contradictions*. This section is much more speculative. What is proposed is really a framework for undertaking further research.

In *liberal* welfare regimes, such as the US and, in the last decade, the UK and New Zealand, the dominant welfare threats to competitiveness are not those of disincentives, crowding-out, state redistribution, regulation and other leading issues in current debates. The dominant threat is of inequality and its effects: instability in demand, a poor quality educational base and social disintegration. In the US low wages and low benefits have stimulated a high rate of job creation; in the UK they coexist with a high but falling level of unemployment. The policy solution almost universally advocated is investment in education and training to improve the skills base and enhance high-productivity sectors of the economy. The dilemma is that high-quality education cannot coexist with long-term poverty, a growing 'underclass' or major community disintegration. These regimes may well need to increase all forms of social expenditure – on infrastructure, social services and social transfers – in order to realise these gains in competitiveness. The absence of major incompatibility threats provides the economic leeway for this to happen but the interest coalitions fostered within liberal welfare regimes militate against this solution.

The problems facing *conservative* welfare regimes, characteristic of the original six members of the European Community and newer continental member states, are very different. They are high and rising social transfers and their effects: high social security charges and non-wage labour costs which cannot always be compensated for by high productivity; discouragement of new service sectors with resulting low employment participation rates, especially among women and young people; labour market inflexibility and an extensive hidden economy which undermines tax revenues; and public sector deficits and rising debt (Esping-Andersen, 1995).[11] It is in these countries that several of the predictions of incompatibility theorists bear fruit. The recommended solutions are to deregulate the labour market, to cap insurance benefits, particularly future pensions as in Italy, and to divert social spending towards more productivist ends. The dilemma is that these solutions threaten the interests of the powerful organised sector of the economy and the breadwinner/familist model of welfare which underpins this.

In *social democratic* welfare regimes, such as Sweden and Denmark, state spending is high on both transfers and social services, unemployment was low (until the 1990s in Sweden) and participation rates particularly for women remain very high, while inequality and poverty are low. The twin threats to this regime today are high rates of taxation and high non-wage labour costs threatening domestic capital supply. The recommended solutions include some cuts in benefits and extension of quasi-markets and private provision. Compared with the previous two regime types many of the policies are in place for a productivist welfare state – indeed, the idea was developed in Sweden. The dilemma which remains is that to free resources for further investment in human capital further cuts may be necessary in social transfers; these may undermine the corporatist institutions and consensual policy-making on which the system partly rests.

Japan and the dynamic new market economies of East Asia such as Taiwan, Hong Kong, Singapore and Korea, may represent a fourth welfare regime. They combine low levels of state social spending with developed functional alternatives in the corporation, the family and the private market. A high degree of employment security, a relatively equal distribution of income and low tax levels permit or encourage high levels of savings which contributes to economic security and growth. The basic threats to this apparently successful system stem from the effects of growth on women's employment, family care functions and the birth rate. A growing double burden on women, especially as the supply of 'grandmother welfare' declines, may create pressure for more state services. At the same time, the falling birth rate is creating a rapidly ageing population placing greater demands on social transfers. Again, the solution points to a more productivist orientation for state policy, but this will require higher taxes which may undermine the self-financing nature of present forms of private welfare.

Three conclusions flow from this admittedly brief and speculative sketch. First, different welfare regimes exhibit different configurations of effects on performance and structural competitiveness. A problem in one may be a solution in another. Second, and despite this contingency, the general goal to which all need to direct themselves is a welfare state which gives due weight to 'productivist' considerations. In this sense the Scandinavian welfare pattern still comes closest to a rational resolution of these dilemmas. Third, in all regimes powerful interest coalitions will resist measures to adapt their welfare systems to the competitive require-ments of nations in the new globalised economy.

Notes

1 Published in *New Political Economy*, Vol. 1, No. 2, 1996. This is a slightly edited version.
2 Charting the development of views on the relationship between education and economic growth, Rubinson and Browne (1994) find three similar stages. First, an optimistic belief that education enhances economic perform-ance; next a cynical period beginning in the early 1970s denying any such relationship; now a more prosaic stage emphasising the conditionality of the relationship.
3 I owe these terms to Geoff Hodgson (1984: ch. 8).
4 On this last see Harris (1990) on Britain and Vobruba (1996) on Germany.
5 Different writers within Marxist political economy have expounded both compatibility and incompatibility positions. For a model which tries to integ-rate the two, see Gough (1979), especially chapter 6 and appendix B.
6 Again, we need to recognise that modern levels of taxation stem from all activities of government, not just its welfare activities. However, given that welfare spending is the largest and most dynamic part of state activity, and that social security contributions are linked to part of social expenditure, there is a case for including this effect here.
7 He points out the necessity to distinguish Levels equations in which country levels of GDP are the dependent variables from Growth Rate equations in which it is the rate of growth of GDP that is to be explained.
8 An alternative method is to enter educational and other human capital qua-lities into an aggregate production function to identify their contribution to average annual rates of growth of the economy. Using this method for the 1950s Denison (1979) and Bowman (1980) show education contributed

between 0.25 per cent and 0.75 per cent to economic growth and health and nutrition up to 0.3 per cent (OECD, 1985). However, this methodology has been subject to several criticisms (Rubinson and Browne, 1994).

9   To my knowledge there is little comparative analysis in this area. For the beginnings of one, see Allmendinger (1989). The OECD (1995) have just published an interesting comparative study on the effects of levels of literacy on competitiveness.

10   Critical commentary on his schema is extensive. These focus on: 1. the applicability of his schema to specific countries (e.g. Castles and Mitchell, 1993; Leibfried, 1993), 2. the applicability of his schema to forms of social policy provision other than income maintenance and employment (e.g. Room and 6, 1994); 3. his neglect of gender and its implications for stratification and decommodification (e.g. Lewis, 1993), and 4. his neglect of religion, status and ethnicity in shaping the welfare mix (e.g. Room and 6, 1994). All of these criticisms make valid points, yet, as will be seen, I regard the basic concept of welfare regimes and Esping-Andersen's initial operationalisation of the concept as of first-rank importance.

11   This scenario applies least well to Germany – Esping-Andersen's archetypical conservative welfare state. It is probable that the maintenance of corporatist structures of interest representation and intermediation account for Germany's continuing good economic performance despite the costs and strains of unification.

9
Basic Income: Real Freedom for All?[1]

Philippe van Parijs's ambitious book *Real Freedom For All? What (If Anything) Can Justify Capitalism?* (1995) develops three arguments. First, he backs 'real freedom for all' as the appropriate goal for the left-of-centre in the modern age. Second, he argues that (with modifications) a universal basic income at the maximum sustainable rate is the morally most just and strategically most effective route to this goal. Third, he contends that capitalism provides a more favourable socio-economic framework than socialism for achieving a high basic income and thus maximising real freedom for all.

These are big claims and I will try to address each in turn. The political upshot is a 'resolutely left-wing variant of Rawlsianism' (p. 297), designed to save the 'European model' of capitalism by taking it one stage further (p. 2). The book is situated in the red-green framework of politics still salient in Belgium, where he lives and works, and in other European countries. Yet the book is not an easy read, addressing as it does a formidable range of issues within political theory and philosophy. Feats of mental gymnastics are frequently performed to achieve what some might see as modest or obvious or perverse conclusions. The book is a good example of the perspective and style of the 'September Group', the 'Non-Bullshit Marxism Group', of which Van Parijs is a founder member; or rather, of the methodologically individualist, rational-choice side of that group.

Van Parijs's maximum sustainable basic income has obvious affinities to the right of all persons to the 'optimal sustainable level of need satisfaction', which Len Doyal and I advocate in *A Theory of Human Need*. Similarly his support for basic-income capitalism has something in common with the case I have made for 'socially regulated capitalism' as the best immediately feasible framework for optimised need satisfaction (see Chapter 2). Yet these superficial similarities mask disagreements over policy and analysis which stem from radically different ethical goals and methodologies. I shall try to clarify some of these similarities and divergences in the course of this article.

Theses

Real freedom for all

According to Van Parijs, a free society is one that satisfies three conditions (p. 25): first, there is some well-enforced structure of rights; second, this structure is such that each person owns herself; and third, this structure is such that each person has the greatest possible opportunity to do whatever she might want to do. It is the third condition, 'maximin opportunity', which distinguishes real freedom from formal freedom and it can be understood as follows. The person with least opportunities has opportunities that are no smaller than those enjoyed by the person with least opportunities under any other feasible arrangement. 'The real freedom we need to be concerned with is not just the real freedom to choose among the various bundles of goods one might wish to consume. It is the real freedom to choose among the various lives one might wish to lead' (p. 33). In particular, later on, this includes the ability to choose between work and leisure.

It is clear that Van Parijs's approach is close to that of Rawls, and on several occasions he acknowledges his debt. More generally he likens his approach to that of other left-liberal or liberal-egalitarian or solidaristic conceptions of justice, including those of Dworkin, Sen, Arneson and even Cohen. All share the general postulate of 'equal respect': that 'what counts as a just society should not be determined on the basis of some particular substantive conception of the good life' (p. 28). Only a thin theory of the good is extolled. When discussing how to make different opportunity sets commensurable, Van Parijs rejects assessing them in terms of the welfare levels they enable different people to achieve (p. 50). However by 'welfare' here he means the utilitarian satisfaction of subjective preferences, not the satisfaction of objective needs. Interpreted in this way he rightly points out a key difficulty: that people with more extensive and expensive tastes would be entitled to a greater share of resources than those who have adapted their tastes to their circumstances. This is unjust, except in the case of people with real handicaps, an issue he addresses in Chapter 3.

An unconditional basic income for all

The bulk of the book presents an argument for a universal, unconditional basic income at the maximum sustainable rate as the surest way of maximising real freedom for all (Chapter 2), followed by responses to a complication (Chapter 3) and two critiques (Chapter 4 and 5).

The opportunities component of real freedom for all justifies a radical shift from the traditional welfare state to an unconditional basic income: 'an income paid by the government to each full member of society (1) even if she is not willing to work, (2) irrespective of her being rich or poor, (3) whoever she lives with, and (4) no matter which part of the country she lives in' (p. 35). Different forms of welfare system in some countries of the industrialised world provide a guaranteed minimum income to all or nearly all citizens, of a greater or lesser amount, but none of these is unconditional in all four of the above senses. It is not difficult to see that maximin opportunity requires the provision of basic resources as a citizenship right, but why an unconditional basic income?

The argument for no work test is directly derived from maximizing opportunities: there should be no constraint on the use of one's time in the form of restriction of benefits to those willing to accept employment or training. The second feature – no means testing – uses a variety of supporting arguments (p. 36). First, an *ex-post* means-tested (or negative income tax) system must entail time lags when the poorest groups are vulnerable to real destitution. Furthermore, ignorance or confusion will mean that some fail to claim their due resulting in less than 100 per cent take-up of benefits (frequently a lot less). Second, the uncertainty of conditional benefits restricts claimants' real choices especially in the contemporary world of rapidly changing and flexible labour markets. For example, it may be too risky to give up regular benefits to take a job which may soon disappear or which they may be unable to keep. An *ex-ante* basic income provides a certain material foundation on which life choices can firmly rest. Third, the administrative costs of basic income are much lower than for means-tested benefits and thus, *ceteris paribus*, the sustainable level of benefit is higher.[2]

The final two (un)conditions are less obviously related to real freedom. Van Parijs simply observes that there is no reason to make the basic benefit dependent on household situation and place of residence. Having ruled out welfare outcomes as a criterion, it is no argument that there are economies of scale from living in a household with others or that it costs more to live in London than the Orkneys. Opportunities to live where or with whom you want are maximised by giving the same benefit to everyone.

The level of benefit should be the highest sustainable amount that could be paid to the members of the society concerned. 'Sustainable' has two components relating to incentives and ecology. Drawing on his earlier innovative work on the 'Laffer curve' with Robert van der Veen, the incentives component dictates that the tax rate set to finance basic income should be that which maximises the total tax yield. How high this is, and thus how high is the sustainable basic income, may well depend on other features of the socio-economic regime, and thus on the capitalism–socialism debate returned to at the end of the book. The complex questions raised by environmental constraints and intergenerational distribution are simply and reasonably dealt with by specifying that the next generation should be no worse off than the present one.

Should the benefit be paid in cash, in kind or some combination of the two? Not surprisingly, Van Parijs contends that opportunity sets will be maximised if it takes the form of a cash benefit. Certain exceptions can be made to take account of collective security (e.g. policing), positive externalities (e.g. basic education and infrastructure) and excessive costs of marketisation (e.g. certain pollution controls). But he prefers to restrict these to a narrow list of market failures. In particular he does not accept that consumer ignorance and irrationality can justify the direct provision of goods and services. So far, so libertarian. Yet Van Parijs recoils from taking this position to its logical conclusion. He opposes an initial endowment on the lines initially advocated by Thomas Paine because of the dangers that misspending in youth will create destitution in old age. He assumes 'a universal desire on people's part, when "in their right minds", to protect their real freedom at older ages against the weakness of their will at younger ages' (p. 47). And at the end of the book he speculates that the experiences of collective crèches and hospitals may be necessary to foster the 'solidaristic patriotism' that such a generous unconditional basic income will require from society's members (p. 231). These qualifications sit uneasily alongside his general belief in the rationality of consumer preferences.

In Chapter 3, Van Parijs confronts the problem that the real opportunities of the worst off will not be maximised if internal endowments are not included, alongside external endowments. Surely a person with disabilities will require a higher basic income than a person without disabilities if real opportunities for all are to be maximised? Once again any 'welfare metric' has been ruled out as a way of handling this, so Van

Parijs, like Dworkin before him, confronts a series of hurdles in distinguishing the seemingly valid claims of the genuinely handicapped from the seemingly invalid claims of those 'with expensive tastes', e.g. a non-musical person with an obsession to play the oboe well. His solution is to apply Ackerman's treatment of genetic features to all internal endowments. 'A's internal endowment (a vector of talents) dominates B's internal endowment if and only if every person (given her own conception of the good life) would prefer to have the former than the latter' (p. 73). This criterion of 'undominated diversity' should hopefully separate out the genuinely handicapped whom nobody would envy from the frustrated oboe players. But Van Parijs recognises the rather absurd corollary: that it would take only one person to prefer, say, blindness to vision, for any extra recompense for the blind to be ruled out. His answer to this is to postulate a large, open, pluralistic society with real exit options and an ubiquitous mass media (p. 83). This would minimise the chances that offbeat preferences would be universal across the social group and thus require transfers to enable everyone to travel to Mecca or to play polo.

It would seem that the principle of undominated diversity acts as a constraint on the principle of a maximum sustainable basic income for all (p. 75). Van Parijs applies the principle not only to 'the handicapped' but also to persons with modest endowments of whatever it takes to make a living in the market at the present time. If no one would prefer to have these modest talents, then he is driven to accept that some form of conditional guaranteed minimum benefit may be the best way of compensating this group of poor people. In other words, means testing, other forms of capability testing and in kind benefits (p. 259, n. 45) may well be the most desirable and effective forms of social policy. Moreover these benefits would have first claim on public revenues which would mean that in all countries less would be left over for basic income. In poorer countries the basic income could well be driven down to zero. Van Parijs's lengthy engagement with the problems of internal assets raised by Dworkin has left his earlier support of basic income peculiarly exposed.

Does basic income unjustly favour the 'lazy' (e.g. the surfer shown on the front cover of the book) and discriminate against what Van Parijs calls, to avoid biased labelling, the 'crazy' (i.e. those who want to get ahead and make money)? In Chapter 4 Van Parijs confronts one set of arguments of this sort. Musgrave (1974) in an early criticism of Rawls argued that implementation of Rawls's maximin favoured those with a high preference for leisure. In a later reply, Rawls (1974) switched to the

opposite extreme by adding leisure to the list of socio-economic advantages governed by the difference principle. The effect of this is to rule out
any entitlement from public funds for the voluntarily unemployed
(p. 96). To avoid this, Van Parijs introduces an argument derived in
different ways from Dworkin and Steiner: an unconditional basic
income does not unjustly benefit the 'lazy' if the 'crazies' use more
external resources than they, which will, generally speaking, be the
case. To endow the two groups with equal external assets will then
optimise the real freedom of neither group. Thus the users of external
assets should be taxed and the proceeds used to finance a basic income
for all.

The next and crucial stage in Van Parijs's argument is to contend that
jobs are the most salient assets in the modern world – more important
than inherited wealth and skills. Assuming that labour markets do not
clear, and thus that unemployment and extreme job inequality are
permanent features of modern political economy, then all jobs should
be auctioned to the highest bidders. In lieu of this, Van Parijs is led to
support, via a series of arguments, an income tax on all earnings at the
rate which maximises the tax yield, not excluding income from self-
employment and interest and dividends. The result of this long digres-
sion is a new justification for the twentieth-century tax state, but with
the revenues supporting an unconditional citizens' income. The argument is heavily reliant on modern theories of the efficiency wage and
sticky labour markets, and is also buttressed by instrumental arguments
for basic income in terms of its effect on labour-market flexibility. Yet
the chapter has been necessary for Van Parijs to provide a moral justification for the same end-result in terms of maximising opportunities and
real freedom.

Van Parijs then turns to arguments concerning exploitation, which,
had he not addressed them, might weigh the dice in favour of capitalism
in the last part of the book. If exploitation is defined in its most general
terms as 'taking unfair advantage of someone else's work' then it is not
at all clear that basic income makes things better and there is a strong
intuition that it will make them worse. In the course of addressing this
critique he provides a dense and wide-ranging survey of recent theoretical writings on exploitation, extracting where possible their normative
implications for basic income. When exploitation is conceived as surplus labour, the ethical implications ('to each according to her labour')
are, he concludes, unattractive since it would favour those workers with
higher productivity due to better capital endowments. Marx himself saw
this principle as inferior to, and eventually to be superseded by, the

principle of 'to each according to her needs'. Van Parijs then takes us through the cerebral pathways of Roemer's theory of exploitation which he (roughly) redefines as follows: A is capitalistically exploited if she would be better off if, *ceteris paribus*, society's means of production were equally distributed. But the *ceteris* cannot be *paribus*, as Roemer recognises. In practice the redistribution would entail costs to efficiency which may well reduce the welfare of the exploited. Real freedom for all is then maximised not by equalising assets and abolishing (Roemerian) exploitation, but by reducing it to the point where a less exploitative situation becomes worse off for the exploited (p. 183). Thus Roemer's approach 'effortlessly converges' with Van Parijs's and can lend support to, rather than undermine, the case for basic income.

Van Parijs spends less time confronting the claims of 'justice as desert', which attracts widespread popular support in judgements about small-scale situations. Why should the Little Red Hen share the bread she made with the other animals who refused to help her? One obvious answer is that in the real world people have arbitrarily unequal opportunities to bake the bread in the first place; another is that she must use scarce resources to bake it (including having a job in a bakery). But a basic income funded from taxation on incomes would rectify (to the maximum possible extent) these problems. If the desert principle is weakened to say that income should be positively related to work effort, rather than strictly proportional to it, then a basic income would contribute to that goal. Nastier jobs would be better rewarded, since the least endowed in the job market would have more bargaining power; unpaid labour would indirectly attract some reward, and yet the more you work the higher your net income. The general conclusion is that basic income would reduce the scope of exploitation in society.

Capitalism, socialism and real freedom

In the final chapter Van Parijs turns to consider whether capitalism or socialism would provide the better framework for maximising basic income and thus real freedom for all. They are distinguished in the orthodox way according to the private or public ownership of non-human means of production. But private ownership for Van Parijs can include, as well as ownership by capitalists employing waged labour, self-employment and worker ownership in cooperatives – an elasticity which might be thought to give it an unfair advantage compared to socialism. He is all too well aware of the problems in making grand comparisons between entire socio-economic regimes: each entails many dimensions other than property ownership; there is an essential relativity between patterns of demand, prices and the availability of particular goods; and so on. His solution is to compare a hypothetical capitalism with a maximum basic income with a similar hypothetical socialism. In doing so he relies not only on theory but on the evidence of the twentieth century, a process which raises interesting problems but which cannot, I think, be avoided.

The rival claims of capitalism and socialism as frameworks for maximising real freedom for all are assessed according to two criteria: efficiency and popular sovereignty. As regards the former, the critiques of capitalism which are surveyed include its tendency to enhance preferences for consumption over leisure; the failures of markets; the expansion of unnecessary activities (advertising and surveillance/control costs); its tendency to crisis; and unemployment. In several cases the criticisms are argued to apply equally to socialism, as with environmental costs or control costs. Others are attenuated, he claims, when basic income is introduced; for example, basic income helps labour markets to clear, thus helping to minimise unemployment, and enables people to choose more leisure if they wish. Yet others could be handled with further institutional modifications to capitalism: for instance, some form of incomes policy and/or a 'workers cooperative economy' to handle 'profit squeeze' tendencies to accumulation crisis. On the other side stand the theory and historical evidence about the dynamic efficiency of capitalism. The upshot is that 'it would be very hard indeed to overturn the strong, empirically supported and theoretically motivated presumption in favour of capitalism's superior economic efficiency' (p 220). It can thus support a higher level of basic income and hence provide more real freedom than socialism.

The arguments around popular sovereignty relate to criticisms that basic income is politically unfeasible or unsustainable in a global capitalist context. Capital can strike or flee the country that ventures down this road, whereas basic income socialism could collectively continue to allocate resources to investment. Even if the level of basic income it could provide is lower than that under capitalism, at least it would be achievable and sustainable. Against this Van Parijs questions whether capital would be so hostile to basic income once its economic benefits were appreciated (the 'new marriage of justice and efficiency'). He also points out that the constraints of international competition will operate on any feasible form of socialism, unless we reverse moves towards a global economy.

Van Parijs concludes by calling for a global basic income: real freedom for all must take the 'all' literally. In the face of profound pressures, constraints and inertia this will require, on the one hand, 'democratic cale-lifting' – the extension of democracy to supranational, ultimately world, levels – and, on the other hand, the fostering of 'solidaristic patriotism' to motivate the potential net contributors to basic income. The struggle for socialism is a dead end; that for basic income capitalism has all to play for.

Critiques

Opportunities and needs

Having summarised the main arguments, let me now treat each of the three themes of Van Parijs's book in turn beginning with real freedom. He rejects the 'welfarist' argument that freedom is enhanced by enabling a person to do whatever she wants to do, as opposed to whatever she might want to do, on the grounds that this enhancement can be achieved through the appropriate manipulation of her preferences. The 'Rousseau solution', of collectively specifying what are desirable preferences, is rejected as inconsistent with a free society (p. 18). He goes on to acknowledge that real freedom interpreted as the size of a person's opportunity set is very close to Sen's approach. Yet in a footnote he also rejects Sen's suggestion that 'the category of capabilities is the natural candidate for reflecting the idea of freedom to do' on the unconvincing grounds that 'I shall want to contrast permissions and abilities as two sets of factors affecting the size of the opportunity set' (p. 240, n. 45). So any objective metric of welfare is rejected.

Yet as Barry (1997) has pointed out this leads to some perverse outcomes. We have noted that the special needs of people with disabilities can only be identified and compensated if everyone in the society would prefer not to be in that situation. This is simply unjust. 'Any discussion of special needs has an ineliminable reference to a normal level of activity. This level is subject to some sort of collective determination.' However, Barry goes on to say that this level 'may be expected to vary, within certain limits, from one society to another'. This immediately raises the problems of relativism and of perverse societal preferences. In China and some other East Asian societies, people with physical and mental disabilities are regarded as bringing shame on their families and are frequently confined, neglected or even put to death. Are we then to respect these collective preferences? And if 'special needs' can be abstracted from the Van Parijs's individualist framework, why not the 'unanimously recognised necessities' (p. 76) of all of us?

The alternative to the methodological individualism of Van Parijs and others close to rational-choice Marxism, is not an equally flawed functionalism or holism but a recognition of the social dimension of individual action. In *A Theory of Human Need*, Len Doyal and I argue that physical health and autonomy are universal prerequisites for any person's successful participation in whatever form of life she finds herself in, or chooses to live in. These basic needs can be and are collectively identified on a global scale, though our understanding of them evolves through time. Their satisfaction requires the provision of satisfiers, whose characteristics can be similarly specified. Van Parijs's aim of maximising the real opportunity sets of all people requires, we would argue, the optimal satisfaction of these objective basic needs. Developing an argument that socially imposed duties imply rights, we conclude that there is a powerful case for social rights – specifically, universal substantive rights to the minimum bundle of satisfiers necessary to achieve that optimal level of basic need satisfaction. Such a welfarist approach overcomes the problems which Van Parijs faces in recognising and compensating special needs without succumbing to the utilitarian problem of 'expensive tastes'.

Furthermore, our approach firmly ties rights to duties whereas Van Parijs generally divorces the two. Again, the starting point is that individuals are born and grow in social environments. We all start off as babies and children and learn what we are capable of in interaction with others in social groups. In turn the cohesion and good functioning of such collectivities requires that certain societal preconditions must be met. These include the production of satisfiers to meet individual needs and the care and socialisation of children. Contributing to such productive work is a constitutive activity common to all cultures. Cooperative labour, including unpaid care work, is a defining feature of all social groups above a certain minimum size. The principle that all able-bodied persons should be enabled to contribute, and should then actually contribute, to the common wealth is a powerful component of intuitions about justice. 'Work' is not simply the antonym to 'leisure' and Van Parijs's liberal neutrality between the two is not morally convincing. Participation in universally socially significant activities, including work, is a crucial contributor to autonomy and human welfare. All able-bodied people should have the right – and the duty – to contribute to these productive activities.

Basic income and the welfare state

Basic income is to be contrasted with conditional state benefits. Van Parijs, like many others, assumes these to be means-tested benefits where eligibility is dependent upon the recent or current resources of he beneficiary. In fact there is another form of conditional benefit far more widespread in the modern world – social insurance, where the benefit is related to both employment status and past contributions paid into the scheme. Both social insurance and social assistance can be more or less hedged around by other categorical conditions, such as those listed earlier. Indeed these categorical conditions also apply to so-called 'universal' benefits like Child Benefit or Disability Living Allowance in the UK. Basic income is unique in doing away with both categorical restrictions (excepting some form or nationality and/or residence qualifications) and means-testing or contribution-testing.

It is agreed by all that basic income would be very expensive. How expensive is strictly impossible to say since its introduction would be an epochal event which would affect most other relevant parameters including the performance of the economy. Purdy (1996) estimates it would require a tax rate of between 33 per cent and 60 per cent. Remembering that all other non-cash government social expenditure, as well as non-social functions, would need to be financed in addition, it is clear that the fiscal feasibility of basic income is, to say the least, uncertain. It would have to provide enormous moral and strategic advantages over current and alternative welfare policies to justify such a risky and costly upheaval.

Let me then consider the advantages over conditional benefit schemes cited by Van Parijs, in particular versions of negative income tax. In doing so, I will draw on a comparative study of social assistance in OECD countries. (Eardley et al., 1996b, ch. 1). In particular, I want to consider whether the Australian model of universal means-tested benefits offers an attractive alternative. Too often comparisons with conditional benefits is based on the US or UK models. But these are but two of seven distinct forms of social assistance we have identified in the OECD world. What we call the US 'public assistance state' – an extensive and inter-related set of means-tested benefits arranged in a hierarchy of acceptability and stigma providing low to very low benefits – is indeed no model to emulate. But in the selective welfare system of Australia (and New Zealand) all benefits are means-tested. If any model can be used as a reference point for the conditional welfare state it is the Australian model.

In brief, Australia provides all citizens with entitlements to a comprehensive set of benefits. These rights are backed by an appeals system which extends to the High Court. The means tests are relatively generous: they provide extensive disregards for assets and earnings and the benefit withdrawal rates of around 50 per cent provide modest work incentives. The means tests apply to husbands and wives or to couples living together as man and wife, but entitlements and payments are made individually so that each partner can receive half the assessed rate in their own right (since 1995 some tests have also been individualised) Basic benefit levels are relatively generous whether measured in absolute terms or relative to Australian average incomes, and they are roughly equal across groups. Various forms of emergency relief are available to meet urgent needs. Since all benefits are means-tested there is little or no stigma attached to claiming them. Administrative costs amount to 3 per cent of the total social security bill. At first glance, some of the more obvious failures attributable to conditional schemes would seem to be absent in Australia.

To what extent does the Australian model maximise real freedom? There are two clear drawbacks. First, the remaining conditions do restrict options and can involve some intrusion into private lives Unemployed people must demonstrate regularly that they have actively sought work during the previous fortnight; data matching and risk-based selection techniques are used to target clients known to have a high correlation with incorrect payment who can then be more closely scrutinised. Basic income would avoid all such surveillance. Second, means-testing is, to use Goodin's (1992) term, 'presumptuous' in the assumptions it makes about people's behaviour and preferences. It is vulnerable to both factual error and social change. In today's world of fragmenting labour markets, where people and families mix and match formal work and informal activity, it becomes ever more difficult to track and assess people's means and thus their entitlements. And to the extent that it forces traditional assumptions about work and family on applicants it restricts the opportunities they can enjoy – as does much contemporary social insurance when it presupposes that 'every-one is either in work or is in a stable, long-term liaison with someone else who is' (Goodin 1992: p. 198). Basic income is the least presump-tuous income support policy.

These are powerful arguments against existing models of welfare and in favour of basic income. Before looking at the downside let me just point out that these arguments are more strategic or consequentialist than ethical. They play a minor role in Van Parijs's book, dedicated as it is to constructing en ethical defence of basic income.

A crucial and attractive part of Van Parijs's case is that in today's world decent jobs are among the scarcest and most valuable of assets. As White (1996) points out, he is in fact arguing that everyone has a right to a job, to a share of the available employment in society, but he is claiming that an ethical way of giving substance to this right is to tax job rents and redistribute them as a universal basic income. However, these two stages of the argument are contradictory. A right to work can be justified in two ways: reciprocity and 'brute bad luck'. The first I have argued above – that every able-bodied person has the obligation to contribute to the community's welfare. If this is so it behoves society to enable people so to contribute, whether through productive or reproductive work. The second justification for a right to work is that people should not be excluded from participating in such socially necessary activities through the brute bad luck of lacking external or internal assets. White argues that both these reasons justify giving people a right to work but do not justify an unconditional basic income – quite the reverse. Basic income directly contradicts the principle of reciprocity by giving benefit to those who choose to surf all day. And it is too indiscriminatory to compensate for brute bad luck since the voluntarily unemployed will receive it alongside the involuntarily unemployed. The appropriate policy is then to give all citizens a real right to work and to tie benefits to such participation.

This connects with another critique of basic income. As Goodin recognises, basic income is also presumptuous. It does not fully recognise that the source of income may provide benefits independent of the income itself. Participation in productive activity, as well as contributing to collective welfare, is a crucial component of self-respect, contributes to cognitive development and provides a site for purposeful socialisation. These benefits from participating in socially significant activities are abstracted from in a calculus of choice between work and leisure. Basic income also assumes that, with a few exceptions, cash benefits are superior to citizenship-based social services and that compensation is more important than prevention of disutilities through regulation. In practice a combination of conditional benefits, job subsidies, training and capital grants may well be more desirable. A needs-based approach supports a more mixed package of policies. What is more, in the light of the horrendous expense of basic income, the reality of a generous basic income would be a welfare state impoverished in all other respects.

More generally, basic income advocates are akin to neoclassical economists in their almost evangelical advocacy of a particular policy. Yet so much policy analysis shows that there is no one-to-one relationship between policy instruments and outcomes. It also shows the importance of inherited institutions and political cultures in selecting policy instruments and in affecting their transformation into welfare outcomes.

Institutions do not figure very much in Van Parijs's book, reflecting again the methodological individualism which underpins his work. Above, I deliberately compare the real-world situation in Australia today with what is still a counterfactual model. Such a comparison is unflattering to the real world and I am not advocating the Australian model as it stands or arguing that it suffers no defects. I have done so to show that even in the inhospitable world of the mid-1990s there were alternatives which perform respectably – including by the light of real freedom – and which are fiscally and politically feasible.

Capitalism(s) and basic income

Much of Van Parijs's defence of the potential of capitalism as the best framework for promoting basic income I find persuasive. After 1989 capitalism is 'the only game in town'. But the game can be played according to different rules and here once again institutional precision is required. One of the attractions of basic income to Van Parijs, I suspect, is that it requires less demanding institutional preconditions than any of the alternatives. However, the discussion in the last chapter begins to disabuse us of this rosy view. Basic income capitalism may well require, we learn, corporatist-style incomes policies and/or a 'share economy' along the lines of Weitzman and Meade and/or even workers' cooperatives, where labour employs capital rather than vice versa. The last is a radical development which many of us would not label as a variant of capitalism, but let that be. The problem is that these institutional specifications are bolted on in an ad hoc fashion to basic income capitalism and the complex relations between these elements and others are not addressed. Fair enough, you may feel, at the end of a long and dense book; Van Parijs cannot be expected to deal with everything.

However this institutional indeterminacy is an integral feature of Van Parijs's whole approach. Real freedom focuses attention on opportunity sets and opportunity sets focus attention on a basic cash income. Somehow all the other messiness of contemporary social policy can be subsumed and tidied away with these conceptual tools. Now some supporters recognise the problems here. Purdy (1996), for example, sees basic income, or Citizens' Income, as a regime; 'an ongoing field of debate rather than a settled programme'. But then its distinctiveness from existing welfare policies is muddied and the one-to-one link which Van Parijs claims with the ethic of freedom for all is broken.

If objective human needs are the subject of our enquiry, then the auditing of socio-economic regimes cannot be so one-dimensional. In

a similar exercise to Van Parijs's comparative evaluation of capitalism
and socialism I found it necessary to use six criteria (Chapter 2). My
conclusion was that a capitalist system which combines state regulation
and negotiated coordination between collective actors is the best feasible framework to secure the optimum satisfaction of human needs
(though I did not also consider other forms of socialism such as market
socialism). Of course my goals and the questions asked differed from
Van Parijs's. The point is that the task of evaluating the contribution of
socio-economic regimes to ethical goals, whatever they are, is likely to
be multidimensional and messy. Similarly the solutions will rarely conform to one policy instrument, whether that be deregulated markets or
basic income. This does not mean that the ethical evaluation of socio-
economic arrangements is too hazardous to contemplate. It does mean
that in the real world of different forms of capitalism there will be more
than one road to its moral reconstruction.

Notes

1. Published as 'Justifying Basic Income?' in the inaugural issue of *Imprints*, vol.
   1, no. 1, 1996.
2. In discussing the extent to which Rawls's difference principle endorses an
   unconditional basic income, Van Parijs also notes that his 'social bases of
   self-respect' are harmed by stigmatising work- and means-testing (p. 95). But
   this case for basic income appears not to follow from his real freedom
   approach. Indeed Van Parijs acknowledges this when concluding that conditional benefits may be more appropriate to compensate for poor internal
   assets, including difficulty in obtaining work.

Bibliography

Alber, J., G. Esping-Andersen, and L. Rainwater (1987) 'Studying the welfare state issues and queries', in M. Dierkes, H. Weiler and A. Antal (eds) *Comparative Policy Research*. Aldershot: Gower.

Alesina, A. and R. Perotti (1995) 'Fiscal expansions and adjustments in OECD countries', *Economic Policy*, October.

Allmendinger, J. (1989) 'Educational systems and labour market outcomes', *European Sociological Review* 5(3): 231–50.

Armstrong, P., A. Glyn and J. Harrison (1991) *Capitalism since 1945*. Oxford Blackwell.

Atkinson, A.B. (1989) 'Social insurance and income maintenance', in *Poverty and Social Security*, Hemel Hempstead: Harvester Wheatsheaf.

Atkinson, A.B. (1993) 'Work incentives', in Atkinson and Mogensen, op. cit.

Atkinson, A.B. (1995) 'The welfare state and economic performance', *Welfare State Programme Discussion Paper* 109, STICERD, LSE, May.

Atkinson, A.B. and G.V. Mogensen (eds) (1993) *Welfare and Work Incentives: A North European Perspective*. Oxford: Clarendon.

Bachrach, P. and M. Baratz (1970) *Power and Poverty: Theory and Practice*. London Oxford University Press.

Bacon, R. and W. Eltis, (1976) *Britain's Economic Problem: Too Few Producers* London: Macmillan.

Baran, P. and P. Sweezy, (1968) *Monopoly Capital*. Harmondsworth: Penguin.

Barr, N. (1987) *The Economics of the Welfare State*. London: Weidenfeld and Nicolson.

Barr, N. (1992) 'Economic theory and the welfare state: a survey and interpretation', *Journal of Economic Literature*, 30: 741–803.

Barry, B. (1997) 'Real freedom and basic income'. Paper presented at a conference on Van Parijs's Real Freedom for All. University of Warwick, 4 May.

Bell, D. (1976) *The Cultural Contradictions of Capitalism*. New York: Basic Books.

Bim, A.S., D.C. Jones and T.E. Weisskopf (1993) 'Privatization in the former Soviet Union and the new Russia', Unpublished.

Block, F. (1977) 'Beyond corporate liberalism', *Social Problems*, 24: 352–61.

Block, F. (1980). 'Beyond relative autonomy: state managers as historical subjects' in *The Socialist Register 1980*, edited by R. Miliband and J. Saville. London Merlin Press.

Blondel, J. (1969) *An Introduction to Comparative Government*. New York: Praeger.

Bollen, K.A. (1980) 'Issues in the comparative measurement of political democracy', *American Sociological Review*, 45: 370–90.

Bollen, K.A. (1983) 'World system position, dependency, and democracy: the cross-national evidence', *American Sociological Review*, 48: 468–79.

Bollen, K.A. (1991) 'Political democracy: conceptual and measurement traps', in *On Measuring Democracy*, edited by A. Inkeles. London: Transaction Publishers

Bornschier, V., C. Chase-Dunn and R. Rubinson (1978) 'Cross-national evidence of the effects of foreign investment and aid on economic growth and inequal ity: a survey of findings and a reanalysis', *American Journal of Sociology*, 84(3): 651–83.

Boswell, J. (1990) *Community and the Economy*. London: Routledge.

Bowles, S. and H. Gintis (1986) *Democracy and Capitalism*. London: Routledge.

Bowles, S., D. Gordon and T. Weisskopf (1989). 'Business ascendancy and economic impasse: a structural retrospective on conservative economics, 1979–87', *Journal of Economic Perspectives*, 3(1): 107–34.

Bowles, S. and H. Gintis, (1994) 'Efficient redistribution in a globally competitive economy', Paper prepared for Colloquium on Social Justice and Economic Constraints at the Université Catholique de Louvain, 3 June.

Bowman, M.J. (1980) 'Education and economic growth: an overview', *Education and Income*, World Bank Staff Working Paper, 402: 1–71.

Bradach, J. and R. Eccles, (1991) 'Price, authority and trust: from ideal types to plural forms', in G. Thompson et al. (eds) *Markets, Hierarchies and Networks: The Coordination of Social Life*. London: Sage.

Brailer, D. and Van R. Horn, (1993) 'Health and the welfare of US business', *Harvard Business Review*, March/April: 125–32.

Burrows, R. and B. Loader, (eds) (1994) *Towards a Post-Fordist Welfare State?* London: Routledge.

Cabrero, G. (1992) *Observatory on Policies to Combat Social Exclusion. Consolidated National Report: Spain*. CEC DGV. Lille: European Economic Interest Group.

Calmfors, L. and J. Driffill, (1988) 'Bargaining structure, corporatism and macroeconomic performance', *Economic Policy* no. 6: 13–61.

Cammack, P. (1989) *New Institutionalist Approaches to Macro-Social Analysis*. Manchester Papers in Politics, Manchester University.

Campbell, J.L. (1993) 'The fiscal crisis of post-communist states', *Telos*, 93, Fall, 89–110.

Carbonaro, G. (1994) *Guarantee of Resources in the Italian System of Social Protection*, European Commission Expert Group on Minimum Incomes, Preliminary Report. Brussels.

Cardoso, F. and E. Faletto, (1979) *Dependency and Development in Latin America*. Berkeley: University of California Press.

Castles, F. (1989) 'Introduction: puzzles of political economy', in F. Castles (ed.) *The Comparative History of Public Policy*. Cambridge: Polity Press.

Castles, F.G. and D. Mitchell, (1993) 'Worlds of welfare and families of nations', in F.G. Castles (ed.) *Families of Nations*. Aldershot: Dartmouth.

Cerami, R. (1979) *Emarginazione e Assistenza*. Milano: Feltrinelli.

Cereseto, S. and H. Waitzkin, (1986) 'Capitalism, socialism and the physical quality of life', *International Journal of Health Services*, 16(4): 643–58.

Chase-Dunn, C. (1975) 'The effects of international dependence on development and inequality: a cross-national study', *American Sociological Review*, 40 (December): 720–38.

Chase-Dunn, C. (1981) 'Interstate system and capitalist world-economy: one logic or two?', *International Studies Quarterly*, 25: 19–42.

Chenery, H. and M. Syrquin, (1975) *Patterns of Development 1950–1970*. London: Oxford University Press.

Clark, R. (1992) 'Economic dependency and gender differences in labor force sectoral change in non-core nations', *The Sociological Quarterly* 33(1): 83–98.

Coase, R. (1937) 'The nature of the firm', *Economica*, 4, 386–405.

Coase, R. (1960) 'The problem of social cost', *Journal of Law and Economics*, 3, 1–44.

Cohen, G.A. (1980) 'Functional explanation: reply to Elster'. *Political Studies* 28(1): 129–35.

Cohen, J. and J. Rogers, (1992) 'Secondary associations and democratic governance', *Politics and Society*, 20(4): 393–472.

Comité des Sages (1996) *For a Europe of Civic and Social Rights*. European Commission DGV.

Commander, S. and R. Jackman, (1993) *Providing Social Benefits in Russia*, World Bank Policy Research Working Paper 1184. Washington, DC.

Commander, S. and M. Schankerman (1996) 'Enterprise restructuring and the efficient provision of social benefits', in OECD, op.cit.

Commission of the European Communities (1993) *Social Protection in Europe*, DG V, Luxembourg.

Commission of the European Communities (1994a) *White Paper on European Social Policy*, Com(94) 333. Brussels: EC.

Commission of the European Communities (1994b) *White Paper on Growth, Competitiveness, Employment*. Brussels: EC.

Commission of the European Communities (1995a) *The Demographic Situation in the European Union*, DG V – Com (94) 595, Luxembourg.

Commission of the European Communities (1995b) *Europe: Social Protection*, DG V, Luxembourg.

Commission on Social Justice (1994) *Social Justice: Strategies for National Renewal*. London: Vintage.

Commissione di Indagine sulla Poverta e sull'Emarginazione (1995) *Verso un politica di lotta alla poverta*, Rome.

Corry, D. and A. Glyn (1994) 'The macroeconomics of equality, stability and growth', in Glyn and Miliband, op. cit.

Council of Europe (1995) *Crime and Economy: Proceedings of 11th Criminological Colloquium*. Strasbourg.

Crouch, C. and W. Streeck (1997) 'The future of capitalist diversity', in *Political Economy of Modern Capitalism: Mapping Convergence and Diversity*, edited by C. Crouch and W. Streeck. London: Sage, 1–18.

Cutright, P. (1965) 'Political structure, economic development and social security programs', *American Journal of Sociology*, 70: 537–50.

Dahl, R. (1961) *Who Governs? Democracy and Power in an American City*. New Haven, Conn: Yale University Press.

Dasgupta, P. (1990) 'Well-being and the extent of its realisation in poor countries' *Economic Journal*, Conference Papers, 1–32.

Delacroix, J. and C. Ragin, (1981) 'Structural blockage: a cross-national study of economic dependency, state efficacy and underdevelopment', *American Journal of Sociology*, 86: 1311–47.

Denison, E.F. (1979) *Accounting for Slower Economic Growth*. Washington, DC: Brookings Institution.

de Swann, A. (1988) *In Care of the State*. Cambridge: Polity Press.

Devine, P. (1988) *Democracy and Economic Planning*. Cambridge: Polity Press.

Dixon, J. and R. Scheurell (eds) (1989) *Social Welfare in Developed Market Countries*. London: Routledge.

Doyal, L. and R. Harris, (1986) *Empiricism, Explanation and Rationality*. London: Routledge.

Doyal, L. and I. Gough (1991) *A Theory of Human Need*. London: Macmillan.

Drover, G. and P. Kerans (1993) 'New approaches to welfare theory: foundations', in G. Drover and P. Kerans (eds) *New Approaches to Welfare Theory*. Aldershot: Edward Elgar.

Dunleavy, P. and B. O'Leary (1987) *Theories of the State: The Politics of Liberal Democracy*. London: Macmillan.

Eardley, T., J. Bradshaw, J. Ditch, I. Gough and P. Whiteford (1996a) *Social Assistance Schemes in OECD Countries: Volume I Synthesis Report*. London: Department of Social Security.

Eardley, T., J. Bradshaw, J. Ditch, I. Gough, and P. Whiteford (1996b) *Social Assistance in OECD Countries: Volume II Country Reports*. London: Department of Social Security.

Edye, D. and V. Lintner, (1996) *Contemporary Europe*. Hemel Hempstead: Prentice Hall.

Ellis, A. and K. Kumar, (1983) *Dilemmas of Liberal Democracies*. London: Tavistock.

Elson, D. (1988) 'Socialisation of the market', *New Left Review*, 172: 3–44.

Elson, D. (1991) 'Male bias in macroeconomics: the case of structural adjustment', in *Male Bias in the Development Process*, edited by D. Elson. Manchester: Manchester University Press.

Elster, J. (1980) 'Cohen on Marx's theory of history', *Political Studies* 28(1): 121–8.

Elster, J. (1985) *Making Sense of Marx*. Cambridge University Press.

Elster, J. and K.O. Moene (eds) (1989) *Alternatives to Capitalism*. Cambridge: Cambridge University Press.

Esping-Andersen, G. (1985) *Politics Against Markets*. Cambridge: Cambridge University Press.

Esping-Andersen, G. (1990) *The Three Worlds of Welfare Capitalism*. Cambridge: Polity Press.

Esping-Andersen, G. (1994) 'Welfare states and the economy', in *The Handbook of Economic Sociology*, edited by N.J. Smelser and R. Swedberg. Princeton, NJ: Princeton University Press, 711–32.

Esping-Andersen, G. (1995) 'Welfare states without work'. Paper presented at Research Committee 19 of International Sociological Association, Pavia, Italy, September.

Esping-Andersen, G. (1996) 'After the Golden Age: welfare state dilemmas in a global economy', in G. Esping-Andersen (ed.), *Welfare States in Transition*. London: Sage.

Esping-Andersen, G. (1999) *Social Foundations of Postindustrial Economies*. Oxford University Press.

Etzioni, A. (1988) *The Moral Dimension: Towards a New Economics*. New York: Free Press.

European Management Forum (1986) *Report on International Industrial Competitiveness*. Geneva: EMF.

Evans, P. (1979) *Dependent Development: The Alliance of Multi-National, State and Local Capital in Brazil*. Princeton, NJ: Princeton University Press.

Evans, P. et al. (eds) (1985) *Bringing the State Back In*. Cambridge: Cambridge University Press.

Evans, P. and J. Stephens (1988) 'Development and the world economy', in *Handbook of Sociology*, edited by N.J. Smelser. London: Sage.

Fawcett, H. and T. Papadopoulos (1997) 'Social exclusion, social citizenship and decommodification: an evaluation of the adequacy of support for the unemployed in the European Union', *West European Politics* 20(3): 1–30.

Feher, F., A. Heller and G. Markus (1983) *Dictatorship over Needs*. Oxford: Blackwell.

Ferrera, M. (1987) 'Italy', in Flora, P. (ed.) *Growth to Limits: The Western European Welfare States since World War II*, Volume 2. Berlin: Walter de Gruyter.

Ferrera, M. (1996) 'The southern welfare states in social Europe', *Journal of European Social Policy*, Vol. 6, No. 1, pp. 17–37.

Finch, J. (1984) 'Community care: developing non-sexist alternatives', *Critical Social Policy*, 9: 6–18.

Finegold, D. and D. Soskice (1988) 'The failure of British training: analysis and prescription', *Oxford Review of Economic Policy*, 4(3): 21–53.

Fisher, A. (1935) *The Clash of Progress and Security*. London: Macmillan.

Freeman, J.R. (1989) *Democracy and Markets: the Politics of Mixed Economies*. Ithaca, NY: Cornell University Press.

Friedland, R. and J. Sanders (1985) 'The public economy and economic growth in Western market economies', *American Sociological Review*, 50: 421–37.

Gamble, A. (1988) *The Free Economy and the Strong State*. London: Macmillan.

Gastil, R. (1989) *Freedom in the World: Political Rights and Civil Liberties, 1988–89*. New York: Freedom House.

Giddens, A. (1979) *Central Problems in Social Theory*. London: Macmillan.

Gilder, G. (1981) *Wealth and Poverty*. New York: Basic Books.

Glassman, M. (1994) 'The great deformation: Polanyi, Poland and the terrors of planned spontaneity', *New Left Review*, No. 205, May/June.

Glyn, A. (1995) *Does Profitability Really Matter?* Discussion Paper, Berlin: Wissenschaftszentrum Berlin für Sozialforschung.

Glyn, A. and D. Miliband (eds) (1994) *Paying for Inequality: The Economic Cost of Social Injustice*. London: Rivers Oram Press.

Goodin, R.E. (1992) 'Towards a minimally presumptuous social welfare policy', in P. van Parijs (ed.) *Arguing for Basic Income*. London: Verso.

Gorz, A. (1982) *Farewell to the Working Class: An Essay on Post-Industrial Socialism*. London: Pluto.

Gough, I. (1972) 'Marx's theory of productive and unproductive labour', *New Left Review*, 76: 46–72.

Gough, I. (1975) 'State expenditure in advanced capitalism', *New Left Review*, 92: 53–92.

Gough, I. (1979) *The Political Economy of the Welfare State*. London: Macmillan.

Gough, I. (1991) 'The United Kingdom', in A. Pfaller, I. Gough and G. Therborn (eds) *Can the Welfare State Compete? A Comparative Study of Five Advanced Capitalist Countries*. London: Macmillan.

Gough, I. (1994) 'Means-testing in the western world', Richard Titmuss Memorial Lecture, Hebrew University of Jerusalem, 31 May. Published in Hebrew in *Social Security*, 43, January 1995: 24–44.

Gough, I. (1997) 'Social aspects of the European model and its economic consequences', in W. Beck, L. van der Maesen and A. Walker (eds), *The Social Quality of Europe*. Kluwer Law International.

Gough, I. and P. McMylor (1995) *Enterprise Welfare in Russia and the Transition to the Market Economy*, CID Studies No. 8. Copenhagen: Copenhagen Business School.

Gough, I. and T. Thomas (1993) *Cross-National Variations in Need Satisfaction*. Manchester: Manchester Papers in Social Policy.

Gray, J. (1992) *The Moral Foundations of Market Institutions*. IEA Health and Welfare Unit. London: Institute of Economic Affairs.

Gray, J. (1999) *False Dawn: The Delusions of Global Capitalism*. London: Granta Books.

Green, F., A. Henley and E. Tsakalotos (1994) 'Income inequality in corporatist and liberal economies', *International Review of Applied Economics*, 8(3): 303–31.

Gregg, P., S. Machin and A. Manning (1994) 'High pay, low pay and labour market inefficiency', in Glyn and Miliband, op. cit.

Habermas, J. (1970) *Towards a Rational Society*. Boston: Beacon Press.

Habermas, J. (1976) *Legitimation Crisis*. Boston: Beacon Press.

Hadenius, A. (1992) *Democracy and Development*. Cambridge: Cambridge University Press.

Hagan, J. (1994) 'Crime, inequality and efficiency', in Glyn and Miliband, op. cit.

Hall, P. (1986) *Governing the Economy*. Cambridge: Polity.

Harris, J. (1990) 'Enterprise and welfare states: a comparative perspective', *Transactions of the Royal Historical Society*, 40.

Hayek, F. (1948) *Individualism and Economic Order*. Chicago: University of Chicago Press.

Held, D. (1995) *Democracy and Global Order*. Oxford: Polity Press.

Held, D., A. McGrew, D. Goldblatt and J. Perraton (1999) *Global Transformations*. Cambridge: Polity.

Hewitt, C. (1977) 'The effects of political democracy and social democracy on equality in industrial societies', *American Sociological Review*, 42: 450–64.

Hewitt, M (1992) *Welfare, Ideology and Need: Recent Perspectives on the Welfare State*. Hemel Hempstead: Harvester-Wheatsheaf.

Hewitt, M. (1993) 'Social movements and social need: problems with postmodern political theory', *Critical Social Policy*, 13(1): 52–74.

Hirsch, F. (1976) *Social Limits to Growth*. London: Routledge.

Hirst, P. and G. Thompson (1996). *Globalization in Question*. Cambridge: Polity Press.

Hodgson, G. (1984) *The Democratic Economy*. Harmondsworth: Penguin.

Hodgson, G. (1988) *Economics and Institutions*. Cambridge: Polity.

Holton, R. (1992) *Economy and Society*. London: Routledge.

Humana, C. (1986, 1992) *World Human Rights Guide*. London: Oxford University Press.

Ignatieff, M. (1984) *The Needs of Strangers*. London: Chatto and Windus.

Ingham, G. (1984) *Capital Divided?* London: Macmillan.

Isaac, J. (1987) *Power and Marxist Theory: A Realist View*, Ithaca/London: Cornell University Press.

Iversen, T. and A. Wren (1998) 'Equality, employment and hudgetary restraint: the trilemma of the service economy', *World Politics*.

Jessop, B. (1994) 'The transition to post-Fordism and the Schumpeterian workfare state', in Burrows and Loader, op. cit.

Jessop, R. (1982) *The Capitalist State*. Oxford: Martin Robertson.

Jones, D. (1999) *Cosmopolitan Mediation? Conflict Resolution and the Oslo Accords*. Manchester: Manchester University Press.

Kanbur, R. (1990) 'Poverty and the social dimensions of structural adjustment in Côte d'Ivoire', *Social Dimensions of Adjustment Working Paper 2*. Washington D.C.: World Bank.

Karantinos, D., C. Ioannou and J. Cavounidis (1992) *The Social Services and Social Policies to Combat Social Exclusion in Greece*, EC Observatory on National Policies to Combat Social Exclusion, National Centre for Social Research, Athens.

Katzenstein, P. (1985) *Small States in World Markets: Industrial Policy in Europe*. Ithaca, NY: Cornell University Press.

Kenworthy, L. (1995) 'Equality and efficiency: the illusory tradeoff', *European Journal of Political Research*, 27 No. 2, pp. 225–54

King, E. and M.A. Hill (1993) *Women's Education in Developing Countries*. Baltimore: Johns Hopkins University Press.

Klein, R. (1993) 'O'Goffe's tale', in C. Jones (ed.) *New Perspectives on the Welfare State in Europe*. London: Routledge.

Kohli, A. (1987) *The State and Poverty in India: the Politics of Reform*. Cambridge University Press.

Kolberg, J. and H. Uusitalo, (1992) 'The interface between the economy and the welfare state: a sociological account', in Z. Ferge and J. Kolberg (eds) *Social Policy in a Changing Europe*. Frankfurt: Campus/Westview.

Kornai, J. (1980) 'The dilemmas of a socialist economy: the Hungarian experience', *Cambridge Journal of Economics*, 4(2): pp. 147–57.

Korpi, W. (1983) *The Democratic Class Struggle*. London: Routledge.

Korpi, W. (1985) 'Economic growth and the welfare state: leaky bucket or irrigation system?', *European Sociological Review*, 1: 97–118.

Krugman, P. (1994) 'Competitiveness: a dangerous obsession', *Foreign Affairs*, March/April: 28–44.

le Cacheux, J. (1996) 'The current situation and key issues for the long term', in OECD.

LeGrand, J. (1992) *Equity and Choice*. London: HarperCollins Academic.

Leibfried, S. (1993) 'Towards a European welfare state?', in C. Jones (ed.) *New Perspectives on the Welfare State in Europe*. London: Routledge.

Leibfried, S. and P. Pierson (1992) *The Prospects for Social Europe*, Working paper series H34 Center for European Studies, Cambridge MA Harvard University.

—— 1995 *European Social Policy: between Fragmentation and Integration*, Washington D. C. Brookings Institution.

Lewis, J. (ed.) (1993) *Women and Social Policies in Europe: Work, Family and the State* Aldershot: Edward Elgar.

Lewis, J. and I. Ostner, (1994) *Gender and the Evolution of European Social Policies* Zentrum für Sozialpolitik, University of Bremen.

Lie, J. (1991) 'Embedding Polanyi's market society', *Sociological Perspectives*, 34(2) 219–35.

Liess, W. (1976) *The Limits to Satisfaction: An Essay on the Problem of Needs and Commodities*. Toronto: University of Toronto Press.

Lindblom, C. (1977) *Politics and Markets: The World's Political-Economic Systems* New York: Basic Books.

Lipset, S.M. (1960) *Political Man*. Garden City, NY: Anchor Books.

Lockwood, D. (1999) 'Civic integration and social cohesion', in *Capitalism and Social Cohesion: Essays on Exclusion and Integration*, edited by I. Gough and G. Olofsson. London: Macmillan.

Lodemel, I. (1992) 'European poverty regimes'. Paper presented at The International Research Conference on Poverty and Distribution, Oslo.

Lodemel, I. and B. Schulte, (1992) 'Social assistance: a part of social security or the Poor Law in new disguise?'. Paper presented at the Beveridge Conference, York.

London, B. and B.A. Williams (1990) 'National policies, international investment, and basic needs provision: a cross-national analysis', *Social Forces*, 69: 565–84.

Lukes, S. (1974) *Power: A Radical View*. London: Macmillan.

McLaughlin, E. (1994) 'Employment, unemployment and social security', in Glyn and Miliband, op. cit.

Mann, M. (1986) *The Sources of Social Power*. 3 vols. Vol. I: *A History of Power from the Beginning to A.D. 1760*. Cambridge: Cambridge University Press.

Mann, M. (1993) *The Sources of Social Power*. 3 vols. Vol. II: *The Rise of Classes and Nation-States, 1760–1914*. Cambridge: Cambridge University Press.

Mann, M. (1997) 'Has globalization ended the rise and rise of the nation-state?', *Review of International Political Economy*, 4(3): 472–96.

March, J. and Olsen, J. (1984) 'The new institutionalism: organisational factors in political life', *American Journal of Political Science*, 78: 734–49.

Markus, G. (1981) 'Planning the crisis: some remarks on the economic system of Soviet-type societies', *Praxis International*, 3.

Marsh, D. (1986) 'On structural power: an empirical test of the structuralist thesis'. Colchester: University of Essex.

Marshall, S. (1985) 'Development, dependence and gender inequality in the Third World', *International Studies Quarterly*, 29: 217–40.

Marx, K. (1926) *Capital*, Volume I. London: Charles Kerr & Co.

Mayhew, A. (1987) 'The beginnings of institutionalism', *Journal of Economic Issues*, 21(3): 971–98.

Mayntz, R. (1983) 'The conditions of effective public policy', *Policy and Politics*, 11: 123–43.

Meade, J.E. (1989) *Agathotopia: the Economics of Partnership*. The David Hume Institute. Aberdeen: Aberdeen University Press.

Mikhalev, V. (1996) 'Restructuring social assets: the case of health care and recreational facilities in two Russian cities', in OECD, op. cit.

Miliband, R. (1969) *The State in Capitalist Society*. London: Weidenfeld and Nicolson.

Miller, D. (1989) *Market, State and Community: Theoretical Foundations of Market Socialism*. Oxford: Clarendon Press.

Miller, J.A. (1986) '*The Fiscal Crisis of the State* revisited', *Review of Radical Political Economy*, 18(1–2): 236–60.

Ministry of Internal Affairs (no date) *Social Assistance and Social Security in Italy*. Rome.

Moon, B. (1991) *The Political Economy of Basic Human Needs*. Ithaca, NY: Cornell University Press.

Moon, B. and W. Dixon (1985) 'Politics, the state and basic human needs: a cross-national study', *American Journal of Political Science*, 29(4): 661–94.

Moran, M. (1988) 'Crises of the welfare state', *British Journal of Political Science*, 18: 397–414.

Morris, M.D. (1979) *Measuring the Condition of the World's Poor*. Oxford: Pergamon Press.

Mouzelis, N. (1999) 'Differentiation and marginalisation in late modernity', in *Capitalism and Social Cohesion: Essays on Exclusion and Integration*, edited by I. Gough and G. Olofsson. London: Macmillan.

Muellbauer, J. (1990) *The Great British Housing Disaster and Economic Policy*. London: Institute of Public Policy Research.

Musgrave, R.A. (1974) 'Maximin, uncertainty, and the leisure tradeoff', *Quarterly Journal of Economics*, 88: 625–32.

Myrdal, G. (1960) *Beyond the Welfare State* New Haven, Conn: Yale University Press.

Negri, N. and C. Saraceno (1996) *Le politiche contro la Poverta in Italia*. Bologna: Il Mulino.

Nell, E. (1984) 'Cowboy capitalism', in E. Nell (ed.) *Free Market Conservatism: A Critique*. London: Allen & Unwin.

Nove, A. (1983) *The Economics of Feasible Socialism*. London: Allen and Unwin.

Nove, A. and D.M. Nuti (eds) (1972) *Socialist Economics*. Harmondsworth: Penguin.

Nozick, R. (1974) *Anarchy, State and Utopia*. Oxford: Blackwell.

Nussbaum, M. (1993) 'Non-relative virtues: an Aristotelian approach', in M. Nussbaum and A. Sen (eds) *The Quality of Life*. Oxford: Clarendon Press.

O'Connor, J. (1973) *The Fiscal Crisis of the State*. New York: St. Martin's Press.

O'Connor, J. (1975) 'Productive and unproductive labor', *Politics and Society*, 297–336.

O'Connor, J. (1978) 'The democratic movement in the United States', *Kapitalistate*, 7: 15–26.

O'Connor, J. (1981) '*The Fiscal Crisis of the State* revisited: economic crisis and Reagan's budget policy', *Kapitalistate*, 9: 41–62.

OECD (1985) The Role of the Public Sector: Causes and Consequences of the Growth of Government, *OECD Economic Studies*. No. 4, by P. Saunders and F. Klau. Paris: OECD.

OECD (1988) *The Future of Social Protection*. Paris: OECD.

OECD (1993) *Country Report: Turkey*. Paris.

OECD (1994a) *The Jobs Study: Facts, Analysis, Strategies*. Paris.

OECD (1994b) *New Orientations for Social Policy*, Social Policy Studies No. 12, Paris.

OECD (1995) *Literacy, Economy and Society: Results of the First International Adult Literacy Survey*. Paris: OECD and Statistics Canada.

OECD (1996) *The Changing Social Benefits of Russian Enterprises*. Paris: OECD.

OECD (1997) *Beyond 2000: The New Social Policy Agenda*. Paris: OECD.

Offe, C. (1975) 'The theory of the capitalist state and the problem of policy-formation', in L. Lindberg et al. (eds) *Stress and Contradiction in Modern Capitalism*. Lexington, Mass: Lexington Books.

Offe, C. (1984) *Contradictions of the Welfare State*, edited by John Keane. London: Hutchinson.

Offe, C. and V. Ronge (1982) 'Theses on the theory of the state', in *Classes, Power and Conflict*, edited by Anthony Giddens and David Held. Basingstoke: Macmillan, 249–56.

Offe, C. and H. Wiesenthal (1980) 'Two logics of collective action', in M. Zeitlin (ed.) *Political Power and Social Theory*. Greenwich, Conn.: JAI Press.

Okun, A.M. (1975) *Equality and Efficiency: The Big Trade-Off*. Washington DC: The Brookings Institution.

Olofsson, G. (1999) 'Embeddedness and integration: an essay on Karl Polanyi's *The Great Transformation*', in *Capitalism and Social Cohesion: Essays on Exclusion and Integration*, edited by Ian Gough and Gunnar Olofsson. London: Macmillan.

Olson, M. (1982) *The Rise and Decline of Nations*. Cambridge, Mass: Harvard University Press.

Parijs, P. van (1995) *Real Freedom For All: What (If Anything) Can Justify Capitalism?* Oxford: Clarendon Press.

Parsons, T. (1960) 'The distribution of power in American society', in *Structure and Processes in Modern Societies*. New York: Free Press.

Pateman, C. (1988) 'The patriarchal welfare state', in A. Gutmann (ed.) *Democracy and the Welfare State*. Princeton, NJ: Princeton University Press.

Penz, G. (1986) *Consumer Sovereignty and Human Interests*. Cambridge: Cambridge University Press.

Penz, G. (1993) 'Comment on Gough', in Drover and P. Kerans (ed.) *New Approaches to Welfare Theory*. Edward Elgar.

Pereirinha, J. (1992) *Observatory on Policies to Combat Social Exclusion. Consolidated National Report: Portugal*. CEC DGV. Lille: European Economic Interest Group.

Persson, T. and G. Tabellini (1994) 'Is inequality harmful for growth?', *American Economic Review* 84: 600–21.

Pfaller, A. and I. Gough (1991) 'The competitiveness of industrialised welfare states: a cross-country survey', in Pfaller et al., *op. cit.*

Pfaller, A., I. Gough and G. Therborn (1991) *Can the Welfare State Compete? A Comparative Study of Five Advanced Capitalist Countries*. London: Macmillan.

Piachaud, D. (1989) 'Social policy and the economy: introduction', in *The Goals of Social Policy*. London: Unwin Hyman.

Pierson, C. (1991) *Beyond the Welfare State: The New Political Economy of the Welfare State*. Cambridge: Polity Press.

Pierson, P. (1995) 'The scope and nature of business power: employers and the American welfare state'. Harvard University. Unpublished.

Plant, R., H. Lesser and P. Taylor-Gooby (1980) *Political Philosophy and Social Welfare*. London: Routledge.

Pogge, T. (1989) *Realizing Rawls*. Ithaca, NY: Cornell University Press.

Polanyi, K. (1944/1957) *The Great Transformation*. Boston: Beacon Press.

Population Crisis Committee (1988) *Country Ranking on the Status of Women: Poor, Powerless and Pregnant*. Population Briefing Paper No. 20. Population Crisis Committee.

Porter, M.E. (1990) *The Competitive Advantage of Nations*. London: Macmillan.

Poulantzas, N. (1969) 'The problem of the capitalist state', *New Left Review*, 58: 67–78.

Poulantzas, N. (1973) *Political Power and Social Classes*. New Left Books.

Powell, W. (1991) 'Neither market nor hierarchy: network forms of organisation', in G. Thompson et al. (eds) *Markets, Hierarchies and Networks*. London: Sage.

Prais, S. and Wagner, K. (1987) 'Educating for productivity', National Institute *Economic Review* 119: 40–56.

Pryor, F. (1968) *Public Expenditures in Communist and Capitalist Nations*. London: Allens & Unwin.

Przeworski, A. (1986) 'Material interests, class compromise and the transition to socialism', in J. Roemer (ed.) *Analytical Marxism*. Cambridge: Cambridge University Press.

Przeworski, A. and M. Wallerstein (1988) 'Structural dependence of the state on capital', *American Political Science Review*, 82(1): 11–29.

Purdy, D. (1996) 'Jobs, work and citizens' income: four strategies and a new regime', *EUI Working Paper, 96/1* San Domenico, Italy: EUI.

Putterman, L. (1990) *Division of Labor and Welfare: An Introduction to Economic Systems*. Oxford: Oxford University Press.

Quinn, D. and C. Inclan (1997), 'The origins of financial openness: a study of current and capital account liberalisation', *American Journal of Political Science* 41(3): 771–813.

Ramprakash, D. (1994) 'Poverty in the countries of the European Union: a synthesis of Eurostat's statistical research on poverty', *Journal of European Social Policy*, 4(2): 117–28.

Rawls, J. (1972) *A Theory of Justice*. Oxford: Oxford University Press.

Rawls, R. (1974) 'Reply to Alexander and Musgrave', *Quarterly Journal of Economics*, 88: 633–55.

Rieger, E. and S. Leibfried (1998) 'Welfare state limits to globalization', *Politics and Society*, 26(3): 363–90.

Rimlinger, G. (1971). *Welfare Policy and Industrialization in Europe, America, and Russia*, 1st edition. New York: John Wiley & Sons.

Ringen, S. (1987) *The Possibility of Politics: A Study in the Political Economy of the Welfare State*. Oxford: Clarendon Press.

Rist, G. (1980) 'Basic questions about basic human needs', in K. Lederer (ed.) *Human Needs*. Cambridge, Mass: Oelgeschlager, Gunn and Hain.

Robbins, D. (1993) *Observatory on National Policies to Combat Social Exclusion: Third Annual Report*, CEC DGV. Lille: European Economic Interest Group.

Roderick, R. (1986) *Habermas and the Foundations of Critical Theory*. London: Macmillan.

Rogers, J. and W. Streeck (1994) 'Productive solidarities: economic strategy and left politics', in D. Miliband (ed.) *Reinventing the Left*. Cambridge: Polity Press.

Room, G. (1990) *'New Poverty' in the European Community*. London: Macmillan.

Room, G. (1993) *Observatory on National Policies to Combat Social Exclusion: Second Annual Report*, CEC DGV. Lille: European Economic Interest Group.

Room, G. and 6, P. (1994) 'Welfare states in Europe and the third sector', in P.6 and I.Vidal (eds) *Delivering Welfare*. Barcelona: CIES.

Rose, R. (1996) 'Evaluating workplace benefits: the views of Russian employees', in OECD.

Rosh, R. (1988) 'Militarisation, human rights and basic needs in the third world', in *Human Rights: Theory and Measurement*, edited by D. Cingranelli. London: Macmillan.

Rowthorn, R. (1992) 'Centralisation, employment and wage dispersion', *Economic Journal*, 102: 506–23.

Rubinson, R. (1977) 'Dependence, government revenue, and economic growth, 1955–1970', *Studies in Comparative International Development*, 12: 3–28.

Rubinson, R. and Browne, I. (1994) 'Education and the economy', in *The Handbook of Economic Sociology*, edited by N.J. Smelser and R. Swedberg. Princeton, NJ: Princeton University Press: 581–99.

Rueschemeyer, D. and Evans, P. (1985) 'The state and economic transformation', in P. Evans et al. (eds) *Bringing the State Back In*. Cambridge: Cambridge University Press.

Rueschemeyer, D., E.H. Stephens and J.D. Stephens (1992) *Capitalist Development and Democracy*. Cambridge: Polity Press.

Russell, B. (1960) *Power: A New Social Analysis*. London: Unwin Books.

Saint-Paul, G. (1992) 'Fiscal policy in an endogenous growth model', *Quarterly Journal of Economics*, 107: 1243–59.

Saunders, P. (1986) 'What can we learn from international comparisons of public sector size and economic performance?' *European Sociological Review*, 2(1): 52–60.

Saraceno, C. (1992) *Observatory on Policies to Combat Social Exclusion. Consolidated National Report: Italy*. CEC DGV. Lille: European Economic Interest Group.

Schmidt, M. (1989) 'Social policy in rich and poor countries: socioeconomic trends and political-institutional determinants'. Paper presented to the conference on *The Welfare State in Transition*, Bergen, 24–27 August.

Schumpeter, J. (1954) 'The crisis of the tax state', in A. Peacock et al., *International Economic Papers: Translations Prepared for the International Economic Association*. New York: Macmillan.

Schumpeter, J. (1976) *Capitalism, Socialism and Democracy*. London: Allen and Unwin.

Sen, A. (1981) *Poverty and Famines: an Essay on Entitlement and Deprivation*. Oxford: Clarendon Press.

Sen, A. (1984) *Resources, Values and Development*. Oxford: Blackwell.

Sen, A. (1987) *The Standard of Living*. Cambridge: Cambridge University Press.

Sen, A. (1992) *Inequality Reexamined*. Oxford: Clarendon Press.

Shonfield, A. (1965) *Modern Capitalism: The Changing Balance of Public and Private Power*. Oxford: Oxford University Press.

Sivard, R. (1989) *World Military and Social Expenditures 1989*, 13th edition. Washington D.C.: World Priorities Inc.

Sjöstrand, S. (1992) 'On the rationale behind "irrational" institutions', *Journal of Economic Issues*, 26(4): 1007–40.

Skocpol, T. (1985) 'Bringing the state back in: strategies of analysis in current research', in P. Evans et al. (eds) *Bringing the State Back In*. Cambridge: Cambridge University Press.

Slemrod, J. (1990) 'Tax Principles in an international economy', In *World Tax Reform*, edited by M. Boskin and C. McClure. San Fancisco: International Center for Economic Growth, 2–31.

Smith, A. (1970) *The Wealth of Nations, Book I*. London: Pelican Books.

Snyder, D. and Kick, E. (1979) 'Structural position in the world system and economic growth 1955–70: a multiple network analysis of transnational interactions', *American Journal of Sociology* 84(5): 1096–126.

Soper, K. (1981) *On Human Need*. London: Harvester.

Soper, K. (1993) 'The thick and the thin of human needing', in G. Drover and P. Kerans (eds) *New Approaches to Welfare Theory*. Aldershot: Edward Elgar 69–81.

Soros, G. (1999) *The Crisis of Global Capitalism*. New York: Little, Brown.

Soskice, D. (1999) 'Divergent production regimes: coordinated and uncoordinated market economies in the 1980s and 1990s', in *Continuity and Change in Contemporary Capitalism*, edited by H. Kitschelt et al. Cambridge: Cambridge University Press.

Spearitt, D. (1990) 'Evaluation of national comparisons', in *The International Encyclopaedia of Educational Evaluation*, edited by H. Walberg and G. Haertel. Oxford: Pergamon.

Steinmo, S. (1993) *Taxation and Democracy: Swedish, British and American Approaches to Financing the Modern State*. New Haven: Yale University Press.

Stephens, J. (1996) 'The Scandinavian welfare states: achievements, crisis and prospects', in G. Esping-Andersen (ed.), *Welfare States in Transition*. London: Sage.

Stewart, F. (1985) *Planning to Meet Basic Needs*. London: Macmillan.

Strange, S. (1986) *Casino Capitalism*. Oxford: Basil Blackwell.

Strange, S. (1988) *States and Markets*. London: Pinter.

Strange, S. (1996) *The Retreat of the State: The Diffusion of Power in the World Economy*. Cambridge: Cambridge University Press.

Streeck, W. and P. Schmitter, (1985) 'Community, market, state – and associations?', in W. Streeck and P. Schmitter (eds) *Private Interest Government: Beyond Market and State*. London: Sage.

Streeck, W. and P. Schmitter (1991) 'From national corporatism to transnational pluralism', *Politics and Society*, 19: 133–64.

Strümpel, B. and J. Scholz (1987) 'The comparative study of the economy: dimensions, methods and results', in M. Dierkes et al. (eds) *Comparative Policy Research*. Aldershot: Gower.

Swaan de, A. (1990) *In Care of the State*, 1st edition. Cambridge: Polity Press.

Swank, D. (1992) 'Politics and the structural dependence of the state in democratic capitalist nations', *American Political Science Review*, 86(1). pp. 38–54.

Swank, D. (1998) 'Funding the welfare state: globalization and the taxation of business in advanced market economies', *Political Studies*, 46: 671–92.

Szelenyi, I. (1978) 'Social inequalities in state socialist redistributive economies', *International Journal of Comparative Sociology*, XIX: 1–2.

Tao, J and Drover, G (1997) 'Chinese and western notions of need', *Critical Social Policy* 50: 5–25.

Taylor-Gooby, P. (1991) *Social Change, Social Welfare and Social Science*. London: Harvester Wheatsheaf.

Therborn, G. (1986) *Why are Some Peoples More Unemployed than Others?* London: Verso.

Therborn, G. (1992) 'The right to vote and the four world routes to/through modernity', in *State Theory and State History*, edited by R. Torstendahl. London: Sage.

Therborn, G. (1996) *European Modernity and Beyond: The Trajectory of European Societies 1945–2000*. London: Sage.

Thompson, G. (1987) *Needs*. London: Routledge.

Thompson, G., J. Frances, R. Levacic and J. Mitchell (eds) (1991) *Markets, Hierarchies and Networks: The Coordination of Social Life*. London: Sage.

Tratch, I., M. Rein and A. Wörgötter (1996) 'Social asset restructuring in Russian enterprises: results of a survey in selected Russian regions', in OECD, op. cit.

UNDP (United Nations Development Program) (1990, 1991, 1992) *Human Development Reports, 1990, 1991 1992*. United Nations.

UNESCO (United Nations Educational, Scientific, and Cultural Organisation) (1991) *Statistical Yearbook*. Paris.

UNICEF (1990) *The State of the Worlds' Children 1990*. New York: Oxford University Press.

UNRISD (United Nations Research Institute for Social Development) (1992) *Qualitative Indicators of Development*. By McGranahan et al. Discussion Paper 15. Paris.

Urry, J. and J. Wakeford (eds) (1973) *Power in Britain*. London: Heinemann.

US Department of Housing and Urban Development (1978) *Insurance Crisis in Urban America* Washington DC: HUD-FIA-315.

Veen, R. van der and P. van Parijs (1987) 'A capitalist road to communism', *Theory and Society*, 15(5): 635–55.

Vobruba, G. (1996) 'The additional use of social policy in the modernization and transformation of societies', in A. Erskine (ed.) *Changinng Europe*. Aldershot: Avebury.

Wallerstein, I. (1974) *The Modern World System*. New York: Academic.

Wallerstein, M. and A. Przeworski (1995) 'Capital taxation with open borders', *Review of International Political Economy*, 2: 425–45.

Weir, M., A. Orloff and T. Skocpol (1988) 'Understanding American social politics', in M. Weir et al. (eds) *The Politics of Social Security in the United States*. Chicago: University of Chicago Press.

Westoby, A. (1983) 'Conceptions of communist states', in D. Held et al. (eds) *States and Societies*. Oxford: Martin Robertson.

Wetherly, P. (1996) 'Basic needs and social policies', *Critical Social Policy*, 16(1): 45–65.

White, S. (1996) 'The Right to Work and the Right to a Basic Income'. Paper prepared for a conference on Van Parijs's Real Freedom for All, University of Warwick, 4 May.

Whitefield, S. (1993) *Industrial Power and the Soviet System*. London: Oxford University Press.

Wilensky, H. (1975) *The Welfare State and Equality*. Berkeley: Berkeley University Press.

Wilensky, H. et al. (1987) 'Comparative social policy: theories, methods, findings', in M. Dierkes et al. (eds) *Comparative Policy Research*. Aldershot: Gower.

Wilkinson, R. (1994) 'Health, redistribution and growth', in Glyn and Miliband, op. cit.

Williamson, O. (1985) *The Economic Institutions of Capitalism: Firms, Markets, Relational Contracting*. London: Macmillan.

Williamson, P. (1989) *Corporatism in Perspective*. London: Sage.

Winters, J. (1996) *Power in Motion: Capital Mobility and the Indonesian State*. New York: Cornell University Press.

Wolfe, A. (1991) 'Market, state and society as codes of moral obligation', in M. Mendell and D. Salee (eds) *The Legacy of Karl Polanyi*. London: Macmillan.

Wood, S. (ed.) (1982) *The Degradation of Work*. London: Hutchinson.

World Bank (1988, 1990, 1991, 1992) *World Bank Development Reports*. London: Oxford University Press.

World Bank. (1992) *1990 World Tables*. World Bank 1992 diskette.

Worswick, G.D. (1985) *Education and Economic Performance*. London: Gower.

Index